Migdal Zophim

&

Farming in the Jewish Colonies of South Jersey

MIGDAL ZOPHIM

The Watch Tower

The Jewish Problem and
Agriculture as its Solution

by

MOSES KLEIN

&

FARMING IN THE JEWISH COLONIES OF SOUTH JERSEY

Articles and early writings by several hands pertaining to the
Jewish colonies of Alliance, Rosenhayn and Carmel

Republished by the
South Jersey Culture & History Center
Stockton University, 2019

Migdal Zophim entered, according to Act of Congress, in the year 1889, by Moses Klein, in the Office of the Librarian of Congress at Washington. Originally printed at the Press of Billstein & Son, Philadelphia. Original photographs prepared by Levytype Co., Philadelphia.

Articles from *The Jewish Exponent, The Jewish Messenger, The New York Herald* and *The Sun* 1882–1907.

This edition published 2019
by the South Jersey Culture & History Center

South Jersey Culture & History Center,
Stockton University,
101 Vera King Farris Drive
Galloway, New Jersey, 08205

Title: Migdal Zophim / Farming in the Jewish Colonies of South Jersey
Authors: Moses Klein, others,
Foreword: Tom Kinsella

Additional material Copyright © 2019
ISBN: 978-1-947889-89-7

The mission of the South Jersey Culture & History Center is to help foster awareness within local communities of the rich cultural and historical heritage of southern New Jersey, to promote the study of this heritage, especially among area students, and to produce publishable materials that provide lasting and deepened understanding of this heritage.

CONTENTS

Migdal Zophim

Farming in the Jewish Colonies of South Jersey

FOREWORD

Migdal Zophim (The Watch Tower)

Deep concern for the fate of Eastern European Jews, driven from their places of birth by the brutal pogroms of the early 1880s, inspired the essays that comprise *Migdal Zophim* (Philadelphia, 1889). Questions and unease run through the early chapters. What solutions could be offered to Jews who endured the harsh legal, and extra-legal, restrictions imposed by the Russian government and populace? What actions should be taken to aid refugees fleeing from anti-Semitism?

Moses Klein, the author of *Migdal Zophim*, and many of his civic-minded contemporaries pondered these questions and answered with the outwardly simple notion of assisting refugees to become "agriculturalists"—farmers. The idea of returning to the land found ready adherents in European Jews familiar with the Jewish nationalist writings of Perez Smolenskin and others. The *Am Olam* ("Eternal People") movement, which began in Odessa in 1881, viewed the creation of agricultural colonies as the solution to *The Jewish Problem*, to use the contemporary phrase.[1] In order to develop self-respect and to achieve acceptance from non-Jewish cultures, Jews needed to return to their agricultural roots.[2] The logic seemed clear: if there was to be an independent Jewish homeland, or independent Jewish colonies anywhere, there needed to be Jewish farmers.

Klein did not publish *Migdal Zophim* in his original three-part conception. A first part, in Hebrew, was to provide "Geographical and Historical" sketches of America; a second, also in Hebrew, would have treated Jewish emigration to the United States; the third part—ultimately, the only portion that was printed—is the text before you. Klein wrote the text in English and supplied sample pages in Hebrew.[3] Russian and Eastern European Jews were the audience for the text as originally envisioned; presumably, it would have served as a guide to those considering emigration. American Jews, who might yet be convinced of the utility of farming colonies and encouraged to support them, were the audience for the text as published.

In the opening essay, Klein addresses the state of Jews who remained in Russia and Eastern Europe, enduring various forms of oppression and bigotry. The Baron de Hirsch, a leading philanthropist, saw education as the solution to this humanitarian crisis. He offered 50 million francs to Czar Alexander III to fund schools for Russian Jews. Klein thought the effort wasted, not because the goal was unde-serving, but because, while Jews might receive better education, the majority of Russians would remain unenlightened:

> We have no security whatever that edu-cation will obtain for the 50,000 Jewish scholars of Baron de Hirsch's 1,000 schools the right of citizenship, and that of settlement in the interior of Russia, or even the right to exercise their edu-cational advantages for securing their independent livelihood in the Czar's domain. (*Migdal Zophim* 13)

To Klein, any such educated Jews would only benefit if they were to emigrate from Rus-sia "to other and more civilized countries, in which their intelligence and industry and their knowledge of art and science will probably be recognized" (13).

Klein did not trust Russia's political climate. He foresaw further difficulties for European Jews: "The political cloud now hanging over the Balkan provinces may also soon introduce a new problem regarding the state of our breth-ren who dwell there" (14). His solution, not surprisingly, was emigration and farming.

"Jews of Palestine," the second essay, sur-veys Jewish enclaves found in contemporary Palestine, then under the governance of the Turkish sultanate. Klein has translated a series of descriptive sketches written in Hebrew by Joshua Stampfer of the Petach Tikvah colony near Jaffa. Stampfer weaves demographic and agricultural statistics together with personal observations and historical details, suggesting the enduring importance of place. The readable prose (translated by Klein) is at times nostalgic, even romanticized. Arriving in the vicinity of Tiberius by caravan on a bright star-lit summer night, Stampfer waxes eloquent as he reaches the summit of Mount Carmel:

> This natural drama gained additional beauty when our eyes were directed toward the level of Gennesaret, which, by reflecting in its silver mirror the mag-nitude of the sky-illuminated bodies, appeared to us as another part of the heavenly globe, and we thought ourselves sailing between two infinite firmaments. It must have been by such a scene, and in such a region, that the "sweet singer of Israel" announced on his harp: "The heavens declare the glory of God, and the firmament showeth His handiwork." (22)

The status of the Jewish enclaves and colo-nies was complex. Some were recently settled, the result of the pogroms of 1881–1882; others were ancient. A few were well established and thriving; some, with substantial Jewish popula-tions, were moribund. The largest community resided in Jerusalem, where the status of the working Jew was very poor and where outside support continued to be needed. Stampfer argues that such support had to be maintained, "until it will be supplanted by aid in the way of agricultural settlements, which alone can solve The Jewish Problem" (29).

The essay "Agriculture as a Solution" is Klein's detailed review of efforts made to encourage Jewish farming in Palestine over the previous twenty years. While not always successful, these efforts prepared the way for further colonization, which Klein recognized as a positive outcome arising from the horrors of the pogroms. He likened the pogroms' impact to that of the French Revolution, which empowered the French people, and the American Civil War, which freed millions of slaves:

> . . . so was modern Jewish colonization brought about by the German, Russian, and Hungarian persecutions, which burst forth from the volcano of anti-Semitism, casting thousands of Israelites to the Eastern and Western diasporas. (36)

These refugees, driven by "the rod of persecution," were hopefully making "a better life in the lands of their dispersion" (3).

These first essays serve as prelude to Klein's great objective, his championing of the New Jersey colonies of Alliance, Rosenhayn and Carmel. Klein had been familiar with the colonies at least since 1883.[4] He knew their challenges, hardships, and successes. As agent for the Association of Jewish Immigrants, he would have been a frequent visitor to the colonies, and in February 1889, his detailed report on the colony at Carmel, reprinted in *Migdal Zophim* (65–83), served as the basis for relief provided to colonists by the Baron de Hirsch Fund.

Twenty early photographs of the South Jersey colonies accompany Klein's text. The images are captivating, although poorly reproduced in the original, and thus here. Colonists stand proudly before their synagogues. Students pose outside their schools. Tailors pause from work: men and women, with children by their side; garment scraps litter the floor and a central, hanging kerosene lamp lights the sewing room. The landscape is often treeless; the colonists had cleared the terrain doggedly. But in some images, the success of the agriculturalists is evident, as in Moses Bayuk's vineyard or the farmlands viewed from the Tiphereth Jisrael Synagogue.

It is difficult not to admire these pioneers as Klein documents their early years. Alongside demographic lists and charts of produce grown, he provides more personal details: the colonists at Carmel contributed $47 to aid the sufferers of the Johnstown flood; no less than eighty farmers from Alliance became U. S. citizens on the same day at the Salem County court house; sixteen families in Alliance did not own land, but worked for other farmers during the summer and sewed in winter.

The penultimate essay of *Migdal Zophim* is a reprinting of an October 1889 article in the Philadelphia *Sunday Mercury* written by a staff writer who spent three days at the colonies, accompanied by Klein. The final "Addenda," a defense of Jewish colonization in Palestine, provides a coda that is uplifting in its conviction. Farming, writes Klein,

> . . . was the occupation of our patriarchs, of our prophets, of our sages; and that which afforded them subsistence, yea, delight,—because it instilled within them the feeling of dependence upon God alone,—ought surely to effect permanent good to their latest posterity. (103)

Farming in the Jewish Colonies of South Jersey

The second half of this volume, entitled *Farming in the Jewish Colonies of South Jersey*, collects a series of essays by Klein and correspondents found in Philadelphia's *The Jewish Exponent*. Klein was a long-time contributor, writing a weekly column, "The House of Israel," under the nom de plume *Hazopheh*, "the scout." Several additional articles and documents pertaining to life in the colonies have also been included, from various sources and by various authors, dating from 1882 to 1907.

The section opens with an 1890 review of *Migdal Zophim* by Myer S. Isaacs, a New York lawyer, judge, philanthropist, and, along with his brothers Isaac and Abram, editor of New York's *The Jewish Messenger*. A report describing conditions at the Alliance Colony follows, submitted to the Hebrew Emigrant Aid Society (HEAS) in 1882, just two months after the founding of the colony, written by superintendent A. C. Sternberg. The rest of the articles and letters appear in chronological order.

We have mentioned that Klein has reproduced an 1889 description of the colonies written by a staff writer for the *Sunday Mercury*. We have reproduced two additional reporters' descriptions from New York newspapers—an acerbic description in Charles A. Dana's *The Sun* (1890) and a quite thoughtful description from *The New York Herald* (1891).

Several of the articles or letters in this section are written by colonists themselves. Moses Bayuk writes two letters in reply to Charles D. Spivakovski's romanticized view of the colonies. Bayuk exhibits both humor and combativeness as he counters the details of Spivakovski's description. J. C. Reis, who arrived in Alliance in 1892, writes several letters championing the cause of the Jewish farmer; this section concludes with his "History of the Alliance Colony" (1907).

We have reproduced a letter from Henry S. Henry to Moses Bayuk, dated December 31, 1884, and a letter from Bayuk to Henry, dated January 1, 1885. Henry, as a trustee of the Alliance Land Trust, which since 1883 had held the mortgages to the land and homes at Alliance, insists that no further aid can be provided to the colony. Bayuk, in his succinct report, states the reasons why more help is needed. Both letters were printed for distribution and appear to be part of an on-going, public correspondence.

Throughout these pieces, the authors bring differing perspectives to recurring themes: the need for local industry to supplement farming; the usefulness (or villainousness) of local building associations; and the problems associated with charity, which Klein describes as "sweet but ill-applied" (71). Many of these articles suggest Americanization as the ultimate goal for the colonists. Others assert that through farming Jews will attain moral stature, and an improvement in their social and financial condition, that will place them on the high road to dignity. Each provide fascinating glimpses of the colonies of Alliance, Rosenhayn and Carmel (with glancing mention of Norma, Brotmanville and Woodbine) and suggest ways that these communities were viewed and understood by contemporaries. Most pieces provide a resounding answer to the recurring question, "Can Jews Be Farmers?"—yes!

Together, the various articles ably describe the very real hardships of the early colonists, men and women with little to no farming experience who struggled to clear the land, afford shelter, and make fruitful the thin soil of South Jersey. It is illuminating, but not surprising, to discover undercurrents of tenacity, pride, and, at times, resentment on the part of colonists, as well as determination, frustration, and, sometimes, self-congratulation on the part of Philadelphia and New York philanthropists.

If Klein were alive today to visit Alliance, Rosenhayn and Carmel, he might well be disappointed. His farmers are largely gone, though not entirely. Industries arrived, as he predicted, and added economic opportunity, but not enough, when combined with volatile farm markets, to sustain community expansion or even to maintain the status quo. Schools, built by community members, taught their students well, and succeeding generations, like so many Americans, left the farms and took up urban or suburban careers and lives.

Attempting to make sense of atrocities committed in the late nineteenth century, and deeply averse to the conditions to which refugees were subjected in urban ghettos, Klein could only envisage farming as the future destiny of Jews "in this blessed country." Instead, descendants of the colonists, drawing on the determination, inventiveness and resilience of their forebears, seized much more varied roles in the ever evolving patchwork of American culture.

Addendum Images

Photographs of the colonies are one of the pleasures of *Migdal Zophim*. We have included several other more recent images of Carmel, Rosenhayn, and the area around Alliance, drawing on early twentieth-century real photo postcards and images provided by community members.

A Biography of Moses Klein

Moses Klein was born May 23, 1857, in Bolekhiv, a city of regional significance in Galicia, and always listed his country of origin as "Hungary."[5] He arrived at the Castle Garden immigration station in New York City on September 26, 1883,[6] and soon after traveled to Philadelphia, where he threw himself into work that benefited that region's immigrant Jewish community.[7]

He first appears in the public record in 1884 as chief interpreter under J. S. Rodgers, Commissioner of Immigration at Philadelphia. Klein was a versatile linguist, with a competence in seven languages, and is described as a faithful and capable official.[8] On September 21, 1884, Klein spoke at the initiatory meeting of the Association of Jewish Immigrants in Philadelphia and by 1885 was employed as agent for the Association. He performed his duties with diligence, sifting through newly arrived "steerage passengers with tremendous care and patience."[9]

Klein's open and altruistic character was not directed solely toward his co-religionists. On April 25, 1886, the steamer WYDALE arrived at Philadelphia with a family of nine Egyptians, headed by a white-haired patriarch, Strief Roumano. The family had taken passage in Gibraltar, requesting that they land at the nearest port to Brazil where a wealthy relative lived. Since the WYDALE's terminus was Philadelphia, upon arrival at that port, the family was little closer to their intended destination. With difficulty they explained their plight to Philadelphia authorities and were only understood completely when Klein arrived as interpreter. He sorted through conflicting details and helped set a resolution in motion; then "Mr. Klein took the wanderers to his own house, where he cared for them for fourteen days."[10] The captain of the WYDALE, meanwhile, engaged passage for the family to Brazil on the steamer COLORADO. A newspaper article describing the event concludes with the patriarch Roumano standing on the deck of the soon-to-depart steamship shaking hands with Klein and stating: "All have been so good and so just in aiding the strange and the helpless who were cast upon their shores. God bless you."[11]

Klein was well regarded in his position as agent for the Association. A newspaper account describes his work in 1886:

> He is a gentleman of great ability, and his monthly reports are not only interesting on account of the matter they contain, as to the disposal of those who arrive at this port from foreign shores, but also they are literary productions of merit. Not satisfied with his work here [in Philadelphia], he has obtained permission from the Board of the Association to go forth into the country, and interest people in the smaller towns in the work of the Society, and also to make arrangements for obtaining employment for some applicants.[12]

As agent for the Association, Klein played an important role assisting members of the Carmel colony in 1888–1889. After the death, in 1888, of writer and philanthropist Michael Heilprin, who served as promoter and supporter of Carmel, Rabbi Sabato Morais successfully appealed to the Baron de Hirsch Fund for assistance for the struggling colony. It was Klein who made recommendations for the disbursment of $5000 to needy colonists.[13] Klein's report on Carmel during this period is reproduced in *Migdal Zophim*.

Klein's duties for the Association included writing tracts that spoke plainly of the limited opportunities for Jewish immigrants in the Philadelphia and South Jersey region, countering the narrative of grand opportunities supposed to exist in America. Louis E. Levy, then president of the Association of Jewish Immigrants, reported in late 1889 that decreasing numbers of immigrant Jews were arriving, partly because political persecution had been relaxed in some parts of Europe, but also because of

> . . . articles published in *Hamagid* [the first Hebrew language weekly, targeting Russian Jews in particular], of Lyck, from the pen of the agent of the association, Mr. Moses Klein, which have been extensively commented upon by the other Jewish periodicals of the Slavic countries and have been reinforced by the publication of warnings by Chief Rabbi Adler, of London, against emigration to England.[14]

In 1890, George Randorf succeeded Klein both as agent for the Association and as interpreter to the United States Commissioners of Immigration.[15] Klein, nevertheless, maintained his connection to the Association, serving as one of its directors at least until 1896.[16]

In 1894, the United Hebrew Charities of Philadelphia, a New York organization that had first opened an auxiliary branch in Philadelphia in 1886, named Klein as its superintendent.[17] The charity had experienced serious funding imbalances in 1893, exacerbated by the extreme winter weather of 1892–1893, and Edward L. Rothschild, the charity's president, had called for changes: "We must . . . search out the means by which charity may be administered worthily—but justly."[18] Two major alterations were effected during 1894. First, the organization tasked Klein with implementing an improved system of charitable distribution and aiding in its oversight. Second, the charity would no longer provide access to monetary relief at its Philadelphia office. Needy immigrants might apply for assistance at the office, but aid would only be disbursed, "after proper investigation . . . to deserving applicants at their homes, excepting, alone, in cases of emergency."[19] Throughout each of the ensuing years, Klein would assess hundreds of needy Philadelphia families, making thousands of visits. A newspaper account describing his annual report for 1895 serves as an example of the extent of his duties. The report

> . . . showed that rent and support to the amount of $12,586.36 had been distributed to 4,716 families, comprising 24,080 persons; 30,027 buckets of coal had been distributed, and 102½ tons in half-ton quantities; shoes and clothing had been provided for 614 persons;

railroad transportation for 597, and ocean transportation for 16. The society had furnished medical service to 8,063 patients, and had provided hospital treatment for 197. Mr. Klein, in his admirable report, referred to the dangers of crowded tenement houses, which he designated as one of the crying evils of the time, the remedy for which was still an unsolved question.[20]

President Max Herzberg, in his annual report for the United Hebrew Charities in 1900, commented:

> When it is remembered that practically none of the $20,000 expended for relief was paid out at this office but delivered to the recipients at their homes, some idea can be formed of the vast amount of labor entailed upon our Superintendent, Mr. Moses Klein, he having made 6706 visits for the purpose of distribution, as well as of investigation, the number of new cases requiring such investigation being 353.[21]

Such a workload could not be sustained. Herzberg's 1902 annual report records:

> Mr. Klein's arduous duties have been performed at a sacrifice to health and

comfort, and only those who have performed similar services, who have visited the poor at their homes, in dark and damp cellars, in dirty garrets and narrow alleys, can appreciate the physical labors that are connected with making over six thousand calls a year. Those who know Mr. Klein need not be told that the work has been a labor of love with him, and it only remains for me to say that the work has been well performed.[22]

Klein suffered a physical breakdown, and although his association with the United Hebrew Charities appears to have lasted to the end of his life, he remained active as superintendent only through 1901–1902.[23]

During the summer of 1890, the Russian government was once again threatening to promulgate the harsh edicts that had led to the pogroms of 1881–1882. Klein spoke as an authority on the matter to the Philadelphia press,[24] and joined with concerned Russian-American Jews at a meeting on August 6, 1890, held at Charles D. Spivak's home. "Representatives of Russian Jewish societies had been summoned to take action in regard to the threatened enforcement of oppressive laws in Russia against its Jewish inhabitants." Klein was elected chair of the meeting with Dr. Spivak secretary.[25] Two weeks later, after considerable organization, discussion, and active debate in the Philadelphia Jewish community, the Jewish Alliance of America was launched on August 20.

Klein's contributions were considerable —"Mr. Moses Klein made a masterly speech at the B'nai Abraham, with the result that five delegates were sent by them to the convention."[26] He was elected vice-president of the new organization and the members quickly began to organize a mass meeting to be held on September 21, 1890, to bring together a larger number of interested parties. At that meeting Klein, ever the linguist, made his comments in German to an audience of 900 at Wheatley Dramatic Hall in Philadelphia, stating that "until the present time the curse that had rested upon the Jews was that of division and disunion. It was time that they should unite in behalf of a good movement such as this."[27] The first national convention of The Jewish Alliance was held on February 15, 1891, in Philadelphia, where Klein once again addressed the convention.[28] By December 1891, he was traveling the east coast, acting as agent for The Alliance, organizing new chapters, and attempting to find new centers for immigrants to settle.[29] He told a newly organized branch in Scranton that within "about a year . . . [The Alliance had organized] 35 branches and about 7500 members."[30]

Although the Jewish Alliance of America was short-lived, Klein's association with the society further demonstrates his dual beliefs: that Jewish immigrants should be settled away from the overcrowded cities of Boston, New York, and Philadelphia and that establishing immigrants in farming communities was a respectable and suitable way of life.

Klein's love for the Hebrew language and its literature was lifelong. "[He] was a zealous devotee of modern Hebrew and contributed to Hebrew periodicals here and abroad."[31] He spoke at the inaugural entertainment of the Hebrew Literature Society in 1887;[32] and he was elected president of the society for the study and preservation of the Hebrew Language in 1890.[33] Not surprisingly, his interest extended to support and encouragement of Hebrew writers who arrived in Philadelphia, including Ezekiel Leavitt, the Hebrew poet. At Klein's suggestion, Leavitt visited and lived, for a time, in Philadelphia.[34]

Closely related to Klein's love of literature and language was his support for learning, which illustrated the influence of the Jewish *Haskelah* (Enlightenment) upon his beliefs and actions. His obituary states that he was:

> . . . a student and loved Jewish learning. He never forgot the privations he suffered in his student days, and always endeavored to help along friendless Jewish students. His house was open for all the Maskilim that came to Philadelphia, where they were always certain of a hearty welcome and sympathetic help.[35]

His contributions to the community in this way were numerous. In 1886, in an early notice of Klein, the Philadelphia congregation of the new Adath Jeshurum Synagogue elected him teacher.[36] Ten years later, in 1896, he made a strong plea for increased support for Philadelphia's "Talmud Torah" (Hebrew free school): it was attended by 300 children, stated Klein, "and if the means for its enlargement were at hand could readily accommodate 5000 children."[37] In 1898, he was elected to the executive committee of the Philadelphia section of the Jewish Theological Seminary Association.[38] In that same year, he assisted in a drive to found a chair of theology in the Jewish Theological Seminary in memory of Rabbi Sabato Morais.[39] Throughout his career, Klein strove to improve education for Jewish immigrants.

In the final twelve years of his life, intermingled with his work for the United Hebrew Charities and efforts to improve the intellectual life of the Jewish community, Klein became an active supporter of Zionism. His obituary describes him as "a lover of Zion before Herzl, before Zionism as such was known. His book attests his hopes for regeneration of his people; to this his whole heart was given."[40] In 1897, Theodor Herzl, a fellow Hungarian, summoned the first Zionist congress to Munich.[41] In June of that year, Klein wrote in impassioned support of Zionism and the upcoming conference, quoting Isaiah: "How beautiful upon the mountains are the feet of the messenger that bringeth good tidings; that publishes Peace; that proclaimeth to Zion: thy God reigneth!" He elaborated:

> No words of the vernacular could express more clearly the real object of the Zionists and the coming Conference of Munich than the verse quoted above. The sole object of the Zionists and their prospective Conference is the transplanting of outcast Israelites from barbarous countries to the Land of the Covenant. Here they shall erect peaceful homes shaded by orange trees and vines. Here they shall promote agriculture and industry, and cultivate religion and science. . . . The ideal of Zionism being one of those sacred heirlooms which linked scattered Israel together and has endowed our people with a spirit of unparalleled heroism to resist the grinding-mill of Time, is certainly entitled to a hearing at the close of the nineteenth century.[42]

Rapidly, Klein became immersed in the movement. He was elected for a three-year term to the board of directors of *Ohave Zion* (Friends of Zion) in November 1897. He was a delegate to the October mass meeting of the New York Zionist societies.[43] He attended several of the annual conventions of the Federation of Zionists.[44]

Klein was active at both the national and local levels, holding numerous positions of importance.[45] True to his generous nature, he did not fail to support the younger adherents of Zionism. In 1902, the Rose of Sharon Society and the Philadelphia Junior Zion Society held a combined picnic in Fairmount Park. Moses Klein was in attendance along with his wife, who served as one of the four chaperones.

> The picnic was a great success, being more successful than any previous one undertaken. The Zionist League song was sung at the table. . . . A fund, amounting to $3.50, was created, and Charles W. Levy, Jr., made treasurer. Two dollars of it was paid to Mr. Klein for the purpose of having the name of Dr. Herzl's father inscribed in "The Golden Book." The remaining $1.50 was retained by the treasurer as a nucleus for future outings.[46]

Klein was married to Bertha "Goslar" Klein by 1887.[47] She attended charitable functions with her husband, and, in 1892, is mentioned as a member of the S. S. Society, a sewing society: "Sewing for charitable purposes and the taking up of literary readings are the *raison d'etre* of the organization. . . . The meeting last week took place at the home of Miss [sic] Klein."[48] Together, Moses and Bertha had a daughter Carrie, who would marry Dr. Elkan

Henly Yunker of Philadelphia, two years after Klein's death.[49]

Moses Klein died from tuberculosis on June 10, 1909, at age 52.[50] As has already been related, Klein's health had begun to decline sometime around 1901 and a notice in *The Jewish Exponent* described him as "suffering for many years from a distressing illness."[51]

Julius H. Greenstone, in his obituary for Klein, and Dr. J. H. Landau and Rabbi Charles I. Hoffman, in their remarks upon his life, commended Klein's sense of idealism, his utter devotion to charitable work, his love of Judaism, Jewish institutions, and the Hebrew language. Greenstone wrote,

> His heart was full of tenderness and affection for his fellow-creatures, and the many years of constant contact with poverty and misery in his official capacity as the agent for the United Hebrew Charities did not dull his sense of pity and sympathy.[52]

Landau stated that men like Klein give the lie to the proverb, "As rich as a Jew," which Landau suggested will pass away and be replaced by the "truer and nobler proverbs, 'Learned as a Jew' and 'Pious as a Jew.'"[53]

Hoffman, Klein's long-time friend, assessed the man:

His was the purest strain of charity. He considered he knew the cause of the poor. He needed no science to inform, no cold and cheerless system to repress; his own heart was his unfailing monitor, and it was nourished upon the breast of mother Israel alone. It beat in unfailing sympathy with the unfortunate and the oppressed. The milk of human kindness never ran dry within his breast. Even when assailed, even when deceived, even when repaid with black ingratitude, he never would turn accuser. He was a martyr to his restless, unwearied devotion. His was the noblest product of our faith—a pure heart.[54]

Hoffman rejoiced in his friendship with the man and cherished his memory: "I can well remember when I first saw him a stranger, robust and strong. His nature was the same then as now."[55] The sentiment is one that Klein might have held in hope for the many Jewish immigrants that he assisted through the years. If they did not arrive in America robust and strong, Klein hoped and believed that over time they would grow toward that condition, especially if they took up the vocation of farming.

Tom Kinsella
Professor of Literature
Stockton University

Notes

1 "Smolenskin, Perez," *Encyclopaedia Judaica*, http://www.encyclopedia.com/religion/encyclopedias-almanacs-transcripts-and-maps/smolenskin-perez. Ellen Eisenberg, *Jewish Agricultural Colonies in New Jersey 1882–1920* (Syracuse, NY: Syracuse University Press, 1995); Eisenberg states that the *Am Olam* movement started in Odessa in the spring of 1881 (26).

2 Joseph Brandes, *Immigrants to Freedom: Jewish Communities in Rural New Jersey since 1882* (Philadelphia: University of Pennsylvania Press, 1971), 18–19.

3 Klein's sample pages in Hebrew have not been reproduced in this edition but original copies of *Migdal Zophim* are available for study in the Department of Special Collections & Archives, at the Bjork Library, Stockton University.

4 Klein writes in *The Jewish Exponent* (Philadelphia), "A few days ago it was my privilege to pay one of my customary annual visits of 14 years to the three Jewish settlements," August 13, 1897 (this text, 186).

5 Klein's date of birth is recorded on his death certificate, issued by the Commonwealth of Pennsylvania. Place of birth established by the Hamburg State Archives, Staatsarchiv Hamburg, *Hamburg Passenger Lists, 1850–1934* [database on-line]. Provo, UT, USA: Ancestry.com Operations, Inc., 2008.

6 Klein's arrival at the Castle Garden immigration station in New York City is documented by the National Archives and Records Administration.

7 Klein's country of origin plus some biographical details are given in Henry Samuel Morais, *Jews of Philadelphia* (Philadelphia: The Levytype Co., 1894), 354.

8 *The Philadelphia Inquirer*, June 2, 1894, 5. *The Jewish Exponent* (Philadelphia), June 10, 1887, 6, states that "Mr. Klein speaks seven languages, and he wishes that he could speak fourteen, especially when his duty calls him to aid in the inspection of a Red Star steamer from Antwerp, which brings many more nationalities than the ships from Liverpool."

9 The inauguration of the Association of Jewish Immigrants in Philadelphia and Klein's contribution is detailed in *The Jews of Philadelphia*, 131–35. Klein's performance of duties is described in *The Philadelphia Inquirer*, October 10, 1885, 2; *The Philadelphia Inquirer*, November 2, 1885, 2; Quotation from *The Jewish Messenger* (New York), November 6, 1885, 5; *The Jewish Exponent* (Philadelphia), April 15, 1887, 13; *The Jewish Exponent* (Philadelphia), June 10, 1887, 6; *The Philadelphia Inquirer*, November 5, 1888, 2. The annual report of the Association of Jewish Immigrants for 1886 states that Klein visited 85 steamships, which arrived at the port of Philadelphia, *The Jewish Messenger* (New York), November 12, 1886, 5. The Association, also known as the Association for the Protection of Jewish Immigrants, later joined with the Hebrew Immigrant Aid Society as HIAS Pennsylvania.

10 "Happy Arabians," *The New York Herald*, May 16, 1886, 15.

11 Ibid. See a second article describing the plight of the emigrants, and of the captain of the

WYDALE in "Destitute Emigrants," *The Times* (Philadelphia), April 27, 1886, 1. For details on a similar situation, in which Klein assisted Dr. Daniel Kuhliman, a Prussian physician who landed in Philadelphia destitute and without aid, see "A Persecuted Wanderer," *The Omaha Daily Bee*, August 23, 1887, 6.

12 *The Jewish Messenger* (New York), April 9, 1886, 5.

13 Brandes, *Immigrants to Freedom*, 61–62.

14 *The Jewish Messenger* (New York), November 15, 1889, 6. Louis Edward Levy (1846–1919) was a prominent member of the Philadelphia Jewish community. He and his brother Max Levy (1857–1926) patented the Levytype photochemical engraving process and established the Levytype Company, which prepared the original photographs for *Migdal Zophim*.

15 *The Jewish Messenger* (New York), January 31, 1890, 6.

16 *The Philadelphia Inquirer* announced that Klein was elected as director to the Jewish Immigration Society in 1890 and 1892; this is clearly a misnaming for the Association of Jewish Immigrants: *The Philadelphia Inquirer*, November 17, 1890, 3; *The Philadelphia Inquirer*, November 14, 1892, 3. The following are notices of Klein's election to the board of directors of the Association: *The Jewish Exponent* (Philadelphia), November 6, 1891, 6; *The Jewish Exponent* (Philadelphia), November 17, 1893, 6; *The Philadelphia Inquirer*, November 26, 1894, 1; *The Jewish Messenger* (New York), November 30, 1894, 3; *The Jewish Messenger* (New York), November 29, 1895, 6; *The Jewish Messenger*

(New York), December 4, 1896, 6.

17 *The Jewish Messenger* (New York), April 4, 1886, 5.

18 *The Jewish Exponent* (Philadelphia), May 19, 1893, 2.

19 Klein's hiring by the United Hebrew Charities is announced: *The Jewish Messenger* (New York), May 25, 1894, 2. Changes to UHC are described: *The Jewish Exponent* (Philadelphia), May 17, 1895, 1–2.

20 *The Jewish Messenger* (New York), May 17, 1895, 6. See also *The Jewish Exponent* (Philadelphia), May 17, 1895, 1, where Klein makes clear: "The items 'Families aided with rent and support,' and 'Individuals comprising these families' represent the number of times aid was given to applicants, and not the actual number of families; five individuals being the average number to each family. The total number of families [served over the year] was 720, added to which number were 217 travelers, or a total of 937."

21 *The Jewish Exponent* (Philadelphia), October 5, 1900, 1.

22 *The Jewish Exponent* (Philadelphia), October 10, 1902, 7.

23 *The Jewish Messenger* (New York), May 25, 1894, 2; *The Philadelphia Inquirer*, June 2, 1894, 5; Henry Samuel Morais, *The Jews of Philadelphia*, 354; *The Jewish Messenger* (New York), May 17, 1895, 6; *The Jewish Exponent* (Philadelphia), September 18, 1896, 6; *The Jewish Exponent* (Philadelphia), January 29, 1897, 2; *The Jewish Messenger* (New York), October 8, 1897, 6; *The Jewish Exponent* (Philadelphia),

September 15, 1899, 4; *The Jewish Messenger* (New York), September 27, 1901, 3.

24 *The Jewish Exponent* (Philadelphia), August 8, 1890, 3.

25 *The Jewish Exponent* (Philadelphia), August 8, 1890, 6.

26 *The Jewish Exponent* (Philadelphia), August 22, 1890, 6.

27 *The Jewish Exponent* (Philadelphia), August 22, 1890, 6; *The Jewish Exponent* (Philadelphia), September 12, 1890, 6; *The Jewish Exponent* (Philadelphia), September 26, 1890, 5, 6.

28 *The Jewish Exponent* (Philadelphia), February 20, 1891, 1.

29 *The Jewish Exponent* (Philadelphia), May 8, 1903, 4.

30 *The Jewish Exponent* (Philadelphia), December 4, 1891, 4, 6.

31 *The Jewish Exponent* (Philadelphia), October 14, 1932, 4.

32 *The Jewish Exponent* (Philadelphia), October 7, 1887, 12.

33 *The Jewish Messenger* (New York), June 6, 1890, 6; *The Jewish Exponent* (Philadelphia), June 6, 1890, 5.

34 *The Jewish Exponent* (Philadelphia), October 14, 1932, 4.

35 *The Jewish Exponent* (Philadelphia), June 18, 1901, 11.

36 *The Philadelphia Inquirer*, November 1, 1886, 3.

37 *The Jewish Exponent* (Philadelphia), February 28, 1896, 7.

38 *The Jewish Messenger* (New York), March 4, 1898, 6.

39 *The Jewish Exponent* (Philadelphia), January 7, 1898, 2.

40 *The Jewish Exponent* (Philadelphia), June 18, 1909, 11.

41 Herzl planned to meet in Munich, but under pressure from local Jewish opposition changed the venue to Basel, Switzerland. "Zionist Congress: First Zionist Congress & Basel Program," *Jewish Virtual Library*, https://www.jewishvirtuallibrary.org/first-zionist-congress-and-basel-program-1897.

42 *The Jewish Exponent* (Philadelphia), June 4, 1897, 2.

43 *The Jewish Exponent* (Philadelphia), November 12, 1897, 8.

44 Klein was a delegate to the second annual convention of the Federation of Zionists at Baltimore in 1899, but to "general regret," did not attend (perhaps was not *able* to attend), *The Jewish Exponent* (Philadelphia), June 23, 1899, 1; *The Jewish Exponent* (Philadelphia), April 12, 1901, 8; *American Jewish Yearbook*, vol. 4 (1902–1903) 101; *The Jewish Exponent* (Philadelphia), May 30, 1902, 9.

45 Klein attends meeting of the Philadelphia Zion Society, April 1899, *The Jewish Exponent* (Philadelphia), April 21, 1899, 8; serves as secretary pro tem at third annual meeting of the Philadelphia Zion Society in 1900 and is elected as co-secretary for the following year, *The Jewish Messenger* (New York), November 16, 1900, 6; announced as speaker addressing "a mass meeting and Zionist demonstration" to be held in Philadelphia on December 23, 1900, *The Jewish Exponent* (Philadelphia), December 7, 1900, 8; Klein is member of the committee organizing

the fourth Convention of the Federation of American Zionists, to be held in Philadelphia in June 1901. Klein is acting as chairman pro tem, *The Jewish Exponent* (Philadelphia), April 12, 1901, 8; Klein is chairman of the Press and Literature Committee for the upcoming 1901 Philadelphia convention—the committee "has sole charge of notifying the press of all the actions of the Convention Committee," *The Jewish Exponent* (Philadelphia), May 24, 1901, 8; attends meeting of the Junior Philadelphia Zion Society, June 9, 1901, *The Jewish Exponent* (Philadelphia), June 14, 1901, 7; elected corresponding secretary of the Philadelphia Zion Society in 1902, *The Philadelphia Inquirer*, October 28, 1902; addressed the meeting of the Philadelphia Zion society on September 14, 1902, *The Jewish Exponent* (Philadelphia), September 19, 1902, 10; at the annual meeting of the Philadelphia Zion Society, October 26, 1902, "An interesting and encouraging letter from Moses Klein, who has been seriously ill during the past three weeks, was read," *The Jewish Exponent* (Philadelphia), October 31, 1902, 10; Klein attended the inaugural meeting of the Doresh Da'ath Society, October 5, 1907: "The most interesting remarks of the evening, if judged by the attention accorded them, were those of Mr. Klein, who told how Dr. Rubin,

26 years ago, began his successful endeavors to make the Jews of Galicia more ardent Jewish nationalists and enthusiastic Galician patriots"; the next meeting of the society was to convene at Klein's residence, *The Jewish Exponent* (Philadelphia), October 11, 1907, 11.

46 *The Jewish Exponent* (Philadelphia), July 11, 1902, 10.

47 We have not located a record of the marriage of Bertha Goslar to Moses Klein. Carrie S. Klein, their only child, was born March 2, 1887, as established by her death certificate issued by the Commonwealth of Pennsylvania. The first mention found of Mrs. Klein in the press is *The Jewish Exponent* (Philadelphia), January 23, 1891, 2.

48 *The Jewish Exponent* (Philadelphia), November 18, 1892, 6.

49 *The Jewish Exponent* (Philadelphia), June 16, 1911, 11.

50 Klein's cause of death is listed as pulmonary tuberculosis on his death certificate.

51 *The Jewish Exponent* (Philadelphia), June 18, 1909, 4.

52 *The Jewish Exponent* (Philadelphia), June 18, 1909, 11.

53 Ibid.

54 Ibid.

55 Ibid.

Migdal Zophim

The Tower of David at Jerusalem.

INTRODUCTION

The Tower of David

"Soldiers! From the summit of those pyramids thirty centuries look down upon you."

If Napoleon, when he encamped before the pyramids, could inspire his soldiers with the memories of a past with which they had no historic connection whatever, how much more significant for us as children of Israel, must be the *Migdal David*, the Tower of David, whose battlements still stand, after a lapse of thirty centuries, as monitors of that heritage of a living faith and of national glory which our forefathers have bequeathed to us!

Not in Egypt's sandy deserts doth
    David's Tower stand;
Nor imaged beast nor idol form
    is graven on its walls;
On Zion's height it rears aloft o'er
    all the Holy Land;
Its very stones are sacred shrines,
    and temples are its halls.

The Tower remains, a relic of our glorious past, bearing testimony now, as in David's time, that *the Eternal is Israel's Banner; its Redeemer liveth!*

Like the torch on the watch-tower of old, this work is intended as a beacon to the exiles of Israel hastening from the rod of persecution, to point for them the way to a better life in the lands of their dispersion.

Moses Klein

PREFACE

The following pages, dealing with the Jewish Problem of today, were originally intended to form the concluding (third) part of a work, entitled *Migdal Zophim* ("The Watch Tower"), which I had designed publishing in both Hebrew and English; the first part (in Hebrew) being devoted to "Geographical and Historical Sketches of America," and the second part (also in Hebrew) treating of "Jewish Emigration to the United States." The chief object I had in view was to benefit those to whom the Hebrew language alone appealed—principally Israelites who live within the domains of the Czar of Russia, in Galicia, in Roumania, and in countries of the far East. But I have been deterred—temporarily, it is hoped—from fulfilling my cherished wish by the lack of an amount sufficient to guarantee me against losses incidental to the publication of the work.

The Jewish Problem, and agriculture as its solution, have engaged for years my serious thought and constant study. Hence, I have deemed it my sacred duty to bring the subject to the attention of Jewish communities, and especially to those philanthropists who have the Jewish cause and the welfare of Israel at heart. This I have attempted to do, notwithstanding the personal sacrifices and pecuniary losses demanded of me.

The present part of my work is published exclusively in English, and the facts therein given have been collected from the most reliable sources, while many of them are results of my own investigations.

The publication of the two other portions—including a Hebrew translation of the present part—will necessarily depend upon the material encouragement the author will receive.

The numerous illustrations accompanying this book have been especially made by the Levytype Company, of Philadelphia. These will convey to the reader some idea as to the state of the colonies herein described.

Moses Klein

1806 Marshall Street,
Philadelphia, Pa., U. S. A.
5650–1889

The Jewish Problem

I. Jewish Education in Russia

The trouble in Russia during the years 1881–82 sent a thrill of horror throughout the world, but the sympathy was as temporary as it was intense; and the condition of our co-religionists in Russia and Roumania is just as bad today as it was at that time, the only difference being that we now have an opportunity to study how they are situated and to suggest a remedy. But before the remedies are suggested, let us study the condition of our brethren who are imprisoned in the large cities of those countries, for the mere knowledge of their condition and circumstances may suggest a remedy.

"Willst den Dichter du verstehen?
*Musst in Dichter's Lande gehen."**

Barditchov had in 1887 a Jewish population of one hundred thousand souls, among whom were two thousand tradesmen, and these employed eight thousand hands. The employees were very destitute, and lived in filthy basements, which, together with their wretched food, exercised a fatal influence upon the health of their children. The mental condition of these children was then also very low, and there exists

_____

* Would you understand the poet? You need to go to the poet's country.

no reason to believe it has since improved. The whole town supported but one public school, which was divided into two sections, and was attended by 348 pupils, amongst whom there were 150 Jewish children. At the opening of the new school season, among the 51 new scholars, 15 boys and 11 girls were of Jewish birth. Such are the *educational facilities* that the Czar's government offers to his subjects, and the *ungrateful Jew* still complains of his brothers' ill-treatment in the Czar's domain.

It is true that the Jews have two schools of their own, one of which counted in 1886 twenty-five children, and in 1887 one hundred; the other, called *Talmud Torah*, had 315 children, who received instruction in Hebrew from eleven teachers, and in Russian from two. They were also instructed in arithmetic. In the latter school the poor children in winter receive warm clothes and shoes, and some obtain one meal a day. This institution is maintained at an annual cost of 2,800 roubles, obtained by a tax on *Kosher* meat, which article of diet the humble Jews enjoy only on Sabbath. It is true also that about two hundred and fifty teachers keep their own schools or *Chedarim*, and give lessons in private houses from the Hebrew alphabet to the *Gemarah*.

But can all these supply the educational necessities for 100,000 Jews, not to speak about the subjects of other denominations? A government whose policy is constantly directed towards ameliorating the condition of other peoples, specially those of European Turkey and of some Asiatic countries, but that neglects its cardinal duties to its subjects at home, must soon feel the inevitable results of its own weakness.

II. Important Needs Sadly Lacking

The Kishenov correspondent of the Odessa *Listock*, writing to that journal in 1887, remarked: "Kishenov has a Jewish community of over seventy thousand souls, with but one organized school, containing ninety children." To remove this evil, the correspondent suggested that an appeal through the above journal to the Jewish public, which is known to be generous, could soon influence the Jews to devise means for erecting schools. From the income of the Jewish meat tax alone, he maintained, six or seven schools could be established and maintained, without any assistance from the government's funds.

While we agree with the above correspondent that the "Jews are generous"—a quality which has distinguished Israel since the period of the first philanthropist, *Abraham Ha'Ibri*—we cannot endorse his suggestion; for, as we know, the tax on *Kosher* meat is generally appropriated for the maintenance of communal institutions; such as synagogues, ministers, hospitals, homes for the aged, orphan asylums, and cemeteries. The six schools, in addition to the above institutions, could only be sustained by raising the tax on *Kosher* meat, which, even at the present time, is exacted chiefly from the poor, the lamentable condition of whom will be shown in the next paragraph. A small sum of the government's funds, towards which four millions of Jews contribute proportionately more than any other class of the Czar's subjects, ought certainly to be granted for the training and education of young Israel—members of the next Russian generation.

The Kief *Slova*, speaking about Jewish poverty, says: "The city of Slatapoll has a population of two thousand Christians, and twelve thousand Jews. The whole city bears a Jewish appearance. But let not the fact of the industry and commerce being totally in Jewish hands deceive readers into the belief that the Jews are wealthy. On the contrary, poverty and starvation rule there, and the support of the community depends chiefly upon ten wealthy and generous Jewish families."

In consequence of the government's transferring the two cities of Taganrog and Rostow to the Don Cossack district, where the number of Jewish inhabitants is restricted by law, there was an exodus of Jews, whom the law compelled to leave these—their native homes—to the city of Marjupoll. The authorities there, possessing no special law to prevent the settlement of newly-arrived Jews, then adopted an ordinance, according to which a Jew may be permitted to settle there only "by the votes of four hundred native citizens."

You see, intelligent reader, under what circumstances the privilege of voting is granted the Russian people by their *liberal* government!

III. Jews Engaged in Russian Commerce

The following statistics, reproduced from the Kief *Slova*, will throw light on Jewish influence on Russian commerce. The city of Kief contains in all 5,936 taxable houses, worth 63,792,629 roubles, with an annual government and city taxation of 386,118 roubles; 113 of these establishments, worth 4,686,140 roubles, belong to Jews, who pay a tax amounting to 33,902 roubles.

The number of Christian merchants in the Government of Kief is 944, with an annual business transaction amounting to 31,355,700 roubles, and with an income of 1,671,787 roubles. Six hundred and twenty-two of them reside in the city of Kief, and transact business amounting to 22,954,130 roubles, with an annual income of 1,049,700 roubles; while the Jewish merchants of that government number 974, with an annual business of 34,840,960 roubles, and an income of 1,653,607 roubles. Only 113 of these reside at Kief, and transact business amounting to 19,044,340 roubles, which affords a yearly profit of 662,800 roubles.

It is remarkable that while in the city of Kief the Christian merchants number 509 more than the Jewish merchants, in the county of Kief and surrounding villages, however, the latter are 539 in excess of the former; and yet the mobs of 1881 were not directed against the large number of Christian merchants of that city, but only against the few Jews, whose lives and property receive no protection, notwithstanding the taxes they pay and the services which they render to their so-called Russian fatherland.

IV. Training Schools for Jewish Children

During the year 1885 one hundred and thirty-four Jewish schools, embracing 6,932 male and 2,227 female children, with 264 male and 22 female teachers, were maintained by the Government of Russia; while 2,966 schools, with 9,550 male and 5,545 female scholars, instructed by 1,581 male and 140 female teachers, were supported chiefly by the Jewish communities, and some of them by prominent private individuals. Of the numberless *Chedarim* no statistics are given. Suffice it to say, that the government desires to educate 4,000,000 subjects by sending 9,159 of that number to schools; which total would hardly reach the number of scholars attending our public schools in a city of 50,000 inhabitants—a lamentable *Armuth Zeugniss* for Russia, indeed!

People of other nationalities, *enjoying* such *educational facilities*, would, in all probability, know as much of their own language as the species of bird called parrot. But the Jews, in spite of these *facilities*, have furnished St. Petersburg with 500 lawyers, physicians, and journalists. Not less than 300 Jewish students lately applied for admission to the University of Moscow; 60 to that of Charkow; 60 to Kief, and many to the University of Warsaw. Almost all were refused,—because—they were Jews! and for that reason we meet about 320 Russian and Polish Jewish students at the high schools of Paris; over a hundred at the Vienna University; and a similar number at the various high schools of Germany; nay, we find even a "humble Russian Jewish emigrant," Dr. Herman Shapiro, as Professor of Mathematics at the University of Heidelberg; another mathematician and astronomer, Leon Rogusnee, at the French Astronomical Observatory; also Antakolsky, the greatest sculptor; Rubinstein, the world-renowned composer and pianist; Slonimsky, the Russian mathematician; Levanda, the Russian Auerbach; J. L. Gordon, the Hebrew Heine; Frug, the promising Russian Byron, and a host of others. "*Mi Bara Eleh?*"—Who created all these illuminating stars on the dark horizon of Russia? Truly, "*Ha'am haholechim Ba-Choschech, Rau Or Gadol!*"—"*In zu dunkeln und geheimen Grunde ruht, tief verborgen, oft des Menschen Geist.*"

V. Baron de Hirsch's Donation to Galicia

In Galicia, a country in which political barriers were leveled some decades ago, the education of the rising Jewish generation is also in a low state, owing to the prevailing poverty. It is true that statistics usually show more progress among the Jews there, when compared with that of their Polish and Ruthenian neighbors.

There are, for instance, 313 attorneys-at-law in the 13 general districts of Galicia, 107 of whom are Jews. There are also 458 physicians, of whom 120 are Jewish; 1,336 midwives, of whom 479 are Jewish. And if we consider the relation that the 620,000 Jews bear to the nearly 6,000,000 Galician inhabitants, then we can show that the Jews, notwithstanding their humble condition, are by far more advanced in civilization than the main body of the Galician nation.

But the material condition of the masses of Jews, huddled together in the cities, is, by far, lower than that of their Christian fellow-citizens, who are distributed throughout the villages and farming districts.

The statement that Baron de Hirsch intends to erect industrial and educational schools in Galicia, comes, therefore, to us as a ray of hope, that we may live to see many a Krochmal, a Rapoport, and a Letteris; also artisans of every description springing forth from among the Jews of that country.

VI. Baron De Hirsch's Offer to Russia

Baron de Hirsch's offer to donate the colossal sum of 50,000,000 francs to Russia will, if accepted, inaugurate, some say, a new epoch in Jewish history. Others go even further, and predict that the acceptance of that gift means the solution of The Jewish Problem. But there are a number of far-sighted men who, with all their gratitude to the great philanthropist, cannot endorse either of the two opinions expressed above. I, myself, who have just hailed with satisfaction the step taken by Baron de Hirsch toward erecting educational and industrial schools for the Jews of Galicia, cannot favor the Baron's generous proposition to Russia, nor can I anticipate an equally happy result for the Jews of that country, proceeding from the Baron's colossal gift. I am forced to such conclusions, not because the Jews of Galicia are in any way superior to those of Russia, but because the accident of birth has placed the former in a country where they have enjoyed for some decades equal rights with their Polish neighbors; while the Jews of Russia are debarred from many rights, and are continually exiled from place to place.

The theory established in medical science that remedies applied to cure a certain disease of patients residing in one climate may prove injurious to the same diseases when attacking those in other lands, can be well applied to this remedy for the Jews of Galicia and Russia. We have no security whatever that education will obtain for the 50,000 Jewish scholars of Baron de Hirsch's 1,000 schools the right of citizenship, and that of settlement in the interior of Russia, or even the right to exercise their educational advantages for securing their independent livelihood in the Czar's domain.

At the time of the Russian exodus, when thousands of Russian outcasts were sent from Brody to America, I publicly deplored that action of our philanthropists, for they were throwing their money into the sea. In the present instance, although it is individual charity, which no outsider has any right to criticize, still I cannot suppress my views, and I must say freely that, in my humble opinion, the sole benefit these 50,000 scholars will derive from their education will reach them only after their emigration from Russia to other and more civilized countries, in which their intelligence and industry and their knowledge of art and science will probably be recognized, notwithstanding their Semitic origin. But such a small benefit will hardly pay the interest of the 50,000,000 francs invested for it.

Whether I am right or wrong in my opinion, history will tell, and I have no more to say at present on this subject, except to express my deepest regret that our philanthropists seldom consult the prominent Jews of Russia, such as Rev. Dr. Swabacher, of Odessa; Dr. Harkavy, Herr Zederbaum, of *Ha Melitz*; Herr Slonimsky, of *Hazephira*; Herr Fin, of Wilna; Dr. Cantor, of *Hayom*; the editor of *Ha Maggid*, and the Rabbis S. Mohliver and J. Spektor. I am sure that an interchange of views at a conference consisting of these distinguished gentlemen, who live and associate with the afflicted, and whose hearts are with their unfortunate brethren and kinsmen, would be more successful in suggesting the proper remedy for the evil condition of the Jews, than any other suggestion in the world; and I earnestly implore all those engaged, either in individual or public charity, to draw into their counsels men of practical experience who live or have lived among the sufferers themselves, and whose suggestions may, therefore, be of great benefit. The exercise of mercy will then be rightly influenced by the teachings of personal experience; for then, and then only, will the object of charity be fulfilled.—*Ma'ase Zedakah—Shalom!*

VII. The Result

Twenty months elapsed since *The Jewish Exponent* of December 16th, 1887, gave publicity to my views as expressed in the preceding article. Great and noble men, who were conferring in regard to Baron de Hirsch's splendid proposition to the Russian Government touching education—viz., Chevalier Emanuel F. Veneziani and Count Tolstoi—have passed into eternity. The Czar, realizing, probably, the danger to his government of iron rule resulting from the spread of knowledge among the masses, has declined to accept the Baron's colossal gift, and thus THE JEWISH PROBLEM, as far as concerns Russia, still remains unsolved.

The political cloud now hanging over the Balkan provinces may also soon introduce a new problem regarding the state of our brethren who dwell there. Those of our people who still remember the shocking outrages inflicted by the Cossacks on Jewish men and women during the last Russo-Turkish war, should be prepared for another problem, differing, however, very slightly from that of Russia, already presented.

The Jews of Palestine

Introductory Remarks

Without wearying the reader with a study of THE JEWISH PROBLEM, as confined to Europe, let me rather present another picture,—viz., a series of descriptive sketches, written by Herr Joshua Stampfer, of the colony *Petach Tikvah*, near Jaffa, Palestine, which series I have translated from the Hebrew. These give a careful, correct and complete analysis of the state of our brethren who sought refuge in Palestine from persecutions they had to endure under various tyrannical governments in different parts of the world.

I. Jerusalem

Small and insignificant was the number of Jews in Palestine ten years ago, despised and degraded by their Mohammedan and Christian neighbors. Outside the limits of Jerusalem they did not dwell in more than half a dozen places; but the Russian persecutions of 1881–82, followed by similar riots against Jews of other lands, forced many of them to seek homes in Palestine. The Jews are no more as few as they were, for we count now over 36,000 souls, distributed in over twenty different towns and villages. The larger portion are naturally at the Eternal City—viz., Jerusalem, which has a Jewish population of 20,000 souls, 9000 of whom form the *Sephardic*, while 11,000 comprise the *Ashkenazic* portions of the community.

Sephardim

The descendants of the Spanish Jews exiled by Ferdinand and Isabella, who found shelter in Moslem lands, still cling to the old Spanish-Jewish school and liturgy which prevailed during the medieval ages; hence the national pride of our Hispano-Portuguese brethren, who style themselves *Sephardim* (Spaniards). Many of them are natives of Turkey; others are from Morocco, Algiers, Tunis, Tripoli, Egypt and Yemen. These are called *Ma'arabim* (Western) and *Temanim* (from Yemen). All except those from Turkey speak the Arabic language, while still others that come from the Caucasus, Bokhara, Babylon, Persia, and Greece speak the Gruzian, Persian, or Greek tongues. The Hispaniols, being natives of Turkey, and large in numbers, enjoy official distinction from the Turkish Government. Thus the *Chacham-Bashi* or Chief Rabbi is decorated by the Sultan with the *Medjidie* Order. One of the Navon brothers is Deputy State-Attorney; the other is one of three aldermen representing the three religious elements of the city—viz., Jewish, Mohammedan, and Christian.

The *Sephardim* have four synagogues and about eleven minor houses of worship and *Yeshiboth*; also schools for Hebrew teaching, and for Arabic reading and writing. Their benevolent institutions are a hospital, and a home for widows, which are maintained by revenues from houses belonging to that community. The revenues, however, are decreasing. They also maintain a *Tamchuy* (restaurant) wherein the destitute receive two meals each Sabbath.

There is a peculiar contrast between our *Yemen* brethren and those coming from the Caucasus; for while the former are physically undeveloped, and are a type of persecution, the latter are well built and strong; and during all my travels through the four continents of Asia, Africa, Europe, and America, nowhere have I found Hebrews of such splendid physical development, except in Salonica.

The material condition of the Jews from the Caucasus is far happier, too, than that of their *Temanim* (Yemen) brethren; for some of the former, such as the Joseph Kukio family, own real estate worth near one million francs; others control the dry goods business, importing directly from Manchester, England, instead of purchasing from middlemen at Bayreuth, as their Spanish predecessors in this line of trade were apt to do. The *Temanim*, on the other hand, notwithstanding their bright mental faculties and their great familiarity with Talmudical lore, have to earn their bread as common laborers, and by carrying water in the city. During my recent visit to Jerusalem I met two such *Temanim*, water-carriers engaged for a long

time in a very deep conversation on the topic of "Reward and Punishment," each sustaining his views by numberless quotations from *Talmud, Midrash, Zohar*, and many Cabalistic and scientific works. Their spirited discussion, which re-echoed round about, seemed to me as if they had transferred God's air into an infinite library, and the leaves of the whispering plants into book pages, containing all their deep arguments on that important subject.

Such are thy water-carriers, O Jerusalem!

Ashkenazim

The first settlement of *Ashkenazim*, or German Jews, at Jerusalem was in the first decade of the thirteenth century, when a group of several hundred rabbis from the Rhine districts and England made a pilgrimage to Palestine, under the leadership of Rabbi Jehudah Ha-Chasid, who purchased a considerable amount of property at Jerusalem, still bearing the name *Chorbath Rabbi Jehudah Ha-Chasid* (Ruins of Rabbi Jehudah the Pious). With the decline of that Jewish settlement, the above property became a part of the Turkish Government's estates, until certain old documents were recovered and presented by the late Sir Moses Montefiore to the Supreme Court of the Sultan at Constantinople. The claim was decided in favor of the *Ashkenazim*, who, soon after the granting of the *firman* (permit), erected the magnificent synagogue Beth Jakob, which is one of the finest structures in Palestine, and the globe of which, made of massive stone, is surpassed by only two of its kind in Europe.

This *Ashkenazic* community, numbering eleven thousand souls, is composed of co-religionists from Russia, Poland, Galicia, Roumania, Hungary, Germany and Holland, and is again subdivided into two distinct bodies called *Parushim* and *Chasidim*. Lithuanian, Hungarian, German and Holland Jews constitute the former division—*Parushim*; while those coming from Southern Russia, Poland, Galicia and Roumania form the latter division—*Chasidim*.

Parushim

The *Parushim* (Pharisees) of today have as little connection with the historic sect of the same name as have the *Sephardim* Hispaniols with the *Chasidim* of Moldavia, who style themselves *Sephardim*. The name is simply derived from that of Rabbi Israel Parush, author of the *Peath-Hashulchan*, who quitted the city of Safed on account of the earthquake which occurred there in the fourth decade of the present century. He re-established the remnant of the old *Ashkenazic* community of Jerusalem, which was then almost out of existence.

Some years later, the newly revived *Ashkenazic* community, finding itself endangered by an increase of the *Chasidim*, sought refuge for its party by adopting the name *Parushim*, in honor of its regenerator, Rabbi Israel Parush, who succeeded in rekindling the extinguishing light of the old *Ashkenazic* Jews in Jerusalem.

The *Parushim* form both in number and influence the most prominent part of the *Ashkenazic* community. Their central synagogue, Beth Jakob, in the *Chorbath Rabbi Jehudah Ha-Chasid*, has already been referred to. In addition to this imposing structure, they have about thirty minor synagogues and *Bate-Midrashoth*. The *Parushim* maintain schools attended by a large number of pupils; a hospital containing twenty-four beds, wherein medical advice and medicine are furnished free to outside patients; a free loan office for the poor; a Home for Orphans; a *Hachnasat Orechim* (Pilgrims' Home), and a Home for the Aged.

Chasidim

This community was established at Jerusalem thirty years ago, and has one large synagogue called Tifereth Israel, and fifteen minor houses of worship and learning. This sect—*Chasidim*—owes its origin to Rabbi Israel Ba'al Shem Tob, of Mezibeth, Russian Poland, who founded it on Cabalistic teachings.

General Benevolent Institutions

Of the 20 general benevolent institutions, we will mention only those of *Ezrat Nidachim* (Help to the Outcast), *Nachlat Jisrael* (for colonization), and *Chesed L'Jisrael* (for lending money to the poor without interest). There are also several institutions erected by individuals, such as twenty houses for the poor by R. David Reis, of Janova, Poland, and others.

Benevolent Institutions Established by Co-religionists from Abroad

The new hospital erected and enlarged by the Rothschild family contains room for fifty patients. Dr. I. Gregory d'Arbella is its superintendent.

A school for girls, containing about two hundred and fifty scholars, is maintained by the Rothschilds.

The industrial and educational school of the *Alliance Israelite Universelle*, with about two hundred scholars, who make great progress in art and general education under the supervision of M. Nissim Bechar, has already been referred to.

The school for girls established by Herr Herz von Lemel, of Vienna, through the influence of Ludwig August Frankl, has lately been united with the orphan asylum which was established by Herr M. G. Levy, of Berlin, and which has received since additional support of 40,000 marks from a Jewish lady of Frankfort, and 10,000 marks from Mr. Jacob H. Schiff, of New York. Thirty-six orphans are sheltered in that institution, and about seventy other children receive instruction under its roof from the superintendent, Dr. W. Herzberg.

Seventy-three houses were erected by German and Hungarian Jews and given to the destitute free of rent. They are under the direction of Rev. Dr. Ezriel Hildesheimer, of Berlin.

Thirty-four houses, bearing the name *Mishkenoth Shaananim*, were erected for the poor by the late Mr. Judah Touro, of New Orleans; and forty other houses were established for the *Temanim* by Jerusalem and English co-religionists.

Trades, Building Societies and Artisans

The domestic trade of Jerusalem and Palestine is in the hands of the *Sephardim*, while the export and import trade, which was started by *Ashkenazim*, is still carried on by members of that community.

Jewish building associations are conducted by the *Ashkenazim*. These associations, by erecting more than one thousand dwelling houses in the vicinity of Jerusalem, have contributed much toward the growth of the city, as well as toward the health of its population. This enterprise on the part of the societies, *Meah Shearim, Eben Jisrael, Beth Jakob, Mishkenoth Jisrael, Beth Jisrael, Beth Joseph* and *Sucath Shalom*, is the best refutation of the charge of "idleness" usually brought against Jews of Palestine by their own brethren. Show me, unprejudiced reader, any city of the world where a thousand houses have been constructed—not merely by Jewish capital, but by Jewish carpenters and laborers—as are seen here in the neighborhood of Jerusalem, built during the last fourteen years. If you know of any such place erected solely by Jewish means and Jewish labor, please name it, and earn my thanks. But you are silent, dear brother, and still you have seldom a word in defense of your "idle" co-religionists of Jerusalem. How do you account for this?

In fact, the supply of Jewish artisans of every description exceeds four times, at least, the demands of Jerusalem and Palestine. It was for this very reason that Superintendent Bechar, of the industrial and educational school at Jerusalem, received orders to store up and not to sell articles manufactured by his pupils, in order to avoid their competition with similar goods manufactured by old Jewish artisans of Jerusalem who have to support large families.

Publications

Four Hebrew publications are issued at Jerusalem—viz., *Chabazelet*, by J. Frumkin; *Hazebi*, by Ben Jehudah—weekly papers devoted to Jewish and secular events; *Hamisderonah*, a monthly, by M. Hirschensohn, devoted to the investigation of rabbinical lore; and *Jerushulajim*, by A. M. Lunz—an annual, conveying a vast amount of information concerning Judea of antiquity, and Palestine of today.

Prominent Hebrew periodicals of Europe, such as *Hamagid* of Lyck, *Der Israelit* of Mainz, *The Jewish Chronicle* of London, *Hameliz* of St. Petersburg, and *Hazephirah* of Warsaw, are represented at Jerusalem by their special correspondents. An excellent annual calendar is also published here by the renowned scholar, M. Adelman, which deserves to be in every Jewish home.

Each of the above periodicals appeals to a different reading circle; and the careful observer must admit that they are in every sense civilizing agents, not alone in Palestine, but throughout the Oriental and European-Jewish world.

II. Hebron

Five hundred *Ashkenazim* and an equal number of *Sephardim* form the Jewish community of Hebron. There are six synagogues; three belonging to the former class and three to the latter. The society for granting loans to poor people without interest named *Chonen Umalveh* is maintained by the *Sephardim*, and the *Gemilut Chesed* (Benevolent Institution) is maintained by the *Ashkenazim*.

Followers of the renowned Rabbi Schneier Salman, of Lodi, author of the work תניא, were the pioneers of the present *Ashkenazic* community, which still adheres to the principles laid down by him. They are usually known by the letters ד״בח, which signify *Chochmah, Binah, Da'ath* (Wisdom, Understanding, Knowledge).

Trade in products of the soil is their chief occupation. They are the link combining labor and capital, for they purchase from the peasants of the villages that lie between Hebron and Gaza (a distance of thirty-six hours' journey) the fruit of their toil, and place it in the markets. But there are also among them some money-lenders.

This place is frequently visited by multitudes of co-religionists, who make a pilgrimage to the *Me'arat Hamachpelah* (Cave of Machpelah) to shed tears at the sepulchres of our nation's patriarchs. The attitude of the Hebron Jehudim toward all such crowds of pilgrims is very praiseworthy. Their free and liberal hospitality has proven them worthy successors of Abraham, our father.

III. Tiberias and Its Neighborhood

Nowhere in all my travels was I so deeply impressed with natural scenery as I was when in the vicinity of Tiberias for the first time. It was in the middle of a bright summer night that our caravan reached the summit of Mount Carmel. The heavens above us, pure as crystal, illuminated with a galaxy of stars the procession of the Queen of Night. The sight surpassed in its majestic splendor any similar illumination I had seen. This natural drama gained additional beauty when our eyes were directed toward the level of Gennesaret, which, by reflecting in its silver mirror the magnitude of the sky-illuminated bodies, appeared to us as another part of the heavenly globe, and we thought ourselves sailing between two infinite firmaments. It must have been by such a scene, and in such a region, that the "sweet singer of Israel" announced on his harp: "The heavens declare the glory of God, and the firmament showeth His handiwork." It must have been this holy spot that filled the heart of *Ben Amoz* with the deepest emotion when he awakened Israel by his inspiring proclamation: *Seu marom 'Enechem Uru mi Bara Eleh!*—"Lift up your eyes toward the heaven and see who created these!" Even Tancred must have received his inspiration here.

Daylight, too, sheds glory upon that region; for oleander trees from thirty to forty feet in height, surrounded by flowers, myrtle, and the fruit of *Genezer*, which adorn the shores of that sweet sea; the line of the Jordan River, crossing along the Gennesaret like two blue threads until it empties into the Dead Sea; the hot mineral springs coming forth from the foot of the mountains at a distance of forty feet from the seashore; the castle erected by Ibrahim Pasha on one of these twelve mineral springs—all these circumstances give to that district the appearance of the Garden of Eden.

Tiberias is noted as the burial-place of Rabbi Jochanan Ben Zakai, Rabbi Akiba, and several other *Tenaim* and *Emoraim*, as well as of Maimonides. It is, therefore, no wonder that Jewish philanthropists have been many times ready to save this city from decay. Don Joseph Nassi, of Naxos, rebuilt it once, and Abulafia of Smyrna rebuilt it a second time. It stood the siege of the Governor of Damascus, which was strenuously resisted by the Jews, until the Governor died at the gate of that city, and the soldiers left the camp on the day of *Hosha'anah Rabbah*. In memory of this event, they read annually the *Megilath Tiberje*.

Fifteen hundred and sixty *Ashkenazim* and fourteen hundred and forty *Sephardim* form the Jewish community of Tiberias, with ten houses of worship for the former and six for the latter.

Near the sepulchre of Rabbi Meir, *Ba'al Nes*, the Jews established a magnificent pilgrim-house, and a house of worship for co-religionists suffering from rheumatism who seek a cure at the hot springs of Tiberias. The Society *Bikur Cholim* was instituted to render assistance to sick co-religionists from every part of the country until their health is restored. The Jews of this city are engaged in domestic trades. They all live in undisturbed harmony together; and this is their actual strength; for "Israel's blessing," says the Talmud, "depends on *Shalom*."

The Libavich Farm

On the Jordan shore, near Tiberias, there extends a huge plot of fertile ground of about one thousand *dunem* (three *dunem* comprise an American acre), belonging to an American citizen, Mr. Jacob Libavich. The place is called in Arabic "Bridge of Jacob's Daughters."

The Village of Chitin

This village is situated on an elevated hill bordering the Sea of Gennesaret, at a distance of two hours' journey from Tiberias. The numerous gardens and orchards found here are sheltered from the burning sun by a high mountain. The place is greatly in want of skillful gardeners. Three of the gardens belong to Rev. A. Wachs of Kalisch, Poland, who bought them for the cultivation of *Ethrogim.*[*]

---

[*] It is with the deepest regret that we announce the recent demise of that distinguished rabbi in Israel. May his soul rest in peace!—M. K.

The Village of Pakien

At a distance of five hours' journey from Tiberias there is situated Pakien, which is mentioned in the Talmud. It has a Jewish population of about thirty farming families, who, in dress, habits, and language, are like the Arabic Mohammedans. They are also field owners like the other farmers, but are very poor, and are occasionally even oppressed by the alderman of the village. The Jews of Tiberias improve from time to time the lamentable condition of these, their brethren, by advancing them money without interest on their crops. These families are strict observers of the Mosaic Law, and they keep a *Shochet* from Tiberias.

The Village of Shapurem

Two hours' journey from Pakien the village of *Shapurem*, or *Shaf-Amer* (in Arabic), is situated. There are about forty Jewish families of the ancient Palestine stock, as described above. Their land contains many olive trees, and their condition is a little better than that of the Jewish inhabitants of Pakien.

IV. Safed

Safed is situated on a high mountain that still bears on its top ruins of the fort of Jotapata, which fell into the hands of the Romans after a long and desperate defense by Flavius Josephus. About forty years ago the city was visited by a tremendous earthquake, and the ruins caused by it have been only partially removed, through the neglect of both the government and the community. The good health of its inhabitants, which is superior to that prevailing in Jerusalem, is attributed chiefly to the excellent climate.

Four thousand eight hundred and fifty souls comprise the *Ashkenazic* congregation of that city, and thirteen hundred constitute the *Sephardic*. The former has, in addition to the great synagogue (which is supposed to be the synagogue of Rabbi Isaac Luria, the expounder of the *Cabalah*), about thirty minor houses of worship, and the latter has only five.

There are two hundred and twenty-two artisans engaged in forty-seven trades, and two hundred and sixty-one merchants engaged in eight different industries. There are four benevolent institutions. One is a *Hekdesh* exclusively for Russians and Roumanians, and a second Home exclusively for the Galician poor. The Roumanians maintain a school—*Talmud Torah*—containing forty-five pupils, with four teachers. Lately the combined communities instituted a United Relief Association, called *Jeshu'at Jisrael*, for the purpose of educating children, curing the sick, and caring for aged co-religionists.

But this organization is still in its infancy, and whether it will ever pass that stage and become an elevating factor in the deplorable state of the *Chasidaic* community is a question of time. The state of affairs prevailing there shows no progress whatsoever, even as a result of the above new organization, and none will be made unless the undertaking will be encouraged by co-religionists from abroad. To the credit of the young generation, be it stated here that a large number of young men of the *Ashkenazic* community are struggling to obtain government land, which they would cultivate; but alas! they are too poor, and without *bagshish* (bribery) you can accomplish little with Turkish authorities. How long Herr S. Shulman, with his brave companions, will have to struggle to reach their noble aim, Heaven knows!

M. Jacob Nebo is the agent of the French Consul at Safed, and M. Gerson Nebo represents the Consul of Persia. Both belong to the *Sephardic* community.

The Village of Meron

At a distance of two hours' journey from Safed lies Kefar-Meron, known as the burial-place of Rabbi Shimeon Ben Jochai and of several other distinguished authors of the *Talmud*. The fields of four thousand *dunem* surrounding that place belong to M. Isaac Eba, of Safed. M. Elias Farber, however, recently bought one thousand *dunem* of the former, and has settled himself in agricultural life among the Arabian farmers.

This undertaking of Herr Farber, as well as the young men's struggle to become agriculturists, is the only good impression we take with us from the city of Safed.

V. Haifa

Voyagers on the Austrian steamers, when landing at the port of Haifa, can hardly believe that they find themselves far off from the European continent; for not only do they find here two fine hotels with modern conveniences, but the greetings of the Templars (a religious sect who emigrated from Wurtemberg, and whose principal belief consists in regenerating the holy soil of Palestine); the beautiful streets shaded by rows of graceful trees; the fine houses surrounded by gardens and vineyards—all might easily cause them to think that they are at some spot along the Rhine or Danube districts.

At the time the Templars settled there (about twenty-four years ago), some of our *Sephardic* co-religionists of the Turkish metropolis, becoming tired of the annoyances to which they were subjected in Constantinople, and of the tendencies of materialism, selected Haifa as their place of residence. They, together with the Roumanian-Jewish immigrants, number today nine hundred souls, and have two synagogues and two schools—one established by the *Alliance Israelite Universelle*, and the other by the Roumanians. They are engaged in various trades.

Some are money-lenders. What a poor liveli-hood, when compared with the prosperous lives of their farming neighbors—the Templars!

VI. Gaza

Gaza is situated on two hills, and the val-ley between divides the city into two sections. Its climate is salubrious, and its twenty-four thousand inhabitants are physically very strong. Besides the Mohammedans, there are only about eighty Christian families, with two churches, and one hundred and twenty Jews, who worship in a private house. In the street called *Chart al Jehud* (Jewish street) the Catholic Jesuits have erected a church on the site of an ancient synagogue. One of the marble pillars of that synagogue, containing the following inscription in Hebrew: *Hamalach hagoel Othi mikol ra', hu Jezakeni la'alot L'Jerushalayim* ("The angel that saved me from all evil may aid me in going up to Jerusalem"), now adorns the Jesuitic church. Gaza is a large commercial centre, owing to the numberless caravans that go and come from Palestine to Egypt, and it only needs enterprising Jews to open therein an export and import trade with Europe. The city is only three-quarters of an hour's distance from the seashore, and the construction of a road and port would be a great material advantage.

VII. Shechem

Shechem is as old as our race; for it was visited by our father, Abraham. The general assembly of all Israel to receive the last instruc-tion from Joshua was held here. It is also the burial-place of Joseph. At the time of Titus, the Roman general and afterward emperor, the ruins were rebuilt by the Romans. Shechem has since been called Naplouse (Nablus in Arabic*). In 1120, Baldwin II, Emperor of Constanti-nople, summoned to this city all the princes to attend a conference.

Shechem is situated in a valley which sepa-rates Mount Gerizim from Mount 'Ebal. The foot of Mount Gerizim is covered with houses, sur-rounded by gardens and vineyards. The volumes of water that flow from fountains irrigate gardens and the soil, and pass through channels to without the city, where they empty into a stream, which pursues its course to the river Jordan.

Shechem, being situated at the junction of several roads which lead to Jerusalem, Jaffa, Salt (principal city of the Jordan district), Tiberias and Damascus, could easily be made a com-mercial centre; but the "curse of Mount 'Ebal" seems to have more effect on its lazy inhabitants than the "blessing of Mount Gerizim." Its pop-ulation of about fourteen thousand inhabitants,

_____

* That Nablus is Shechem is evident from the *Midrash Rabba*, on Numbers, chapter xxiii.

representing Mohammedans, Christians, and Jews, are all, like their Samaritan neighbors, at a standstill in everything that concerns progress. The Jewish community here, of both *Sephardim* and *Ashkenazim*, comprises only one hundred and twenty souls, and the Samaritans number one hundred and sixty members.

The Samaritans are descendants of captives whom the Assyrian conqueror, Sennacherib, brought from the isle of Chuta to settle in desolated cities of *Shomeron*, after he had overthrown the kingdom of Israel, and carried away its people into exile. Here they adopted some principles of Israel's faith, such as the existence of God, the prophecy and laws of Moses, which they practiced in common with their inherited idolatry. "They feared the Lord, and worshiped their gods" (Kings ii. 17). In course of time their belief underwent various changes, and their dogmas of today are constructed from several religions, and from Eastern philosophical speculations. They reject the belief in all the prophets after Joshua; more so do they reject Jewish traditions; they deny the sanctity of Jerusalem and its Temple, but offer their sacrifices on Mount Gerizim, with peculiar ceremonies, a so-called High Priest officiating. Near their residences, in the southwestern portion of the city, stands their house of worship, which is never entered by any one unless the shoes are taken off. Their prayers are composed of praises, songs, history of the Creation, a selection of verses, chapter of *Vehaja Im Shamoa*, and of supplications. Their books consist of the Five Books of Moses (with a Samaritan translation), a Book of Joshua (different, however, from that universally accepted), and several other writings, chiefly commentaries on the Law of Moses. They are in possession of an ancient Scroll of the Law, written on parchment, which, according to their claim, has the peculiarity not only of having been indited by Abishua' ben Pinechas, grandson of Eleazar, son of Aaron, the first High Priest, but that of exceeding in age (according to universal reckoning) the creation of the world by about 4770 years! But scholars—and experts at that—have shown that this writing dates back not more than seventeen or eighteen hundred years. The Samaritans observe many of the Jewish ceremonies, such as circumcision, and *Shechitah*. They keep the Sabbath. Of their festivals, three are celebrated with numerous sacrifices, offered by their High Priest on an altar on Mount Gerizim.

The object of our writing does not permit us to dwell any longer on that peculiar sect. We therefore proceed on our journey.

VIII. Akka and Sidon

Akka has one hundred and fifty *Sephardim*.

In Sidon there are one hundred and fifty families, numbering eight hundred *Sephardim*.

The Jews here are engaged in different trades. M. M. Levy is a banker and M. Jacob Pakii is a prominent silk merchant.

IX. Jaffa

Twenty years ago, when I first visited this fortified city, it looked like a lifeless *pusta* of Hungary. There was nothing in its poverty-stricken population, or in its miserable streets, wretched buildings and filthy surroundings, that would justify the least hope for the regeneration, during the present century, of that ancient city. But what are human calculations in the presence of Providence's activity? And what is our limited shortsightedness against civilization's progress? Two wealthy *Sephardic* co-religionists, Sir Mimon Emiel and Sir Ahran Majel, were instrumental in bringing about a state of progress by purchasing the largest portion of the fortification. Many large streets have been added to the city. With the fragments of the destroyed wall, new and beautiful buildings were erected. This improvement of the city soon attracted a large, enterprising population, and it has now become a commercial centre and seaport that has a great future before it. There are also other factors that have contributed much to the material growth of Jaffa, and these will be described when we treat of the colonies.

One thousand souls comprise the *Sephardic* community, and there are five hundred of the *Ashkenazim*. The *Sephardim* own three synagogues, while the *Ashkenazim* worship in private houses. The latter have a *Talmud Torah* school containing thirty-five pupils. There are many artisans among the people; also a number of money-lenders; five hotel-keepers; four import and export brokers, and four exchanges. Sir Isaac Amzalag is Consul for Great Britain; his son, Sir Joseph Amzalag, is Consul for Portugal; and Joseph Amojal Bey is Consul for Persia.

With Jaffa we have completed our journeys in the old Jewish communities of Palestine. We will now return to Jerusalem for recreation.

X. Recreation

This was the concluding word of our last chapter, after we had completed our journey in several ancient cities of Palestine. Indeed, few are the men engaged in any pursuit of life who do not long for rest, or who should ignore the importance of recreation; those who know no limits to work and take no rest from labor are the enemies of their callings; for, by undermining their physical and mental faculties through unceasing labor, they become unfit to work and are responsible to God, the Author of work and rest, and to His executive power, Nature. Recreation does not signify disturbance of work or negligence of duty; on the contrary, by turning ourselves away for some time from our daily vocations, to imbibe fresh air at summer resorts, or to find enjoyment in social circles, we gain strength which enables us to pursue our line of duty with redoubled vigor.

We have returned safely to Jerusalem. But are we now enjoying the desired recreation? Or does our brethren's condition at Jerusalem permit us to seek pleasure or even to look for rest for ourselves? Am I better, nobler, more refined, than my pious co-religionists who stand yonder by the *Cothel-Ma'arabi* (Western Wall), praying to God to grant peace to scattered Israel in every clime, rest to the wandering Jew, and regeneration to Judea and Jerusalem? Am I more deserving of recreation than the thousands of my brethren who contributed incalculably by their untiring work toward the advance of Jerusalem, as we have shown? Let us not forget, my friends, that with all the progress of Jerusalem in recent years, the fact cannot be denied that a very large number of persecuted co-religionists from Russia, Roumania, Morocco, Arabia, Babylon, and other places, have been added to its Jewish population; and these our brethren, who make Jerusalem a universal exhibition of persecuted Israel from all over the globe, have, by their zeal for work, increased competition among Jewish laborers to such an extent that the wages for a day's work paid to an artisan or laborer average from a half franc to one and a half francs (from ten to thirty cents in American money) per day, and with these earnings fathers have to sustain families, sometimes numbering eight or ten souls. Can anybody seek recreation under such circumstances?

Even at such starving wages, the prospects of Jewish artisans, outside of the cities of Jerusalem, Jaffa, and Haifa, which contain European inhabitants, are poor indeed. The Arabs are *producers* and not *consumers*; bread and herbs form their diet for the whole year, while meat and rice are enjoyed by them only during their two annual festivals, which are known as *Kurban-Byram* (Wedding) and *Ramazan* (Covenant of Abraham). Wine and alcohol are excluded from these festivals, for the Arabs are strict prohibitionists. These combined circumstances, and not idleness, of which they are falsely accused, are the actual causes for the prevailing poverty among Palestinian co-religionists. The *Chalukah*, which is somewhat on the same plan as that adopted by the United Hebrew Charities in America, should therefore not be withheld from the poor of Jerusalem and Palestine, until it will be supplanted by aid in the way of agricultural settlements, which alone can solve THE JEWISH PROBLEM and secure to the "Wandering Jew" the promised recreation. *Habaim Jashresh Jaakob! Jaziz Uparach Jisrael, Umaleu Pene Tebel Tenubah!* "The time will come when Jacob will take root, Israel shall blossom and bud, and fill the face of the world with fruit!"

XI. General Table of the Jewish Population of Palestine Cities and Farming Settlements

Ancient Cities	Jewish Population
Jerusalem	20,000
Hebron	1,000
Tiberias	3,000
Safed	6,150
Haifa	900
Schem	120
Gazza	120
Akka	150
Sidon	800
Jaffa	1,500

New Farming Settlements

Petach Tikvah	412
Jehud	50
Rishon L'Zion	190
Nachelat Reuben	30
Mazkereth-Bat-Jah	185
Gederah	87
Zichron Ja'acob	515
Rosh Pinah	178
Jesod Hama'ala	65
Kostina	50
Total	35,502

Ancient Colonies	Jewish Families
Pakien, about	30
Shapurem, about	40
Total	70

Adding to the above number, the pupils at the agricultural school of *Mickve Jisrael*,* near Jaffa, and the many families scattered in other places and farming settlements, I feel justified in my statement "that we count now over 36,000 souls."

In view of Mr. Stampfer's having referred to the agricultural school, *Mickve Jisrael*, near Jaffa, the following excerpt from a paper, written by me, and describing the workings of the *Alliance Israelite Universelle*, will convey some information about the founding of the above school, and what it has accomplished. The full paper was published by *The Jewish Exponent*, of Philadelphia, in its issue of February 24th, 1888.

---

* This school, notwithstanding unjust criticism, which has been passed upon it, has been the real means of promoting agriculture among modern Jews.

Agriculture as a Solution

The Mickve-Jisrael Agricultural School

The late Charles Netter visited, in August, 1868, the city of Jerusalem. After his return to Paris, he suggested to the Central Committee of the *Alliance* that the many applications for work on farms, which he had received from our starving brethren of Jerusalem, convinced him of their willingness to till the ground; but, since the mere assertion of their willingness was no evidence that they would become practical farmers, he therefore thought that an agricultural school for training young Palestinians in farming for a period not exceeding three years was everything that was needed; for such pupils might be the best mediums for extending practical farming amongst all the Jews under the Sultan's government.

He also suggested the following twelve rules for the government of such a school: 1st. Instruction in agriculture shall be given by an experienced and competent farmer, and secular knowledge by another teacher. 2d. The number of pupils admitted to the school shall be ten annually. 3d. The training shall last three years, and after the third year, no less than thirty shall be at the school. 4th. The pupils shall receive food and clothing. 5th. The applicant for admission must not be under the age of thirteen years, nor more than sixteen. He must be physically healthy, and acquainted with Hebrew, elementary studies, arithmetic, Arabic, and with one European language. Preference shall be given to pupils educated at the *Alliance* schools. 6th. The benefits of the school shall be given to applicants irrespective of creed or religion; but their number shall not exceed those who, in addition to their education, are supplied at the school with the necessaries of life. 7th. Any Jewish community of any country shall be entitled to send pupils to that school, with the understanding that it will bear all the expenses which the school will make on such a pupil. 8th. The scholars will have to pass an examination annually, and after the third examination they shall receive a certificate according to their merits. 9th. After the second year, a plot of ground shall be purchased sufficient to maintain ten families of farmers. This ground shall again be sold to such Hebrew families who will take upon themselves the care of the young farmers who will leave the school. Should such Hebrew buyers, or hirers, not be found, then the soil shall be cultivated by the students of the school, with the aid and supervision of the *Alliance*, and they shall have their proper share of all the products. 10th. The Superintendents shall search among our people for men capable and willing to work on farms; they shall also employ on the farm such Israelites as have no work; and they shall lend their support by furnishing trained farmers to those co-religionists who are engaged on farms of their own. 11th. The foundation and supervision of the establishment shall be in the hands of the Director, who represents the Orient at the Central Committee of the *Alliance*. 12th. An account of the educational and material advancement of the establishment shall be presented annually to the Central Committee for publication. The funds necessary for the investment shall be raised from annual subscriptions, donations, and contributions; while the products of the soil, and the income from selling or renting out portions of the land, shall be invested again in the increase of the *Alliance* property.

This plan, with all its details, was approved and adopted unanimously by the Central Committee, which devoted 100,000 francs for its realization; and M. Charles Netter was entrusted with the erection of the school. At the general meeting of the *Alliance Israelite Universelle*, held on January 14th, 1869, the president, M. Adolphe Cremieux, announced the adoption of M. Charles Netter's plan by the Central Committee, in glowing oratory, from which we translate the following:

"Religious freedom raises its voice throughout lands. It subdues its enemies everywhere, and comes forth victorious. With the fulfillment of this, our ardent desire, we concluded to establish an agricultural school for Jewish youth in the land whence we were brought out, on the spot which was, in ancient times, blessed with prosperity, and is yet an asylum for some of Jacob's children, and a magnetic centre of Israel's eye and heart. A Friday afternoon at the *Kothel Maarabi* (Western Wall of the Temple) will fill your heart with the deepest emotion at the touching scene of Jews shedding tears at the wall, all which is left of their Holy Sanctuary, like our weeping ancestors by the rivers of Babel. Here you will soon convince yourself that that land is still recognized by our brethren to be God's Chosen Land. It is for that reason that we venture to recommend the vicinity of Jaffa. The cultivation of its land may be difficult, but the soil is very fertile, and promises to tillers a good return for the selection of the school. This holy spot will inspire our brethren of the present age with love for agriculture, the pursuit of our ancestors, who were a people devoted to agriculture and sheep-raising. Israel has always recognized God's favor towards the tillers of the ground. But the land, The Eternal saith, cannot be sold; it must be returned at the Jubilee. This soil was once a beautiful spot, of fruitful fields, crowned with mountains of pines and vines, and pouring forth streams of milk and honey. The ground in the vicinity of Jaffa is still fruitful, and yields tenfold. Its products are sent to the Egyptian markets. The road on which Moses and Israel were journeying forty years, can now be made in a few hours. A steamship laden with Palestinian products at the port of

Jaffa in the morning, anchors in the evening at the ports of Suez, or Ismaila. The voyage from Palestine to Egypt is now made in eight hours. The pupils of an agricultural school, cherishing good hopes for their labor, will continue to work diligently on farms, and thus after a few years a new road will be opened to Israelites, from all parts, in the Land of Promise. From here (Jaffa) the pilgrims will proceed to Jerusalem, which is not very far from the former place, and behold New Jerusalem appearing in its brilliant attire! It is true that at the beginning it will be a limited and narrow sanctuary; still, even this will in future wipe away the tears from Israel's eyes so often shed on the stones of the Holy Temple, and will induce Israel to pray to the Heavenly Father, and then re-establish the sanctuary on the mountain of Zion, in honor of The Eternal God, like that of ancient times. Israel will then come and rejoice at the feasts and solemnize the holy festivals. Our successors will see The Great Day which the poet of fire has sublimely described.

> The trumpet's peal both loud and clear
> From Zion's heights shall ring,
> The Temple's walls with flowers decked
> Salvation all shall bring.
> Jerusalem's gates shall open wide
> To welcome Israel's host,
> The altars of the living God
> First fruits again shall boast,
> Of Israel's faith, belief and hope
> In God, their rock and trust.

An eloquent appeal was issued on March 26th, 1869, by the Central Committee, and M. Netter, who was designated to take charge of the erection of the school at Jaffa, and its administration, exercised great zeal and labor for over a year, until he obtained from the Sultan of Turkey a *firman* for the Government soil, near Jaffa, granted to the *Alliance Israelite Universelle* to be used for the erection of an agricultural school under certain conditions. On this soil the agricultural school called *Mickve Jisrael* was established.

That the experience of twenty years has not realized M. Netter's anticipated hopes, is due to the following facts: 1st. To find among the Jewish youth of Palestine boys possessing all the qualifications as required in Article 5 of M. Netter's plan was an utter impossibility at that time. 2d. The wisdom of M. Netter himself was suggested in Article 11 of his plan, "that the administration of the school must be in the hands of such a member of the Central Committee as represents the Oriental Jewish element." Had this been complied with, less distrust and more confidence in the school would have been displayed among leaders of the Palestinian Jewish communities, whose narrow-mindedness, in those days, stigmatized every new improvement coming from German or French sources as un-Jewish; while the same ideas, if they had emanated from among themselves, would probably have been received with appreciation. 3d. The time in which the *Chalukah* flourished was not suitable for this object. Any father who would dare to send his children to the agricultural school instead of to the *Cheder*, would soon be deprived of his share of the *Chalukah*. For these three reasons, the Directors were obliged to take children from any source, which action, in some cases, did not reflect credit on themselves and the school.

But, *En lach dabor she'en lo sha'ah*—"There is not a thing in existence that has not its time." The life-long dream of Sir Moses Montefiore (to see Eastern Jews engaged in farming), the excellent plan of Charles Netter, the eloquent address of Adolphe Cremieux, and the 100,000 francs donated by M. Goldschmidt towards maintaining the above agricultural school, have finally resulted in the establishment of thirteen agricultural settlements, embracing about three thousand Jewish souls. These colonies, as we will presently show, are all on the road to success, and being established both in Palestine and in America, they point to the fulfillment of the ancient prophecy: *Asidah Eretz Jisrael Shetitpashot bechol Ha-Aratzoth*—"The Land of Israel (Jewish farms) will be extended in all countries."

Jewish Colonization

Like many great movements, Jewish colonization owes its cause to a phenomenon of history. The French Revolution freed that country from despotism; the American Civil War raised millions of slaves from the condition of chattel, and rendered them independent citizens; and so was modern Jewish colonization brought about by the German, Russian, and Hungarian persecutions, which burst forth from the volcano of anti-Semitism, casting thousands of Israelites to the Eastern and Western diasporas.

Colonization was their guiding star to the East, and Mammon to the West. And these different aims developed a constant struggle between Hebrew journalists and philanthropists. The former were in favor of colonization in Palestine; the latter, of emigration to America.

Hard was the task of the advocates of the Palestine colonization scheme; great were the obstacles and severe were the attacks they had to endure from their opponents, who endeavored to direct the stream of emigration solely to America, where peddling and tailoring became the only occupations of the immigrants.

But, being men of resolution, and knowing that colonization would be the only safety for the future of Israel and of Judaism, these journalists fought like brave soldiers; and some of them, like the editors of *Hamagid* and

Haschachar, died like heroes, while engaged in the holy battle for Israel's true emancipation. They have gone; but their views are now realized in the following practical colonies, which are daily advancing,—to the honor and prosperity of our people.

In this table I refer only to the colonies started, or revived, since the persecution of 1881–1882; while those started before that time such as the Agricultural School *Mickve Israel*, and Rabbi Wachs's and Rabbi Liboviz's large properties—which look as fair as Paradise—are omitted.

The impulse that permeates most of these colonies is that given by that noble and practical Jewish philanthropist, Baron Edmund de Rothschild, who, by encouraging agriculture on business principles, has contributed incalculably toward the elevation of Israel. It is largely through his liberality that history will announce to the world its verdict in favor of Jewish colonization. This country, too, had a few far-seeing men, whose eyes were not dazzled by commercial glitter, and who with an ardent desire and burning love strove to encourage Jewish colonization in America. Foremost among them was the lamented Michael Heilprin, to whom some American-Jewish colonies owe their existence.

As to the question whether Jews will adopt colonization when peddling and tailoring are open before them, I would merely mention the *Alliance* Colony at Vineland.

Table of Jewish Colonies in Palestine

Names of Jewish Colonies in Palestine	Their size in dunems	Families	Souls	Houses	Stables	Cattle	Wagons	Vines	Olive, fig, almond & orange trees	Managers
Petach Tikvah	14,084	69	412	41	26	335	30	350,000	3,000	Mr. Bloch
Jehuda	160	12	50	11	2	108	2	2,000	200	Mr. Gutman
Rishon L'Zion	6,600	35	190	30	30	96	20	2,000,000	10,000	Mr. Bloch
Nachalat Reuben	1,500	11	30	10	5	42	5	25,000	8,000	Mr. R. Lehrer
Mazkeret-Bat-Yah	5,500	18	185	18	18	127	18	—	1,500	Mr. Ettinger
Gederah	3,000	15	87	15	15	50	15	50,000	2,000	Mr. M. Pines
Zichron Ya'acob	10,000	86	515	86	86	288	86	100,000	15,000	Mr. Ben Shîmul
Rosh Pina	5,600	32	178	32	32	350	20	18,000	3,000	Mr. Ossovetzky
Jesod Hama'ala	2,400	15	65	5	10	37	3	—	—	Mr. Ossovetzky
Kostinia	4,000	5	50	20	20	10	5	—	—	Mr. Bloch
10	52,844	298	1762	268	244	1443	204	2,545,000	42,700	

To illustrate this, I beg to quote from the December report of 1884 to the Association of Jewish Immigrants the following paragraph:

The question of the *Alliance* colonists grows daily more serious, and I fear that its solution will be starvation and death, which we Philadelphians, as near Jewish neighbors to that dreadful scene, will have to atone for according to the ancient religious prescription of *Egle-Arufah*, and acknowledge that "our hands did not shed this blood." Have mercy on these unfortunate beings; save their lives by supplying them with temporary relief and permanent work before it will be too late.

This appeal was not in vain; for on the following Friday, Mr. Alfred T. Jones, President, and Mr. Simon Muhr, Treasurer of the above Association, appealed to our community through the *Jewish Record*, which appeal was generously responded to, and about $7000 contributed were spent by these gentlemen, who, on their frequent visits, supplied the colonists with all the necessities of life and work, and thus preserved that colony for the honor of our community and Israel at large.

Thus Jewish colonization has developed gradually, within a few years; and it lies in the power of our community to ensure its further development on business principles. It was from this city that the Liberty Bell proclaimed "liberty throughout the land, and unto all the inhabitants thereof"; and let it be again our community of Philadelphia that announces Jewish independence, by extending agricultural life among our people.

May the God of Israel bless such efforts!

Jewish Colonies in America

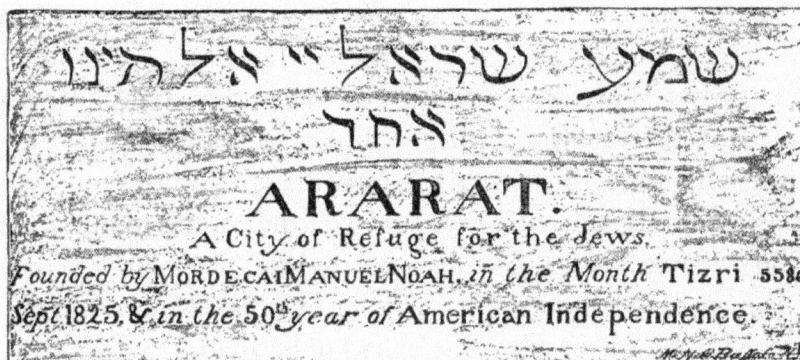

Major Noah's Memorial Stone.

A Relic

A very curious incident connected with early Jewish settlements in the United States was the scheme projected by the distinguished American scholar and statesman, Major Mordecai Manuel Noah. That gentleman, who figured so prominently in our country's history during the first half century of this Republic, conceived the plan of a permanent Jewish settlement on Grand Island, situated on the Niagara River. Mr. Noah grew enthusiastic over his plan, and even succeeded in enlisting the sympathy of some New York capitalists. With the assistance received, 17,381 acres on Grand Island were purchased by him for the sum of $76,280. For five years he agitated the matter, but as no immigration to that spot could be induced, his efforts were met with no permanent success. However, he was not discouraged; and he erected in 1825, amid ceremonies, on the spot destined for the colony, a monument of brick and wood. This monument has since worn away; but the corner-stone has been preserved, and is at present in possession of the Buffalo (New York) Historical Society. The cut given above represents the corner-stone and its inscription. We have not been able to ascertain whether the omission of the letter ׳ (yod) in the second Hebrew word, and of the entire fifth word (The Lord) occurred in the original inscription—which, however, it is scarcely possible to believe—or whether these Hebrew characters were erased over course of time.[*]

_____

[*] For a sketch of Major Noah and his remarkable career, see *The Life and Times of Martin Van Buren*, by William L. Mackenzie; *Eminent Israelites of the Nineteenth Century*, by Henry S. Morais; *The Hebrews in America*, by Isaac Markens; Appleton's *Cyclopædia, or American Biography*, etc.

The Hebrew inscription on Major Noah's memorial stone is translated: "Hear O Israel, The Eternal is our God; The Eternal is One" (see *The Jews of Philadelphia*, 1894, 212).

An Early Settlement

An evidence of an early attempt at an actual settlement is afforded by the experience of a number of Israelites who, in 1837, left the city of New York and retired to a village in the township of Warwarsing, Ulster County, New York State. The movement appears to have been started by Moses Cohen, who emigrated there, with his family, accompanied by about twelve other families. The place was called *Shalom* (Peace), and the new settlers built farms there. Most of those who retired here remained until 1842. Upon their leaving, others arrived. During this period all followed agricultural pursuits, and a number of them also engaged in trading. Some manufacturing was likewise carried on. The settlers labored earnestly, but after five years of constant effort, the enterprise had to be abandoned. The time was, doubtless, not yet ripe for successful Jewish colonization among us.

The Alliance Colony

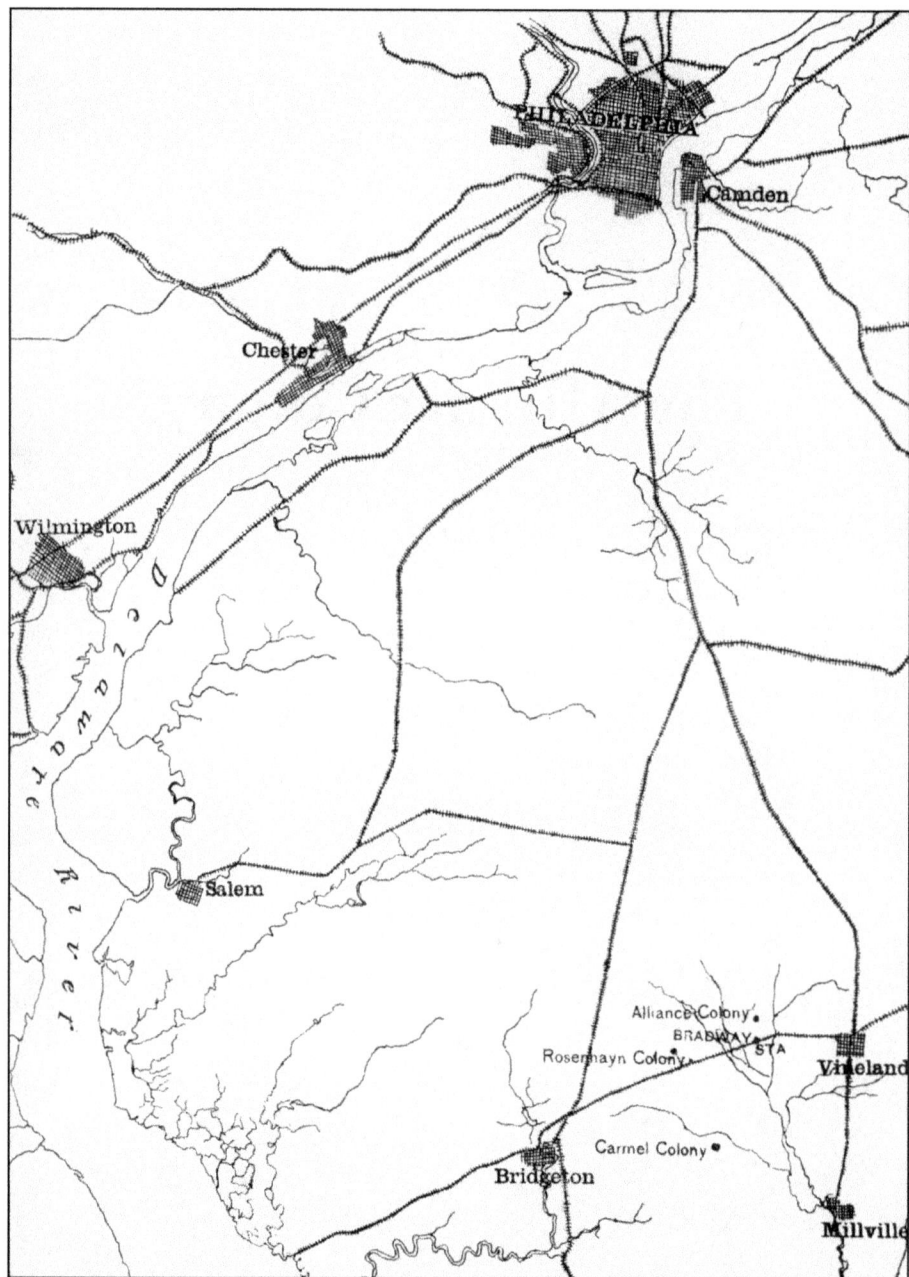

Map of Southern New Jersey showing location of the three Jewish Agricultural Colonies.

The Alliance Colony

The sandy spot of New Jersey where the three Jewish colonies are now located, and which once formed a bed of the sea (as geological research has shown), forcibly reminded me of the Divine command given to Nature, as described in the first chapter of Genesis: "Let the waters be gathered together, and let the dry land appear." There seems to have been here also an obedience to the will of the Creator; for, as in the Biblical narrative, the earth here, after being separated from the sea, became productive; here also grass, herbs, and trees were first visible; and here, likewise, the soil of what once appeared like a sandy desert was rendered fertile by human labor, aided by the workings of Nature. Such were my impressions after my first visit to the *Alliance* Colony.

I do not propose to write here a full history of the colony—viz., the life of the community, as an aggregate of human beings; for this would require deeper study than what I can give to it. If, by a historical narrative, I would be required to trace the present course of events to their original source, it would necessarily involve some researches into the recent past, dwelling on the awful horrors in Russia, and would eventually carry me beyond the scope of the present writing. My aim is to recount the chief events connected with the origin of the *Alliance* Colony, and its rise to the position it now occupies—being the pioneer of all Jewish colonies in America.

When *Alliance* will have passed through all the varied stages of development it will then be the task of the historian to work out the subject in all its bearings. For my own part, if I succeed in presenting the main facts, which have contributed to the success of the colony,—referring at the same time to a few others which are essential to its future welfare,—I will consider my object accomplished.

I. Locality and History of the Settlement

Alliance is situated in the State of New Jersey (in a triangle of which the three growing cities of Bridgeton, to the south, Vineland, to the east, and Millville, to the southeast, form the corners), and at a distance of forty-three miles from Philadelphia, to the north. In 1882, the year of its present settlement, it bore unmistakable signs of an early but neglected cultivation. The 43 families, that formed the settlement in the spring of 1882, hailed from almost as many cities, principally of Southern Russia,—such as Odessa, Kief, Elizabethgrad, etc. They were brought over to *Alliance*, and lodged by the Hebrew Emigrant Aid Society (now the *Alliance* Land Trust of New York, composed of such

"Castle Garden" at Alliance (formerly the Cigar Factory).

zealous and untiring workers as Messrs. Henry S. Henry, Isaac Eppinger, L. Gershel, and Rev. Dr. F. de Sola Mendes) in three large buildings erected for the temporary use of the farmers.

Immediately after their arrival, the whole area of land, purchased from the Messrs. Leach Brothers, was mapped out and divided into lots of fifteen acres or thereabout for each family, and leased to the people, under contract, for a term of ten years. The hard work of clearing the land, uprooting stumps, planting berries, and cultivating the soil began at once, under the guidance of an experienced person, employed for this purpose.

Vineland and Bridgeton being inaccessible to the farmers for want of a horse and wagon, the store of the Messrs. Leach Bros. was the sole means of supplying the colonists with the necessities of life, at the society's expense. Meanwhile, the Messrs. Leach were busily engaged in erecting houses,—comprising of two rooms and a cellar,—also in constructing wells,—which were not completed until early in 1883, when two of the three huge buildings were completely torn down; the remaining one being left for a cigar factory, which was subsequently established, in accordance with the suggestion of Mr. M. Mendel, of New York.

This last institution must not by any means pass unnoticed, as it disclosed an important step on the part of the society, having in view the possible advancement of the colony. The fact of its having been short-lived was due neither to mismanagement, nor to any cause that might have rendered its existence impossible; but to certain peculiar circumstances, under which even its limited career must be regarded as remarkable. Given an aggregate of human beings, coming from a part of Europe where the darkness of ignorance prevails, and who had, besides, the misfortune to depend, for a certain period, solely on the benevolence of a society, in order to obtain their victuals and raiment, the failure of the cigar factory is at once accounted for.

II. Practical Work. A Critical State of Affairs. Philadelphians to the Rescue

A more successful experiment was the establishment of a shirt factory, which lasted a year, after which the cigar factory building (now bearing the name of "The Factory; or, Castle Garden,"—the latter appellation being given by reason of its occupancy by new settlers, free of rent) was transformed into a temporary House of Worship. But the interval between the establishments of the two factories was a time of hardships and difficulties, which would have been unendurable, were it not for the generous relief afforded by Philadelphia Israelites. The colonists were in despair, and the scenes presented at that period were heart-rending. The

Farm Lands at Alliance Colony. View from the Tiphereth Jisrael Synagogue.

Home of the Association of Jewish Immigrants, the *Jewish Record* office, and the jewelry store of H. Muhr's Sons, were for several months in danger of becoming asylums for *Alliance* colonists.

It was chiefly through the energetic efforts and constant labors of the late Mr. Alfred T. Jones, and of Mr. Simon Muhr,* that the alarming difficulties were tided over and the colonists rescued from the dangers that threatened them. (See reference to this event in our article on "Jewish Colonization.")

Since that memorable time, sewing on machines has been the chief means of support to the farmers during the winter, and is even at the present date a valuable auxiliary to successful farming on virgin soil, under existing circumstances.

This timely aid bore golden fruit, and the colonists were enabled through it to transform their barren soil into a smiling garden, and thus succeeded in attracting the sympathy of the London Mansion House Relief Committee, who had entrusted the New York Committee with adequate funds to secure the soil for the colonists under certain conditions. This was the means of re-establishing the relationship between the New York Committee and the colonists.

---

* Several ladies and gentlemen, viz., Dr. M. Jastrow, Jr., Mr. Louis E. Levy, Mr. Jacob Miller, Miss Esther Baum, Mrs. A. T. Jones, and Mrs. Charles I. Phillips, afterwards co-operated with the above named gentlemen in securing for the colonists employment and clothing.

The first products of the soil shipped from *Alliance* to New York brought a moderate return, and the crop of 1887 yielded a still fairer income. Thus the stability of the settlement was permanently secured.

III. Synagogue Erected.—Other Facts

The members of the community having at first been mostly concerned with the all-important question of procuring a livelihood, and having partially solved that problem, turned with gratitude to their Creator, realizing the need of a suitable House of Worship to offer their prayers unto Him. This sentiment was spontaneous, and on the 29th of July, 1888—the anniversary of the day on which the colonists first set foot on our free shores—the present fine building *Eben Ha 'Ezer* was dedicated to the Worship of The One God, in the presence of a number of prominent gentlemen from New York, Philadelphia, and Washington. It was then that the right of the farmers to their property was generally recognized, and on the same visit to the colony, the directors of the *Alliance* Land Trust apprised the farmers of this decision, and the issuing of deeds at once proceeded, to the joy of the settlers. Among the donations given to the synagogue on that occasion were $500 from Mr. Jacob H. Schiff, of New York (half of which, however, was intended

The Synagogue Eben Ha 'Ezer at Alliance.

for the library at the colony), and $100 from Mr. M. Mendel, of New York. A. S. Solomons, Esq., of Washington, expressed his readiness to carry out the colonists' wishes with regard to the establishment of a post office at the colony, and in November of the same year it was opened, with Mr. G. S. Seldes, one of the farmers, as postmaster. This appointment was a fortunate step towards the future progress of the colony.

IV. Table of Births, Deaths, and Marriages

Births

Male	94
Female	48
	142

Deaths

Adults	4
Children	9
	13

Marriages

Marriages	32

V. Table of Ages

	Male	Female
Under 1 year	4	3
From 1 to 10 years	40	37
From 10 to 20 years	55	36
From 20 to 30 years	57	48
From 30 to 40 years	66	60
From 40 to 50 years	43	42
From 50 to 60 years	13	20
From 60 to 70 years	4	1
	282	247
Total	529	

Besides these there are sixteen families living in the colony who do not own any land, but derive their maintenance from working for the farmers in summer and operating on sewing machines in winter; also twenty-eight American Christian farmers on 1,573 acres of land, all of whom are well-to-do, and some of whom are wealthy.

VI. General Statistics

Land belonging to Jews, acres	1400
Soil cultivated	889
Houses	92
Barns	63
Wagons	39
Horses and mules	32

Interior of the Synagogue Eben Ha 'Ezer at Alliance.

Cows.....................................59
Grocery stores 3
Clothing stores..............................2
Blacksmith shop 1
Butchers' shops...........................3
Shoe store....................................1

VII. Vocations

Postmaster..................................1
Doctor 1
Teachers 3
Shochatim.................................2
Painters 2
Carpenters and builders.....................5
Shoemakers 3
Butchers 3
Tailors (custom) 2
Machine operators, about..................150

VIII. Institutions

Synagogues*..............................2
Library†...................................1
Post-office................................1
Night school.............................1

---

* 1. *Eben Ha 'Ezer*; 2. *Tiphereth Jisrael.*

† *Alliance Israelite* Library.

IX. Improvements

As shown by the statistical statement, some grocery, shoe and clothing stores, and butcher and blacksmith shops were opened. The repairing of the streets and roads and the opening of a new public school (the school which the children now attend is somewhat too far removed from the colony and is rather overcrowded) are expected to take place some time during the next spring. Another synagogue was dedicated in 1889.‡ The *Alliance Israelite* Library is the last institution I will name before concluding my, cursory review.

X. Profits of the Crop

That the *Alliance* colonists are laboring nobly to accomplish their difficult task becomes manifest when we glance at the yieldings of the soil.

Dr. William Kallman, one of the colonists, who prescribes for the sick while tilling his sixteen acres of land, has realized during the present year (1889):

---

‡ Whether the reason for establishing another public school in the settlement also applies to a second synagogue, is hard to tell. To me it appears that there is more *'Ezer* and *Tiphereth* in a community worshiping The One God, in one synagogue, than in a small community divided in two groups.

From strawberries....................................$75
From blackberries....................................60
From raspberries.....................................30
From corn 60
From sweet potatoes...............................20
From peaches 12
From ninety-eight gallons of
grape wine..100
Total..$357

Some of the colonists have even realized more than the above; but the average return for the present year to each colonist has amounted to about $280.

This comparatively small income is due to the extremely unfavorable season caused by the heavy rains of the summer; otherwise, the crop would have been much larger, and would have yielded more than double the above average. However, the amount stated does not include the value of vegetables stored up by the farmers for their own use, nor the products of the six thousand peach, pear, apple and plum trees, which were very light, owing to the trees being young, but these will doubtless bring a goodly return next summer.

XI. Citizenship

The twenty-second of October, 1889, marked a new departure in the history of the *Alliance* Colony, for on that day not less than eighty farmers received their second naturalization papers at the county court of Salem, by which they became citizens of the United States. This distinction is of as high importance as that of a governorship in the czar's domains.

The colony may derive large benefits from this step. It will stand upon a firmer political footing, and its importance will, doubtless, be recognized by the State of New Jersey, in constructing roads; by the general government, in erecting a public school house; and by the railroad company, in adopting the name of "Alliance Station," as a substitute for the present "Bradway Station." All of these measures will contribute to the growth of the colony. The new citizens will learn the needs of organization, and will thus be enabled to silence dangerous elements among them, and promote the material and moral elevation of the people who form the *Alliance* settlement.

A distinguished Russian, who, at our instance, went over to Salem to witness the event just described, remarked thus on his return: "Of all the varied scenes which America affords, none can be of greater interest for the Muscovite visitor than the sight of Jewish farmers of Russian birth rejoicing under the blessings of a free citizenship of this glorious republic—a privilege for which their co-religionists of my country have so long struggled, alas! in vain." May the time soon come when our unfortunate fellow-believers in Russia may see the light,

when free air and space will not be the possession of a few, but the unlimited privilege of
every creature of the same God!

Mr. Bayuk's Vineyard at Alliance.

The Rosenhayn Colony

The Rosenhayn Colony

This colony, started under discouragements, is now progressing favorably, and while it has by no means engaged the same attention or received the same help as its sister colonies in New Jersey, it is assuming a position of permanence, largely due to the labors of its own inhabitants, who recognize the advantages of agriculture, and strive hard for success.

I. Situation and History

The colony is situated midway (five miles) between Vineland and Bridgeton, near which cities the colonies of *Alliance* and Carmel are respectively located. The history of Rosenhayn began in 1882, when six Russian Jewish families were settled by the New York Emigrant Aid Society in the upper section and a number of others in the lower portion of Rosenhayn. They started to cultivate the soil, and to erect some houses. But the attendant hardships were so numerous that those settled in the lower district were compelled to abandon their object and quit the place. They sought to obtain aid toward building up a settlement, but no success attended their appeals at that period. In 1887, however, when the success of the *Alliance* Colony had become well known,

several other people repaired to Rosenhayn, contracted for some land there, and resided for a while in a large city nearby, earning their livelihood by manual labor, and gradually paying off the sum required for the purchase.

In 1888, over thirty-seven families bought land under similar conditions. It is to be regretted, however, that by a stipulation in their contracts they are bound to cultivate a certain number of acres of land, and erect a dwelling within a limited space of time; such stipulation necessitating their presence on the farm, and calling for an investment which they cannot at present well afford. But this does not include some whose occupation, being that of sewing on machines, enables them to live near their farms in a large rented building, called "The Hotel," located opposite the railroad station. As a matter of course, they are in want of room, but their overcrowded state has not been attended with dangers, as might be the case in a large city. The people here enjoy plenty of fresh air, and are healthy, notwithstanding their present enforced way of living.

II. General Statistics

The whole Jewish settlement of Rosenhayn comprises an area of 1912 acres (out of a total of 4000 acres.) Cultivated by Jews thus far, 261 acres. (Planted on this land are strawberries,

School House at Rosenhayn.

blackberries, raspberries, corn, grape-vines, and trees.)

Number of Jewish families settled here 67
Houses belonging to colonists 23
(6 built by Jewish carpenters of this place.)
Horses and mules 12
Barns...12
Wagons 12
Cows and heifers 14
Grocery stores 2
Shoe store..1

III. Vocations

Carpenters..4
Painters 2
Shoemakers 2
Custom tailors..2
Machine operators......................................40
Cooper..1
Roofer 1
Tinsmith 1
Stocking-weavers 2

Fifteen of the settlers were employed in farming in Russia.

The average profits from the crop for the present year (1889) to each farmer amounted to $150.

IV. Table of Ages

	Male	Female
Under 1 year	4	5
From 1 to 10 years	32	28
From 10 to 20 years	36	32
From 20 to 30 years	35	39
From 30 to 40 years	20	16
From 40 to 50 years	15	16
From 50 to 60 years	7	5
From 60 to 70 years		3
From 70 to 80 years		1
	149	145
Total	294	

Sixty of the children of both sexes receive instruction at the public school. The colony has a post-office, railroad station, public school, and a drug-store, with attending physician.

V. The Colony's Future

So much for the present. As to the future, considering that the purchase of land was effected on very stringent stipulations, we must not be surprised to find the colonists rather embarrassed. Let us hope that the clouds, pierced by some bright star, will disperse, and that Rosenhayn will assume a distinct feature among her sister colonies.

Mr. Josum's Homestead (one of the original settlers) at Rosenhayn.

Carmel Colony

Carmel Colony's Condition

To the Rev. Dr. S. Morais, Mayer Sulzberger, Esq., and Mr. Simon Muhr, trustees of Baron de Hirsch's fund in aid of the Jewish farmers at Carmel, New Jersey.

GENTLEMEN: Hardly two days had passed after I had consented to Mr. Muhr's request to investigate the state of the people at Carmel, when I received a note from Rev. Dr. Morais, urging me to go to Carmel at once, Baron de Hirsch being inclined to have the money returned to him to Paris, where he might utilize it for some other benevolent purpose, rather than to sanction any further delay in its distribution.

None of my various duties could prevent me from attending immediately to this important mission. I left on the first train for Bridgeton, N. J., and there I hired a team for Carmel. The driver, however, being ignorant of its location, had taken me to Rosenhayn, whence he was directed on the road to Carmel.

While viewing the large extent of bushes, especially the wilderness that separates Carmel from the outside world, I was impressed as a wanderer in the Sahara desert, thinking that, as in ancient times, the next generation of Israelites may enjoy the fruit of this soil; and while I was thus thinking the team reached the colony.

History of the Locality

During the second decade of the present century, when the world was moving slowly and railroads were hardly known in New Jersey, Irving Avenue was the only road combining the traffic of Bridgeton and South Vineland, which cities are separated ten miles from each other. On that road a hotel was established six miles from Bridgeton and four miles from South Vineland, for the accommodation of travelers. After many years the hotel owner committed suicide, leaving a widow with several children. The latter, finding themselves deprived of their father, and unprotected, sold their hotel and other property to the present land owner, Mr. W. H. Miller, who moved from Philadelphia, accompanied by a number of German farming families, whom he hired to clear and cultivate the soil. Mr. Miller had some houses erected for them, but they, seeing no golden harvest before them, left the place and returned to Manayunk, where they had been formerly engaged in some other work.

Thus the spot again became deserted, until a group of seventeen of our persecuted Russian brethren, encouraged and constantly aided by

General View of Irving Avenue at Carmel. (When the town is surveyed into streets some of the names of the latter will doubtless be dedicated to Mr. Heilprin and Baron de Hirsch.)

the noble and practical philanthropist, Mr. M. Heilprin, were settled in 1882 as farmers. They named the colony *Carmel*.

In the course of a few years, about seven of the original settlers left Carmel, but they were soon replaced by Western Russian Jewish farmers, who, owing to the extremely hot climate, had to quit those regions, and were settled by Mr. Heilprin on hired soil at Carmel.

II. The Situation of Carmel

The Jewish settlement called Carmel is situated 6¼ miles from East Bridgeton, 5 miles north from Millville, and 2¾ miles from Rosenhayn station. It covers an area of 864 acres of land, bordering south on the turnpike, and north on the Lebanon River. The soil, although somewhat stony, may still, after proper cultivation, yield more fruit than the sandy spot of the *Alliance* colony near Vineland.

III. Number and Ages of Jewish Settlers

	Male	Female
Under 1 year	5	6
From 1 to 10 years	36	42
From 10 to 20 years	33	39
From 20 to 30 years	25	12
From 30 to 40 years	24	24
From 40 to 50 years	13	9

	Male	Female
From 50 to 60 years	14	4
	150	136

The total number of males and females, 286.

IV. The Sanitary Condition

Notwithstanding the moderate way of living, the children are all bodily well developed and healthy looking. Those who arrive at conclusions from hospital reports, which state that consumption prevails among our Russian brethren, should be referred for information to the Carmel colonists, who within seven years have not lost one single life, except one or two by premature birth.

V. The Soil

The soil occupied by Jewish settlers consists of 848 acres.

Soil cleared by Jewish settlers consists of 124 acres.

Soil partially cultivated or planted by them: 123 acres.

VI. Dwellings Houses

Rented from Mr. Miller..............................7
Erected for them through
Building Associations 19

Group of Homesteads on West Irving Avenue at Carmel.

(Of these nineteen, two Jewish carpenters in the colony erected 6)

Old houses bought with the soil 4

Barns, stables and poultry yards erected by the colonists 25

Synagogue, Post Office, Library and School, owned by Mr. Miller 4

Grocery Stores, owned by the colonists (1 is likely to be abandoned) 3

Butcher Shop, belonging to Mr. Miller 1

VII. Children in School

Number of children of both sexes attending school 82

Teacher of general instruction 1

(There is no Teacher as yet for Jewish instruction.)

VIII. Artisans and Laborers

Carpenters (who erected six new houses) 2

Shoemaker 1

Tanner 1

Saddler 1

Locksmith 1

Butcher that supplies weekly 340 pounds of meat to the colonists 1

Cigar Makers 2

Custom Tailors 3

Workers on Sewing Machines (the tailors included) 63

Nearly all are capable of doing laboring work.

IX. Cattle

Horses belonging to colonists 10

Colt (an excellent one) raised by a colonist 1

Cows owned by them, which supply milk to the colonists 10

Calf raised by a colonist 1

X. Wagons, Ploughs and Implements

The colonists own about 13 Wagons.

The colonists own about 10 Ploughs.

The colonists own about 15 Cultivators.

XI. Produce of the Soil

During last summer, enough corn, rye, buckwheat, vegetables and berries were raised to supply seventeen families for the whole winter. Some have even realized a small amount by selling berries, while the vines and fruit trees planted may probably not yield fruit before another two years.

View of the Synagogue (second from left), School House (fourth from left), and Butcher Shop (fifth from left) on northern side of Irving Avenue.

XII. Classification of the Colonists

(This subdivision contains a list of the colonists divided into four classes, and the aid they are entitled to according to their respective merits in farming, artisanship and general standing, making sixteen among the list as farmers, nineteen as secondary, twenty-one in the third class, and twelve in the fourth class.)

This classification was made after long and careful investigation at the house of each colonist. In addition to this, I have examined the children in English reading and writing; have inspected each room, garret, and cellar. I was pleased to find here some corn, there some rye; in one place buckwheat, in another vegetables,—all of the colonists' production. Where such evidences were not seen, I searched through the farms to see whether the ground was covered with bushes or cleared, whether it was cultivated or planted; and unfavorable as the season in which I visited the colony was, still I could judge of the merits or demerits of the people. Even cattle and poultry showed the industry of the persons who raised them, and I realized the truth of the verse, *Mallefenu, Mi-Bahamoth Aretz! Ume'of Ha-Shamayim Yechakemenu.*

By reason of all this evidence, I deemed it necessary to divide the colonists into the above four different lists.

XIII. Charity and Justice

Having noticed people who became degraded by sweet but ill-applied charity, we must avoid such a dangerous result as far as possible. The following suggestions may help to direct the distribution of the fund in proper channels:—1st. The money should be given to the colonists as a loan on mortgage, and this should be repaid with a small interest. 2nd. The beneficiaries should be given to understand that the produce of the farms produced by their own labor may reduce the amount of the interest. 3rd. The distribution of the fund according to my lists will secure to many the deeds on their ground, and in some instances reduce the heavy dues to building associations. No provision has been made for buying horses, which are indispensable to the progress of the colony. About $400 is required for eight or ten horses, and this amount should be raised by those kind-hearted gentlemen of our community to whom history will ascribe the preservation of the Alliance Colony and colonists. 4th. Should some individual philanthropist or organization be inspired to follow the noble example set forth by Baron de Hirsch to further the scheme of Jewish farming in America, I would recommend the consideration of such cases as were omitted (because the funds were inadequate), before attempting to start new Jewish colonies.

View in the town centre at Carmel—East Irving Avenue.

XIV. Farming Tailors

Fault was found with the colonists for making shirts on a large scale for city manufacturers. The fault-finders seem to consider tailoring a crime, or at least an unworthy occupation for farmers. But they are ignorant of the fact that sewing machinery is, during the winter, an important factor in Pennsylvania farming life; that the Jewish settlers at Carmel had to support large families without any other means; that they could not maintain themselves for a single day by clearing the wild soil. Under such circumstances, we should rather admire than criticize earnest work, both in farming and tailoring. Let those who object to tailoring strive to erect a brickyard, and can, or glass factories, for which the soil of Carmel may be fitted, and many of the colonists will exchange their sewing-machines for hard-labor instruments and their needles for plows.

XV. Farming as a Solution of the Jewish Problem

Now, gentlemen, let us return from Carmel to South and Lombard Streets, of this city, or to Essex, Ludlow and Hester Streets, of New York, and let our hearts and minds watch the mass of humanity thronging their sidewalks. Look at the thousands of pale features moving about like ghosts in the valley of death; some anxious to work for a loaf of bread: others eager for employment, by the earnings of which they may pay the rent of some obscure garret of a tenement house occupied by their starving families; everyone moves, strives, and struggles for work in this battle of life. Alas! Neither the tailors, manufacturers, nor the dealers in peddlers' supplies; neither the *Kosher* butchers and *Matzoth* bakers, nor the *Kosher* saloons and restaurants; neither the hundreds of *Chebroth* and synagogues, nor the thousands of *Maggidim, Schochatim*, and *Melammedim*; neither the booksellers, nor the groups of *Kosher* European steamship agencies; neither the jargon press nor the stage, is able to satisfy these hungry souls. Nor can our charitable organizations supply the demands of these *Neshamoth deazelin' Artelain*. Poor souls! in such a state, there is no brighter future for you in New York than in Wilna; and no more prospect at Philadelphia and Chicago than in Lemberg and Bucharest! *Farming* alone seems to me to be your future destiny in this blessed country, and colonization only can solve THE JEWISH PROBLEM forced upon us for solution by Eastern Europe and Asia.

Respectfully submitted,

M. KLEIN,

Agent of Association of Jewish Immigrants. PHILADELPHIA, February 17, 1889.

Group of School Children at the School House at Carmel.

Notes,—Since the above report was received, the $5000 sent by Baron de Hirsch has been distributed by the Rev. Dr. Morais—as agreed upon by the committee—in different sums among colonists for the purchase of the land, and for other necessary objects relating to the colony.

Dr. Morais has since received from New York, through Hon. Myer S. Isaacs and Dr. Julius Goldman, the sum of $489.15, being a balance of the fund sent by the Mansion House Committee of London, England; also $50 through Dr. Goldman, being the sum bequeathed by a friend. These amounts were expended for the purchase of land, implements, etc., for some other deserving colonists.

Two benevolent Jewish ladies of Philadelphia donated $200 (each $100), which amount served to defray the expense of drawing up legal documents and other papers.

Carmel's Recent Progress

Seldom has a sum of five thousand dollars been more successfully applied, and with better results, than Baron de Hirsch's fund in aid of the Carmel colonists. It has given a remarkable impetus to the Carmelites; it has practically set their affairs on a firm footing. We no longer hear cries of distress; neither are the colonists forced to dwell in tenement hovels of New York or Philadelphia during the wintry season, and eke out a livelihood at the settlement during the milder season. They seem fully content to remain where they are, looking hopefully forward to the time when each may dwell "under his vine and his fig tree," as is the case with hundreds of our co-religionists, who form the Jewish colonies in Palestine, and with thousands of Jewish farmers scattered along the shores of the Somash and Theiss rivers, flowing through Transylvania and Hungary.

During the period succeeding the date of my official report (as given above, and which appeared in a number of Jewish weeklies of the United States) the external as well as the internal appearance of the Carmel Colony has considerably changed. About fifteen hundred additional acres of land have been purchased by Jews, and thirty-six neat and comfortable houses have been erected. The value of land, as will be shown, has very materially increased. The settlers are rapidly becoming Americanized, while the arts of industry and of agriculture are progressing to a marked degree within their midst.

Some Facts and Figures

About fifteen hundred acres of land have been bought by Jews since last February. This purchase, added to the original 848 acres, makes a total of 2348 acres now belonging to Jews at Carmel and elsewhere. The land, which sold in January, 1889, at from $12 to $30 per acre, has

Mr. Miller's Residence and the Post-Office (first from left), and the Library (second from left) at Carmel.

already increased to as much as from $30 to $80 per acre. As an illustration of the above, we may cite the case of a colonist who, not long before, would have parted with his entire land for $40, and has recently sold three of the eighteen acres belonging to him for the sum of $180. The thirty-six new houses referred to were erected at an average cost of $800 each, the work being chiefly done by Jewish carpenters and laborers. Four more houses are in the course of construction, and there are prospects of others being added towards spring. The needed money is obtained on first mortgages from building associations at Bridgeton, New Jersey.

All these events have naturally tended to an increased population. The want of a railroad direct to the colony, however, is greatly felt, and it is hoped a station will soon be established at that point—a step which will benefit all sides.

Mr. W. H. Miller, the postmaster at Carmel, from whom a large part of the land was purchased, has labored earnestly for the welfare of the colony, and the advancement of its interests. But the main credit belongs to the colonists themselves, who have exerted all efforts to render Carmel a prosperous Jewish settlement.

The colonists evinced their feelings of humanity and of real sympathy by contributing the sum of $47 to aid the sufferers by the recent disastrous flood at Johnstown, Pennsylvania.

General Observations

The general state of the Jewish colonies located on the Eastern coast of the United States—as portrayed by us—will have demonstrated to the reader the favorable outlook for Jewish colonization in America. The recent purchase of additional land at the Carmel settlement, by foreign-born co-religionists residing in some of our large centres, also shows that a real desire is manifested by many of our people to become agriculturists; and surely such a desire ought to obtain the moral and practical support of every friend of Israel and of humanity.

The *Jewish Chronicle*, of London, England, in its issue of October 25th, 1889, refers at length to a scheme, proposed by Rev. S. Singer, of that city, in connection with Jewish agricultural settlements in America. This news comes to us as a message of good tidings, and is of itself an evidence of the attention now being given to this weighty subject, the discussion of which is by no means confined to our own country. The remarks of the *Chronicle* we present in full:

"The discourse delivered by Rev. S. Singer at the new West End Synagogue on the First Day of Tabernacles has been printed. The address is a forcible plea for an agricultural life as the only remedy for the evils which afflict the Russian Jew.

Group of Farm-Houses on Second Street at Carmel.

Mr. Singer points out the contrast existing between the commercial predilections of the modern Israelite and the purely agricultural life of his remote ancestors. In respect of its pursuits and of their influence upon its character, 'the overwhelming mass of the Jewish race is in direct conflict with its own most honorable past.' The effects of this unwholesome change are to be seen in 'the hardships, the privations, the squalor, the wretchedness, amid which three-quarters of the Jewish inhabitants of every large town pass through existence.' It follows that if so much mischief is to be cured, it can only be by a revival of those conditions the disappearance of which has produced it. Mr. Singer advocates, then, the settlement of the downtrodden Russian Jews in new countries where the advent of large bodies of agricultural colonists would be welcomed; and among those countries he gives the preference to Canada, with a climate 'similar in some respects, in others superior, to that of the East of Europe,' with its fruitful soil, the perfect security it affords to life and property, and the liberty and justice it accords to all its indwellers. He earnestly bespeaks due consideration for his main idea, which, he mentions, in passing, is engaging the serious attention of Baron de Hirsch. 'One thing,' he concludes, 'appears certain: the social and material regeneration of Israel will not be worked out in large towns, or by the instrumentality of strikes and the like, but will depend in a great measure upon their return to more natural methods of living, and the resumption of their ancient character.'

"These are highly significant words, and they are worth pondering. They suggest a solution of problems which have a far wider scope than the well-being of the Jews only. The overcrowding of towns, with all its attendant economic and moral evils, is a stupendous danger which will soon have to be dealt with, and the only remedy for it seems to lie in the direction suggested by Mr. Singer. A return to a more natural mode of life, the revival of agricultural and pastoral pursuits, if not at home, at any rate abroad, is the only rational means of diminishing the troubles which are pressing with ever-increasing force upon the chief nations of Europe. As Jews it behooves us to do our part toward achieving this consummation by dealing intelligently with the members of our race. They are suffering, in even a greater degree than their neighbors, from subjection to an artificial environment. Take the Russian Jew from his Russian town, or from Whitechapel, for the matter of that, and set him in the midst of an open, rolling country; make him exchange the tailor's needle for the spade, the task of commercially conquering his fellow-men for that of subduing the soil, and you place him on the high road not merely to independence, but to dignity. His poverty and his misery will vanish; but, what

Mr. Steinberg's Farm, adjoining the Eben Ha 'Ezer Synagogue at Alliance.

is at least of equal importance, he will attain to a moral stature which never has been his, and never can be as long as he lives his present life. Every lover of Israel, nay, of humanity, will heartily applaud Baron de Hirsch's farsighted philanthropy if he decides to carry out the scheme he is now cogitating."

Rev. Mr. Singer is undoubtedly correct in his views touching the general condition and life of the Russian Jew, which, as the *Chronicle* states, can only be ameliorated by exchanging "the tailor's needle for the spade, the task of commercially conquering his fellow-men for that of subduing the soil," and that by such means alone will he be placed "on the high road not merely to independence, but to dignity." Many a time we have maintained exactly the same view, and the *Chronicle* but re-echoes us. Agriculture, we have insisted, is, and must be, the only solution of the Jewish Problem. But this very question of agricultural settlements admits of a wide line of demarcation when considering localities. We must beg respectfully to differ with Mr. Singer in his opinion as expressed concerning the advantages of Canada, to which country he gives the preference for the establishment of Jewish agricultural colonies. And these are our reasons: In such parts of Canada where the climate is inviting and the soil fertile, the population is naturally largest; hence, the price of land is high—ranging from $25 to $50 per acre. In such regions where government prairie land can be obtained gratis (on the condition of three years' continuous habitation), the temperature during the winter season, which not infrequently falls to between thirty and fifty degrees below zero, would certainly deter newly-arrived immigrants from settling there. The scarcity of fuel and the occasional visitations of grasshoppers in summer are also among the drawbacks to production. Then, again, these very localities are at such a distance from the market, which alone renders them unfit for settlement.

During the summer of 1888 a large number of Jewish immigrants arrived in Canada, purposing to settle on its soil. The opportunities for obtaining a livelihood were, however, so few that many were forced to leave that country, and repair on foot to large cities of the Eastern coast of the United States. These facts are well known, and were published at that period.

We have recently been furnished with the following complete tables, referring to the number of persons born in the Dominion of Canada, and residing in the United States, and those who are natives of our country, but who dwell in Canada. The figures are taken from the last census (1880–1881) in both countries, and are supplied to us by the Chief of the Bureau of Statistics at Washington, and by the Canadian Secretary of the Department of Agriculture at Ottawa. Proceeding directly from official

A Typical Farm-House (Mr. Gerson's) at Rosenhayn.

sources, they are therefore trustworthy, and instructive as well.

Number of persons residing in the United States:

Born in Canada..................................610,090
Born in New Brunswick.....................41,788
Born in Nova Scotia...........................51,160
Born in Prince Edward's......................7,537
Total...710,575

Number of persons born in the United States and residing in the different provinces of Canada is follows:

At Prince Edward's Island 609
At Nova Scotia 3,004
At New Brunswick 5,108
At Quebec...19,415
At Ontario 45,454
At Manitoba...1,752
At British Columbia.............................2,295
At The Territories 116
Total...77,753

Hence, we see that the excess of Canadians in the United States, over natives of the latter country who reside in Canada, reaches the enormous figures of 632,822. Would it be possible to present a more convincing statement as to the unfitness of Canada as a place for the establishment of Jewish agricultural colonies, when compared with the great advantages offered in the United States? We could even rest our case with these statements, for they are explicit and incontrovertible.

Baron de Hirsch's generosity is remembered by the Carmel colonists with deep gratitude; for it has practically ensured the success of that settlement. It is far from our thought to discourage any scheme which has in view the amelioration of our brethren; but it is sincerely to be hoped that every phase of this all-engrossing question will be duly considered before attempting to form new Jewish colonies. Rather let us seek to give permanence to those already established. The *Alliance* and Carmel colonies have their future insured; it is true, they are in want of various local industries—as substitutes for machine-operating for city manufacturers, which is on the decline—but these will, doubtless, come in the course of their development. Their sister colony, however—that of Rosenhayn—whose soil is likely to yield abundantly, has been struggling hard, and is at present—as has been shown—on a fair road to success; but assistance is needed in order to render it lasting. The settlers there are industrious and enterprising, and were the liberal-hearted Baron de Hirsch, or some other philanthropists, disposed to lend them a helping hand, blessed results would be obtained.

Jewish Farmers

The Agricultural Colonies of Russian Jews in New Jersey*

Away, back in the days of the prophet Jeremiah, the precursors of the barbarians that afterward extinguished the civilization of Rome and plunged Europe into the darkness of the Middle Ages had already begun their encroachments on their more civilized neighbors. At that time the empire of Media was suffering from the incursions of predatory tribes of Scythians, and when Jeremiah threatened Israel with the wrathful visitation of those savage hordes, he little dreamed that 2500 years later the descendants of his people would be fleeing from the oppression of the same barbarous power to find a refuge in a land of promise beyond the seas.

In Jeremiah's day the Muscovite was yet a distant bug-a-boo, and no vision of America appears to have been vouchsafed to the seer. Since then the times have changed a good deal. Liberty now enlightens the world with a steam engine and a dynamo machine, after wasting much valuable time with tallow dips and sperm oil, but the Cossack is still a barbarian and the land of the Muscovite is still in the night.

What wonder then, that with the railroad and the steamship to help him out and with the Scythian driving him, the liberty-yearning Israelite turns his face with longing toward these Western shores? What wonder that those of them that reach here send out their earliest savings to bring along their relatives and friends? That they are anxious to get them out of their Slavic prison-house the Transatlantic steamship lines have learned to their profit; and how well the steamship and railroad companies co-operate with the exiles to increase their numbers is sufficiently indicated by the abundance of emigrant-ticket agencies on both sides of the Atlantic. In that regard the Russian-Jewish immigrants are by no means a separate class. The same thing is true of the Irish and the Huns, the Italians and the Swedes, who are flocking hither, if not under the same stimulus, at least with a like bent to better their condition.

So far as the Jews are concerned, they come in large part for much the same reason as that which impelled the Pilgrim Fathers to Plymouth Rock, and they bring with them today the same indomitable spirit of enterprise and industry as that through which, two hundred years ago, the Puritans made the New England forests to blossom as a rose.

---

* The Philadelphia *Sunday Mercury*, in its issues of October 20th and 27th, 1889, presented descriptive articles under the above heading. These were written by one of its staff, who spent three days with the author in the colonies.

The articles are reproduced as a fitting corollary to that part of this work dealing with the three Jewish colonies in America.

The present wave of Jewish emigration from Eastern Europe took its rise in the Danubian Principalities about 1878, in consequence of the upheaval caused by the Russo Turkish War, and reached its height in 1882, when the Jews in various districts of the Russian Empire were subjected to such barbarous persecutions as evoked authoritative protests from all parts of the civilized world. These persecutions, which proceeded to the length of wholesale murder and rapine, were carried on by the rabble with the connivance of the government, or at least of its local representatives. The cruelties that were practiced, and which were chronicled at the time in the leading English and Continental newspapers by correspondents specially sent to investigate the facts, reveal a degree of social and official corruption among whose concomitant evils the tyranny of the central government was the least. Thousands of Jews were driven from their homes, including tradesmen and artisans in the cities and towns and farmers in the agricultural districts.

In Russia proper the evictions were effected by riotous demonstrations on the part of the lowest orders of the people, prompted by their own avarice and that of the brutal officials who had taken the hint from the fanatic Katkoff, the recently deceased Pan-Slavist leader and editor of a Moscow newspaper. Katkoff was credited with being the direct mouthpiece of the Czar, and as possessing an all-powerful influence at St. Petersburg, both assumptions having sufficient basis to sustain the exaggerated reports that were current among the ignorant populace. As a result of this Pan-Slavic furore the Russian officials in Poland took new measures of repression against the Roman Catholic Poles, whom their Greek Catholic conquerors look upon as traditional enemies and born rebels. So, while the Russian rabble was plundering the Jews, the Russian commissaries, bent on Russianizing Poland, were making it as uncomfortable as possible for the Christian Poles. Meanwhile, under Bismarck's direction, the German authorities in Prussian Poland were carrying out a determined policy, having in view the Germanizing of that province. To this end all the non-German inhabitants of the province, excepting those who were actual natives of the soil, were ordered out of the country. This order of eviction affected a large number of people, most of them natives of Russian or Austrian Poland, who had settled in Prussian Poland at various periods of their lives. Many of these "foreigners" had been brought to the province during childhood by their parents and had "grown up with the country," but all had to go. The mass of the national Poles are either Roman Catholics or Jews, the latter, though greatly in the minority, forming a very considerable number of the population. Between the upper and nether millstones of oppression and repression thousands of both denominations were thus forced out. Some went back to their native provinces, others scattered to different centres of Europe, particularly London, but the majority immigrated to distant parts. Of these emigrants the greater number have come to our shores, but not a few have found their way to Brazil, the Argentine Republic and to Australia.

Over a hundred thousand Slavic Jews have come over here since 1882; but the throng of new-comers is no longer as great as it has been. Whether it will permanently decrease and eventually cease altogether, as has been the case with the Jews from the western countries of Europe, will depend mainly on their political conditions. As these have become ameliorated the number of Jewish immigrants has diminished in proportion, and if the Russian Government, through enlightened self-interest, if from no other motive, can be brought to treat its 3,000,000 Jewish subjects with a more liberal spirit, the present thriving trade in prepaid passage tickets would soon show a material falling off.

Among the Russian Jews, who came to this country in such large numbers in 1882, were a considerable number of individuals who had been farmers in their native homes. To enable these people to continue that avocation here, and with the view of checking the overcrowding that was going on in the cities, a committee of Jewish residents of New York was charged with the task of founding in some practicable manner an agricultural colony which should form the nucleus of future settlements of a like character. This committee, after examining the lands in various sections of the country, chose Southern New Jersey as the most promising locality for the purpose, by reason of its proximity to centres of population and the likelihood of the speediest return for the labor involved. A considerable sum of money was collected for the purpose, and in the summer of 1882 some forty families of Russian-Jewish refugees were settled upon lands allotted to them by the committee at a point about a mile north of Bradway Station, some three miles east of Vineland, on the Southern New Jersey Railroad. Fifteen acres of land were given to each family upon conditions which had in view the eventual repayment of the original value of the land to the trustees of the fund, together with interest at 3 per cent. per annum after the first year. Leases were made out to each of the colonists with these provisions, but it is needless to say that but a very few of the settlers were able to comply with the stipulations even after the second and third years. Many of them required outside aid continuously, and a number of the original settlers finally gave up their undertakings and betook themselves to the cities.

The majority of them, however, fought their way through several years of privation to a more or less successful mastery of their circumstances, and today three communities of Jewish farmers

Tiphereth Jisrael Synagogue at Alliance.

are fast proving here what has long ago been demonstrated in various sections of Europe, particularly in Hungary and Transylvania—that the Jews can succeed as well at farming as they do in commerce or the arts.

II.

Within a comparatively recent geologic period the level expanse, which covers the southern portion of New Jersey, was below the surface of the sea. The siliceous soil is now covered with a thick growth of pine woods and scrub oak, and on these sandy bottoms, interspersed with tracks of gravelly loam, well adapted for truck farming and wine culture, the Jewish agricultural colonies of New Jersey have been planted.

The three colonies are known as Alliance, Carmel, and Rosenhayn, all situated in the triangular district of which the towns of Vineland, Millville and Bridgeton form the corners. The forty families originally settled at Alliance by the New York committee have been increased to about a hundred by the addition of newcomers from the cities and from abroad, and the two other colonies, planted after Alliance, have increased in like proportions until now, when the total number of souls embraced in the three communities is over one thousand.

Alliance was so called after the great Jewish charitable association whose branches ramify into all quarters of the globe, and which is known as the "Alliance Israelite Universelle," its headquarters being in Paris. This society was originally instituted for the purpose of directing organized efforts towards ameliorating the political conditions of the Jews in the Slavic and Mohammedan countries of Europe and Asia, and to its influence are directly traceable the stipulations of the Treaty of Berlin by which the political disabilities of the Jewish inhabitants of the Balkan provinces were removed. The society has latterly directed its efforts toward affording a more liberal education to the impoverished masses of these people, and in that connection has particularly fostered the establishment of agricultural schools and colonies. The "Alliance Universelle" has a flourishing branch in this city, presided over by Mr. Moses A. Dropsie, and this branch sends an annual contribution of two dollars per member to the central body in Paris.

The Funds for the Establishment of the Colony

The funds for the establishment of the colony at Alliance were originally contributed by the Hebrews of New York City. Later on, when the colony required further aid to sustain it during its struggling infancy, the New York committee turned over the tentative charge of the colony to a new board, composed of several

Tailors working at "Castle Garden" at Rosenhayn.

members of the old committee and a number of residents of this city [Philadelphia], prominent among whom may be mentioned Mr. Simon Muhr, Mr. Moses A. Dropsie and Mr. Mayer Sulzberger. These gentlemen were materially aided by the Jewish Emigration Society of this city, its president, the late Alfred T. Jones, and a number of his coadjutors, including: Dr. Morris Jastrow, Jr., Miss Esther Baum and Mrs. Charles Phillips, making repeated collections of money, clothing and other requirements for the settlers, and as frequent visits to the colony for the purpose of distributing the needed aid.

The privations of several successive winters were thus relieved, and further aid was afforded to the colonists by the establishment of a cigar factory,* which afforded a means of livelihood to many of them during the winter months, while others eked out their meagre earnings through shirtmaking and other similar occupations. Sewing-machines for this purpose were furnished to the more needy settlers through charitable organizations here and in New York, but quite a number of them were able to buy machines for themselves, paying for them out of their earnings. Finally, some three years ago, after the less capable colonists had been gradually weeded out and those remaining were beginning to manifest a capacity for

* The cigar factory ceased to exist long before the Philadelphia parties referred to came to the front and aided the colonists. M. K.

self-maintenance, a concerted effort was made to effectively establish the settlement on a firm footing. To this end the London Society, having in charge the "Mansion House Fund," collected to aid the refugees passing through England, sent over $10,000, which amount was applied to paying off the remaining liens upon the land and houses of the colonists, due to the previous owners, Messrs. Leach Bros., of Vineland. These gentlemen had greatly aided the progress of the undertaking by their liberal treatment of the impoverished settlers, among whom were a number of later comers, who had purchased their holdings directly from them.

It is, perhaps, needless to remark that these newcomers form the majority of the more successful inhabitants of Alliance, and this is equally true of the neighboring colonies of Carmel and Rosenhayn. Quite a number of the original colonists who were carried through the storm-and-stress period of the settlements by charitable aid, have indeed become self-supporting, and some of them quite comfortably situated, but those who subsequently established themselves with their own means have almost uniformly succeeded in obtaining a satisfactory foothold, and these now comprise the most influential element in the various communities.

One of them, a Mr. Steinberg, at whose house our reporter was entertained, and who, by the way, reminds one strongly of the published

The Young Jewish Element of Rosenhayn.

portraits of the late Russian author, Count Tolstoï, arrived in this country five years ago, and through the Jewish Emigration Society, in whose house he found temporary lodgment, was induced to settle at Alliance. He was an experienced farmer, and his success has been such as to enable him last year to donate to the congregation the land on which the larger of the two synagogues has been erected. Mr. Gerson at Rosenhayn is a similar example of successful accomplishment through arduous labor intelligently directed, and quite a number of other such cases could be cited. Mr. Bayuk at Alliance is a notable instance among the original settlers who succeeded from the start, and Mr. Weissman and Mr. Kuney at Carmel can be cited in the same category.

Alliance now comprises a population of about 500 individuals, who occupy ninety-two houses, spread over a tract of about 1300 acres of land, of which 900 are under cultivation. It contains a post-office, two synagogues and school-houses and a library, and supports a physician, three teachers and a considerable number of artisans. Over 6000 fruit trees are set out, and the colony promises to develop into an important suburb of Vineland, from which it is three miles distant.

Carmel Colony is situated on the old Beaver Dam turnpike, about seven miles east of Bridgeton and five miles northwest of Millville. This settlement owes its origin directly to the personal efforts of the late Michael Heilprin, whose erudition and scholarship, whether as author in linguistic literature, as a journalist on the New York *Nation*, or as revising editor of the *American Encyclopædia*, had acquired for him a world-wide recognition, but whose philanthropic self-sacrifice and constant devotion to works of charity were kept hidden, as far as possible, by his profound and truly inexpressible modesty.

In 1882 Mr. Heilprin, aided by a number of sympathetic friends in New York, among them Messrs. Jacob Schiff, Jesse Seligman and the late Julius Hallgarten, settled a number of the Russian-Jewish refugees, who arrived here in that year, upon lands owned by Mr. W. H. Miller, the present postmaster at Carmel. These lands had been previously occupied by a number of German families who had been brought to Carmel by Mr. Miller, but who had abandoned their holdings and returned to Philadelphia. Of the seventeen families colonized at Carmel by Mr. Heilprin, a few succumbed under the ordeal of the first two years' privations; but these were soon replaced by more capable settlers from among later comers of the refugees. When these had become fairly established, new arrivals began to swell the numbers of the settlers, but the sudden death of Michael Heilprin bereft the colonists of their main support during the infantile stages of the settlement. Such organized support as remained was devoted to fostering the

Jewish Homesteads on Miller Avenue, South Carmel.

growth of Alliance, and to avoid the imminent danger of the settlement failing for want of temporary sustenance an appeal was made through Rev. Dr. Morais, of this city, to the celebrated philanthropist, Baron de Hirsch, of Paris. After some correspondence with the late Chevalier Veneziani, the agent of Baron de Hirsch's charitable dispensations, the baron sent on $5000 for distribution among the colonists.

The money was allotted to the settlers in various amounts in accordance with recommendations made by Mr. Moses Klein, the agent of the Jewish Emigration Society of this city, who had been detailed to make a thorough investigation of the needs of each individual colonist, and the timely aid thus obtained has carried the colony to the point of self-maintenance. Latterly a number of families have settled there with means of their own, and the prospects of the settlement are now very favorable, and will become still more so when the projected railroad between Millville and Bridgeton is built. This proposed road, which would pass through Carmel, is part of a system connecting with railroads on the western shore of Delaware Bay, and running from Salem, N. J., to May's Landing and thence to the seashore.

Carmel now contains upward of 300 of the refugees, who occupy a tract of 848 acres, of which about 300 are cultivated. There are a post-office, a synagogue and school and a library, two teachers and a number of artisans.

No physician is as yet settled here, which leaves a good chance open for some of the superfluous graduates of our numerous medical schools.

Rosenhayn, which is a station on the Southern New Jersey Railroad, forms a halfway point in the ten miles which separate Vineland and Bridgeton. This place is an old settlement, and the Jewish farmers here are mostly such as have obtained their holdings through their own means. It contains about 1000 inhabitants, of whom 270 are Russian Jews. These own 1912 acres of land and have about 300 acres under cultivation. Sixty children of the colonists attend school at Rosenhayn, and in this connection it may be remarked that the rapidity with which the coming generation of these people is being assimilated to the native language, customs and attitude of mind, is simply astonishing. Even characteristics of feature and other ethnological peculiarities seem rapidly to be melting away under the influence of the New Jersey air and soil, and 10 year-old boys and girls who have been here four or five years no longer betray their foreign birth by the slightest trace of accent.

On last Tuesday, 22nd inst.,* about seventy of the Alliance colonists, who had completed the probationary term of five or more years' residence in this Republic, applied for their final naturalization papers to the court at Salem, N. J. They will thus become full-fledged citizens

---

* October 22, 1889.

of the United States and will presently be accounted as factors in State and local politics. As might be supposed, their party preferences are by no means uniform; differences of opinion are more than ordinarily pronounced among these people, and these differences have manifested themselves even in their religious observances. With regard to the latter, the majority are of the most orthodox school, but a strong minority have already introduced innovations upon their older customs, and have arrayed themselves as "Reformers." In Alliance the rival sects have each a synagogue of their own, the religious organizations forming here, as in all primitive communities, the focus of social movement. In this respect all three colonies are alike, although it is only in the largest, at Alliance, that religious differences have developed to the stage of separate organization.

In general the relations of the colonists, to each other and to their Christian neighbors, have been of the most amicable and satisfactory character. In fact, these colonies, combining as they do the solidarity of a communal organization with the complete independence of each individual, afford a rare object lesson to the student of sociology.

Addenda

The Jewish Colonies in Palestine: A Defense

In view of the unfounded statements constantly cropping out, with regard to Palestine, and the results attending Jewish colonization in the Holy Land, we have considered it our duty—even at the risk of delaying the publication of the present work—to correct willful errors which have gained currency in different sections. That the condition of our brethren who dwell in cities of Palestine is not what it should be, that squalor and wretchedness prevail among them, and that their social position in general is below the average standard, we have never attempted to deny. But we do emphatically maintain that the opposite is shown with those who have settled at the colonies, now prospering, and meeting with the approval of the Turkish authorities, as well as the support of their noble benefactor, Baron Edmund de Rothschild.

Ever since the plan of colonizing Palestine was formulated, opponents have been endeavoring by every means to excite the hostility of Jewish communities, and thus render the movement an utter failure.

Happily, they have not succeeded, and the future of the Palestinean colonies is assured, despite their attacks. Even some of the Jewish journals have been used as vehicles for the display of petty feelings, and the בני קרח have endeavored in vain to retard the progress of the colonies, by their misrepresentations, in certain Hebrew papers, in which they have stopped short at nothing to accomplish their purpose and have even attempted to cast odium upon Baron Edmund de Rothschild, who has brought about so much good in this direction, and whose deeds have won for him an honored name in modern Jewish history.

The Palestinean Jewish colonies, far from being failures are, with scarcely an exception, established upon successful bases. The earliest of the modern colonies there, *Petach Tikvah*, was started already in 1872, by prominent Jews of Jerusalem. This was followed by *Zichron Ya'acob* (originally called *Shomeron*) and *Rosh Pinah* (both formed by Roumanian Jews). The outbursts of Russian fanaticism which, in 1881–1882, drove thousands of our unfortunate co-religionists from the cruel country of the Czar, led to the formation of the now prosperous *Rishon L'Zion* colony, by a band of Russian students. The success of these attempts, aided, of course, by Baron de Rothschild, is seen today, when ten Jewish colonies exist in Palestine, the majority of which are on a permanent footing, while four others have been added thereto during the year 1889.

Furthermore, it is well known:

(1) That Baron Edmund de Rothschild individually sustains most of the Jewish settlements, and affords the means for the establishment of new ones in the Land of Promise.

(2) That the British consul at Jerusalem, in his report, dwelt especially upon the excellent state of the *Rishon L'Zion* colony, with its 2,000,000 grape-vines.

(3) That the present Turkish governor of the Holy City, Reshad Pasha, is favorably disposed towards the Jewish colonies, and seeks their advancement.

(4) That the "Sublime Porte" recently granted a *firman* to Mr. Joseph Navon for the construction of a railroad between Jaffa and Jerusalem, where most of the settlements are located.

(5) That the law forbidding any permanent residence of foreign Jews in Palestine is no longer enforced; according to latest advices, this law has been altogether repealed.

(6) That the Sultan has conferred upon Mr. Scheid, Baron de Rothschild's agent, the Order of the *Medjidie*, in recognition of his services in encouraging farming in Palestine.

(7) That the schools at the different colonies have adopted the pure Hebrew as a substitute for the Jargon, so that the sacred tongue is spoken now with as much fluency as the Arabic, or the European languages taught there.

A highly pleasing incident was that of last *Succoth*, when a group of Palestinean Jewish farmers, attired in European garments, repaired, in procession, to Jerusalem, following the custom of our ancestors, who, three times, yearly, visited the Holy Sanctuary, as commanded in our Law. After having offered up their prayers at the *Kothel Ma'arabi* (The Western Wall of the Temple), they attended a representation, by Hebrew school-children, of a Biblical drama, given in pure Hebrew, and describing the deeds performed by Zerubbabel and his compatriots in connection with the restoration of the Jewish State in Palestine. The visit deepened the good impression formed of the colonists, and was by itself calculated to arouse enthusiasm in Jewish colonization, and strengthen its future. Are the hopes of the illustrious Crémieux about to be fulfilled? (See page 34.)

The distinguished Jewish merchant and savant, Mordecai Ben Hillel Ha-Cohen, who, in order to ascertain the actual condition of affairs at the Palestinean Jewish colonies, recently left Russia, and proceeded there, has since written to a friend a general description of four colonies he has thus far visited. This communication was published in a late issue of *Ha-Meliz*, of St. Petersburg, and discloses facts which directly contradict the glaring falsities circulated through the medium of some Jewish journals. Mr. Cohen proves, beyond all doubt, that Jewish colonies in the Holy Land are "living habitations"; that the settlers are sincerely attached to their new homes, and cultivate the soil with eagerness and zeal; that the settlements, far from being wastes, or even villages, present the appearance of cities—thriving and prosperous. He advises all to avoid specious theorizing, and be convinced solely by practical results, which constitute the most irrefutable proof of the existing state of things.

And what conclusion must be drawn from the above statements—briefly as they are told? Simply this—that the Jewish colonists who till the soil of the Holy Land will advance onward and upward; that by pursuing agriculture as their calling, they will uplift themselves, and incite many others of their brethren, in enlightened, as well as in benighted, countries, to emulate their example, and earn their livelihood by the "sweat of their brow." Such was the occupation of our patriarchs, of our prophets, of our sages; and that which afforded them subsistence, yea, delight,—because it instilled within them the feeling of dependence upon God alone,—ought surely to effect permanent good to their latest posterity. Joined to the pursuit of agriculture, the dissemination of the pure Hebrew as a language of intercourse will be attended with inestimable benefits.

We sincerely believe that the time will come when Jewish agricultural colonization will spread throughout the Orient, and that Palestine will be, as in ancient days, the centre of all such efforts.

Then will be fulfilled the glorious prediction of the Prophet Isaiah:

ובנו ממך חרבות עולם! מוסדי דור ודור תקומם,
וקרא לך גודר פרץ, משובב נתיבות לשבת.

"And they that shall be of thee shall build the old waste places; thou shalt raise up the foundations of many generations; and thou shalt be called the repairer of the breach, the restorer of paths to dwell in."

Farming in the Jewish Colonies of South Jersey

Extracts from contemporary newspapers,
Chiefly *The Jewish Exponent*

The Growth of Jewish Colonies Review of Migdal Zophim*

By Myer S. Isaacs

Mr. Klein is favorably known in connection with philanthropic work in Philadelphia directly aiding immigrants from Russia. He has reprinted his interesting papers on the Palestine and New Jersey colonies, and also the article of the Philadelphia *Sunday Mercury* on the Vineland settlements. It is a valuable contribution to the history of these colonies, and the author has preserved graphic illustrations of the beginnings of Alliance, Carmel, and Rosenhayn. He promises shortly a supplementary volume in Hebrew, embracing in part a translation of the present work.

We cannot say that the history of these settlements in New Jersey is fully told; altogether too much stress is laid upon the part taken by Philadelphians in the replenishment of the treasury of Alliance. But it is of far greater importance to tell the story of the struggles of the unfortunate exiles in their praiseworthy effort to attain independence than to seek to award honor to individuals who helped "here a little and there a little" to save the colonies from failure.

In truth, the young and energetic immigrant who is willing to labor and to wait *can* attain independence by farming. He must have some means or be aided at the first stage of his journey. He should not enjoy too much paternal government; that was the cause of the slow progress of Alliance. He should not be made the recipient of charity. The grants of money to enable him to acquire implements of husbandry and to support himself while clearing his land and raising the first crop, should be only a loan and should be secured by a mortgage on his land, so that he will be prevented from borrowing to excess and be spared the temptation of speculating in land beyond his means.

The difficulty is that the immigrant was usually placed upon a plot of uniform area with no example but that of an inexperienced and ambitious neighbor. He was trained on the socialistic plan—every settler must have the identical acreage, cow, sewing machine, and profit accorded to his neighbor, or there will be a revolution. In consequence, the higher moral sense of the settler was not cultivated. He had not grown up with the country. And only last year, when the final step was taken of putting

---

* *The Jewish Messenger* (New York), March 14, 1890, 1. Myer S. Isaacs (1841–1904), the eldest son of the second English-speaking Rabbi in the United States, the Rev. Dr. Samuel M. Isaacs, was a real estate lawyer, judge, philanthropist and, along with his brothers Isaac and Abram, editor of the *Jewish Messenger*. See the finding aid to his records at the American Jewish Historical Society, New York, New York.

the land owner on a business basis as to the future, was there apparent a clear recognition of the colonist's obligations.

At Carmel, the settlement of questions between colonists and benefactor was discouraging. Mr. Klein does not appear to have understood this, and it is to be hoped that when he publishes his Hebrew edition, he will secure accurate information and thus be enabled to teach thousands of intending colonists the limitations of successful agricultural work in America.

Only one man has been found engaged in the work who understood the subject practically and theoretically—Mr. Heilprin. He was modest enough in his greatness of heart and keen intellectual grasp of the problem to know that the givers of money or time needed education as much as the unhappy exiles, their brethren who fled from persecution. And had Mr. Heilprin lived, there seemed to be a certainty of a solution of this serious and important question.

The combination of industrial with agricultural employment has been indispensable, because there were families dependent upon a single inexperienced wage-earner who was a paper farmer, but very energetic and faithful. It is but a temporary expedient. There must be farmers who will study the soil and acquire special knowledge and aptitude. There must be some who strike out for themselves, like other pioneers and build up their own future. Neither Carmel nor Alliance can be pronounced a thorough success as an agricultural settlement, but both are very hopeful in the unmistakable evidence they furnish of heroic fidelity to duty—the establishment on free soil of an independent family life denied most cruelly to worthy citizens in their inhospitable native land.

Report to the Emigrant Aid Society[*]
Vineland, N. J.

Mr. A. C. Sternberg, Superintendent of the Russian colony, has made the following interesting report to the Emigrant Aid Society, which we publish in full:

As Superintendent of the Vineland Agricultural Training School, I beg to submit the following statement of the work performed, and the results achieved by the emigrants in my charge, prefacing this by the assertion that no verbal description can adequately depict the industry, perseverance under difficulties, and energy daily evinced by the Refugees.

One hundred and twenty-five families numbering nearly four hundred and fifty persons, are now in this colony. Nearly all the adult males are employed in agricultural pursuits, which are conducted so as to illustrate consecutively the methods employed in the United States in reclaiming virgin soils from the primitive conditions in which such lands are usually found in this country; that is to say,

* *The Jewish Messenger* (New York), July 21, 1882, 2–3. This early description of the Alliance Colony was made two months after the first settlers arrived.

by first clearing off the sprouts and underbrush from the land, then cutting down the heavy timber (sawing and cutting it up for fuel and winter use), next in plowing and in planting the various crops suited to this latitude, teaching during this latter process the manures adapted to the different products and the methods of their employment, as well as some practical instruction in their chemical constituents.

The soil in this section as you are aware, is well adapted for Indian Corn, Sweet Potatoes, White Potatoes and other vegetables, and it is to the cultivation of these crops we have devoted our attention.

Some of the men who are expert handicraftsmen, we have employed at their respective trades in necessary work at the colony, viz: carpenters, blacksmiths, brick masons, bakers, barbers, etc. Most of the women, having large families of [young] children to care for, have been engaged in domestic avocations: cooking, sewing, washing, etc. They also devote themselves assiduously to keeping their apartments in good order. It is very interesting to observe the individuality perceptible in the fitting up of these apartments, which has been left to themselves, with a view to attain this very result of competitive cleanliness and taste. The materials for the garments made by the women have been supplied by the Society as required upon my requisition.

I take great pleasure in announcing the satisfactory hygienic condition of the colony, only one death having taken place to this date, and this the case of a young child, the disease having been contracted before arrival here. We have not now nor have we had a single case of serious sickness with the above exception. I therefore think myself justified in claiming for this locality exceptionally favorable sanitary conditions, aided of course by good water and constant employment of mind and body of all the colonists.

The conduct of the emigrants with very rare exceptions has been in every respect exemplary; no punishment having been required; an earnest reprimand having invariably sufficed. Considering the number under my charge and the close proximity in which they are housed, and that they are deprived of many comforts beyond our ability to supply, and come themselves from different localities and various views and habits, this is as well a surprising as a satisfactory result.

I cannot otherwise than attribute this result to the uniformity of the religious sentiment thoroughly permeating one and all, which tends to create a sentiment of fraternity between persons hitherto strangers.

The rites of their religion have been in every respect sedulously and strictly observed, no business or labor being permitted to interfere in any way. In no other form of occupation than agricultural colonies, in my judgment, can these be thus so strictly maintained. In our case for example, slightly removed from neighbors, no conflict with other religious practices takes place, and no objection is raised to labor on Sunday in place of Saturday as is our custom.

We are enabled by buying our meat in large quantities, to procure it kosher from a Philadelphia butcher, thus overcoming the great difficulty found by emigrants scattered among small towns in conforming to the dietary laws.

I dwell on these matters because I am convinced, as I know you and the entire Committee are, that upon them depend the happiness of these unfortunate people, and the promotion of their highest interests. Our work here has steadily progressed since its inception, the men working not alone with will, but manifesting an adaptation and endurance much beyond my most sanguine expectation.

In consequence of the prevalent opinion so confidently expressed in many quarters that the Jew would never make an agriculturalist, or in fact be capable of doing any work requiring any endurance, fears were entertained that my labor here would prove futile, and that this colony was doomed to failure.

It is with the highest pleasure that I am enabled to state as the result of my experience here that, during my work as a practical farmer covering a period of over thirty years, I have rarely found beginners who have proved pupils more apt or who made more satisfactory progress than the Refugees here. We have therefore, I conclude, practically controverted (under circumstances sufficiently trying) the outcry so often and so unjustly made that "Jews will not work." It is true that these people have been promised homesteads provided they proved themselves competent to make a living at agriculture, and possibly this inducement has been a strong incentive throughout their labor, and thus enabled them to demonstrate this competency. However this may be, the result at least is plainly manifest. It becomes therefore my plain duty now to intercede for the people under my charge, and to petition the Society to take the necessary steps to provide them as quickly as possible with their own homes in severalty, so as to render them self supporting, and to remove what is always most desirable in such cases, the dependent feeling which the quasi-paternal support of the Society must have developed. The sooner this is done the better for them and for the Society. You know the condition upon which the land we occupy was secured, the price being fifteen dollars ($15) per acre. I would recommend for each head of a family an allotment of fifteen acres, the erection of a small house thereon, the providing of the necessary furniture and agricultural implements (on the most economical basis) and their being assisted for a definite limited time with the necessaries of life; it being plainly understood that at the expiration of such time all further support will be withdrawn. I have carefully examined the matter, and have questioned many of the emigrants as to how they would manage on new land to support their families, and I am quite convinced that they not only fully comprehend the difficulties, but also that they are quite able to grapple with and in the end to solve them. They do not expect to devote their entire time to the cultivation of the land at first, but propose to supplement this by work for themselves and children on contiguous farms, railroads, and in factories, or even when necessary by leaving home for longer periods, always in such cases leaving their families at the colony. In fact, I cannot but believe that they are well able to earn a livelihood if once permanently settled with their families.

The following presents an approximate estimate of the cost of the above plan for each family thus settled:

15 acres of land at $15 per acre,	$225.00
House	125.00
Household furniture	25.00
Small tools	10.00
Supplies for six months	100.00
Incidental expenses	15.00
Total	$500.00

Upon this basis I deem it perfectly safe to predict success for such a plan which I think insures the ability on the part of the colonist to repay the advance above proposed. This advance should be loaned at a low rate of interest, say three percent. per annum, and the term of repayment extended over a period of say ten years in installments, to be made at such periods as they shall be able most probably to discharge such obligations. Of course during the first three or four years, these payments should be as little burdensome as possible, owing to their extreme poverty in the beginning, the necessary work required on new land not being immediately remunerative, their comparative inexperience, and lastly their unfamiliarity with our language.

In this connection I would say, that I am employing two teachers in giving lessons in the rudiments of English to the children, thus preparing them to enter the public schools in the vicinity as soon as the Fall term begins, having made due application for the full enjoyment of school privileges afforded by the State of New Jersey. I may here state that additional buildings are being erected by the Government authorities for this purpose in order to accommodate the sudden large increase occasioned by the establishment of our colony. This instruction is in addition to the religious tuition in the Hebrew language, religion, and literature in which the young pupils manifest astonishing proficiency.

In closing my report, Mr. President, permit me to again impress you with the vital necessity of encouraging our people in the work so admirably begun, and to answer their prayers as quickly as possible, by advancing the means of supplying these suffering unfortunate, and homeless people, at last happy in this broad land of freedom and religious toleration.

Let us demonstrate to the world that this people will become producers, if afforded an even chance so to do.

Let us enable them to worship in the faith of their fathers, so that we may be assured of their prayers and those of their children for generations yet to come.

It is a great work which we are engaged in; it is a great privilege that we have been permitted to assist in it. Let us prove ourselves entirely worthy of the great trust which has been allotted to us and to our generation.

To Moses Bayuk from Henry S. Henry[*]

48 Exchange Place, New York, Dec. 31, 1884

Mr. M. Bayuk and Others, Colony Alliance:

I received the letter addressed to me representing your present condition and wants. I have no money at my disp[osal] and cannot help you further than by representing to others that you require work and that you are willing to work.

Nothing will give us greater pleasure than that you should become independent without our aid; and if you think you can manage this we shall be perfectly satisfied.

We are in correspondence with the Committee in London for the purchase outright of the land occupied by you and now owned by Messrs. Leach; and if they accede to our prayer it is proposed that new contracts be made with all of you who are deserving, whereby you may become owners of the land by paying one-half of its present contract value; or else by paying 3 per cent. interest on this half value for 33 years; you then obtain a deed in your own names for the property. None of you yet have ever paid anything, either interest or taxes, on the land, and if you choose to leave it you are welcome to do so; but you cannot possibly expect us to support you any longer and if you cannot make a living for yourselves and families and see no prospect of doing so, you must go elsewhere, but it must be at your own expense.

You should be aware that business is very bad all over the United States; that many people are out of employ and that wages are not so good as they have been and will be again. It is therefore unreasonable to expect that Mr. Jacobson or anybody else can afford to pay as high wages as he did some time ago. Even at the wages he pays, he cannot sell the segars so as to cover cost.

In conclusion, you should understand that Mr. Eppinger, Mr. Gerschel and myself have done all in our power to help you along, and that we have neither means nor ability to do any more. If we can succeed to get the land for you on such terms as we propose, we shall consider ourselves fortunate; but, beyond that, you can expect nothing further at our hands.

Yours,

H. S. HENRY

---

[*] Letter from Henry S. Henry to Moses Bayuk, dated December 31, 1884. Henry was a trustee of the Alliance Land Trust, which since 1883 had held the mortgages to the land and homes settled by the original Alliance colonists. The letter was printed, presumably for distribution, by the Evening Journal Steam Print, Vineland, N. J. *Courtesy of Marsha Levin Schumer for the Judge I. Harry Levin collection.*

Report on Alliance Colony by Moses Bayuk*

BELOVED:

It has pleased the Lord to over-rule the anger of man toward our race, to find a new home under the care of those who are the founders of Alliance Colony. Believing that those who feel an interest in founding this Colony desire to know directly from the Colonists what has been done, what is now doing, and what may be the prospects for the future, this Bi-Annual Report is hereby respectfully submitted:

The Alliance Colony was founded in 1882 under the auspices of the Hebrew Emigrant Aid Society, of New York. The Colony is situated in what is known as South Jersey, between Vineland and Bridgeton, one mile from Bradway Station, on the New Jersey Southern Railroad. The soil is not naturally rich, but may be made very productive if properly composted and carefully cultivated. In these circumstances, with lack of experience and an almost total want of supplies, it must not be regarded as a

matter of surprise to find that our crops and the results of our skill in management are not what we expected, nor what the founders of the Colony had reason to expect. Still, though very sadly disappointed and in many respects much distressed as to how we are to live, yet we are not disheartened; but, hope, with your continual care and encouragement, to be able to accomplish what may be reasonably expected.

The soil is best adapted to grow fruits, and especially berries; potatoes and other vegetables are also successfully grown. The market is certainly among the best in the nation, and with time and continual care along with the judicious expenditure of additional money, there can be no just reason why our colony should not, in the course of time, become not only self-supporting but moderately wealthy.

When properly enriched and carefully cultivated, the soil may be made to bring a net income of from twenty five, to fifty dollars per acre.

The area of the Colony is one thousand one hundred and fifty acres. Of this one hundred and fifty acres are the common property of the Colony, intended for burial ground, school buildings, factories, etc. The remaining number of acres is divided into small farms of about fifteen acres. According to the contracts each farmer pays $350 within ten years—for the house and well $150, and $15 per acre for the land. During the first four years only the

---

* Printed report on the Alliance colony written by Moses Bayuk, undated, but with handwritten notation dated January 1, 1885. This report seems to be part of an ongoing correspondence between colonists and their trustees. The letter was printed, presumably, for distribution. *Courtesy of Marsha Levin Schumer for the Judge I. Harry Levin collection.*

interest is to be paid; during the six remaining years the full amount is to be paid in equal annual payments.

Care has been taken to state the money basis upon which our hope as a colony is based. We are very anxious to improve every possible advantage this year, in order to be in circumstances as soon as possible to live without the dread of some future calamity, by which we might again be homeless wanderers. Of the sixty-six farms, thirty-three and the common property are already paid for. The contracts are made with Mr. H. Henry, ex-President of the ex H. E. A. S. The remaining thirty-three are not paid for; the contracts are made with Messrs. Leach & Bro., the owners of the land. Owing to what was considered unfavorable circumstances, seventeen farmers left their farms; the remaining forty-nine are doing all they can to improve.

That the reader may know very precisely how we are doing, and something of the privations as well as comforts that have fallen to our lot, as colonists, it may be of interest to state, for the purpose of general information, that on each farm there is a two-story house of two rooms, twelve by fourteen feet, and a well. These houses were built by the committee. At present there is not a house in the Colony that has not been enlarged. In some instances one room has been added, in others two rooms. In addition, every one knows the necessity of a small barn, stable, chicken house and other buildings. Thus it will be seen that with all our want of experience and knowledge of the soil some progress has been made. During the first of the settlement each family, according to the number of men, received eight to twelve dollars a month for nine months and one hundred dollars worth of seed for planting. Each farmer received in addition to the above some furniture, cooking utensils and small farming implements, like axes, saws, grindstones, etc. The second year each received thirty dollars worth of seed. Thanks to Dr. Gottheil and the late Dr. Huebsch, of New York, some forty families were supplied with sewing machines and material for cellars.

We wish to be very explicit in stating what has been done to assist us in getting started in our new home. But it will be remembered by every intelligent reader that we are in a strange land, and by necessary consequence we must have time to gain experience in farming. While true that South Jersey is an excellent fruit growing part of the United States, still the intelligent reader well knows that two or three years must be regarded as too short a time to clear away a forest, plant fruit trees and berries and raise a profitable crop. Thus it will be seen that, under the most favorable circumstances, we have not yet had sufficient time to be getting any real advantage from our farms. Besides, every farmer who has at all succeeded in South Jersey well knows that it takes time to enrich soil, naturally light, in order to get good crops. Then it is a matter of actual fact that the last season in this region was a peculiarly dry and unfruitful year. Even the experienced farmer in many instances did not get a crop large enough to pay for the seed sown. This does not often occur; but just at this time it is exceedingly oppressive to us, to know that with all our labor, expenditure of money and loss of time, we are not in circumstances to go on with our farm work as we must in order to live.

While discouraged in one direction, we cannot but feel encouraged in other directions. Our children are attending public school, and thereby enjoying advantages for which we try to feel thankful. Thanks to Mr. M. Heilgrin and Judge M. S. Isaacs, of New York, we are provided with a teacher of the Hebrew language. Disaster must not be overlooked; five houses have been burned, three only were insured.

At present the Colony consists of forty-nine families—four to six men in a family—total, two hundred and eighty-five. All the Colonists are thrifty, laborious and hard working. Most of the men were traders and merchants in their native home in Russia. The men are healthy and cheerful, owing, it seems, to temperate use of food and abstinence from meat, fish, milk, butter and other nutricious articles of food. Well, it is a fruit growing region. This cannot be said of the women. There is more or less of constitutional distress, accompanied with suffering, which, with better medical attendance, might be avoided. Something, doubtless, may be attributed to exposure. The houses are frail and not substantially built, and, as a consequence, there must be exposure to cold during Winter and to heat in Summer.

These plain facts are stated in order to show that while, as Colonists, we are exceedingly anxious to do all for ourselves that can be reasonably expected, yet with little or no money, having lost all in our native land, and with a forest and naturally poor soil to commence our farming, it could not be expected of us to live without some assistance until we can make our farms productive. Only two years have gone. We have worked hard, we have worked perseveringly amid many trials and much self-denial. With bad seasons, and especially the last season, we have literally nothing on which to lay our plans for the future. True, nominally, we have a home; but a home in a strange land with no money in our purses and no crops, how are we to live?

To avert actual starvation and at the same time enable us, as helpless Colonists, to earn our own living, which we very much prefer to do, two factories were erected; but, as all know, it is not easy to obtain work. One of these buildings was designed to be a sewing establishment; but there was no sewing to do. Consequently the building is now standing idle. The other was intended for a cigar factory. The latter was erected by Mrs. B. Reckendorfer, in memory of her late husband, Joseph Reckendorfer. The wages are the lowest possible figure, so that a good man can earn at an average only about one dollar and seventy-five cents a week.

Now, it is not intended to make any reflections upon any one; but the intelligent reader can at once see that, while some one enjoys the large profit connected with the sale of this luxury, we, as humble refugees, are compelled to work at starvation prices. No man can either live himself or farm his land, much less support a family, at $1.75 a week!

We do not make this statement in any complaining spirit. Very far from it. We are thankful to have a home at all, and under the circumstances would certainly not present our condition to the public if it were not that we sincerely desire to get on with what has already been commenced. It is said that a prudent man foreseeth the evil. We must be mindful of the necessity of providing in time for the emergencies of the future. With our very limited resources in actual money we have not been able to plant all the fruit trees and vines that ought now to be growing. We have no horses to do our plowing and no plows with which to plow, even if we had the horses, and no money to employ others to do our plowing. It is now time to be making preparations, but being without seed and without way to earn money, how can we get along?

We have gained knowledge by experience, and we now want to profit by our experience; and hence present our case in order that patriotic and kindly benevolent people may at least have an opportunity of assisting us.

Without complaint or murmuring, we accept our situation as being necessary in the circumstances to teach us self dependence. We do certainly believe that with our knowledge gained by experience, we may even now begin to do right what we did not know at our first coming. If plants can be purchased for us, or trees and vines, horses and plows, we propose to plant all we can, as we have done in the past. Though in poverty and actual suffering, still, we suffered before and the good Lord enabled us to bear all. So will He do now. Though disappointed and cast down, we are not in despair; though mistakes have been made, it is never too late to do better. Our dependence is on the strong arm of Jehovah; our hope is in the patriotic and benevolent spirit of the citizens of our beloved, adopted country; our reliance is in the perseverance and energy of our own manhood. Others have failed and failed again, and yet in the end have prospered. So may it be—so must it be with us. We wish to remain where we are; we are already warmly attached to our new home, and we sincerely trust that our sad misfortune in the loss of all in our native land may be the means of causing us to feel the more faithfully devoted to our adopted land, where warm hearts bid us welcome to this home of the distressed; and not only welcomed us, but, being without money, naked and homeless, money and a home were kindly offered. For all this we are truly thankful, and only now ask that we may be permitted still to share the hospitality of kind friends until we can walk alone.

We know that it is the glory of this blessed Republic to offer a home alike to all; we know, too, that the citizens of this great nation are warm-hearted and sympathetic. No distress ever appeals in vain to a true son or daughter of this Republic. Only let the distress be real, not pretended. As Colonists, therefore, we respectfully invite any committee to visit us, inquire into our habits of life, our knowledge of labor, our plans for the coming Spring, and home-care and domestic order, and see whether we are doing all for ourselves that we can do with our limited means.

We certainly invite any and all to come. We want information, we need instruction, we desire to be told how to improve our condition.

In closing this Report, we simply leave our case with those who have the struggles and sufferings of our distressed people near to their heart, assured that, when they know our true condition, the help we need will be cheerfully granted. It was so before. When driven from our homes, with the loss of everything, you, as brothers and sisters, gave us all we have: now we come as the adopted citizens of the greatest Republic on earth, and wishing first to offer sincere thanks for all that has been done for us, we can only say, we still need your fostering care, your helping hand and sympathetic heart. Help us in our effort to become independent citizens of our great Brotherly Union! [Date handwritten: "Jan 1 1885"]

Respectfully submitted.

ALLIANCE COLONY

Information may be obtained at the office of the Secretary.

M. Bayouk, N. 34, Alliance Colony
[Address handwritten: "Vineland N. J."]

The Jewish Colony at Vineland in 1887[*]

It was last week when away I went from the tumultuous city, from the din and noise of the busy streets of Brotherly Love to the country, to enjoy the pure air and refreshing breeze; and for a day or two, at least, to give myself perfect rest in the midst of new scenery and new surroundings. Short as my vacation was, I returned buoyant and with a cheerful heart. Not to the sea-shore did I go, neither did I climb mountains nor hills, nor did I eye nature through an artificial telescope from a piazza of a fashionable hotel, or from the portico of a handsome cottage.

The "Maurice River" is a merry laughing brooklet with as fine a sandy shore as you could wish; the potatoes and watermelons are planted on hills, and from the low windows of the double-framed colonists' houses one can behold a sight that would overcome you with joy, a sight that no one since eighteen hundred years could have beheld, should he have roamed over land and valley, and explored this place from *Mizrach* to *Maarab* (sunrise to sunset).

The descendants of those who were driven off their native land; who went into a long exile, during the whole period of which one would in vain look for a bright moment in their lives; despised and persecuted even now in almost every country of the Old World; these descendants are now free men, equal citizens, and honest tillers of the soil. A Jew tills the ground! To me that is a sight that surpasses everything in the line of sight-seeing! Who could have imagined a few years ago that the ideal which, by many, not to say by enemies, was regarded as unattainable and a mere chimera, would be realized and would become a matter of fact, an undeniable reality in this blessed country of America? But here the facts stand in their persuading grandeur, and speak to all in a language of truth. Here a Jew, a real Jew, in flesh and spirit, slowly walks after his own horse, which draws a plough, and you could stand and gaze for hours, how this ploughman—a Jew—lays fallow after fallow, and manages to ingeniously avoid all obstacles in the shape of stumps which are bountifully scattered over the newly-cleared ground. There he stops. He wipes the sweat from his honest brow, takes a draught of cold crystal well-water from the hands of his chubby boy, and with a few encouraging utterances to his own horse goes on with his work. There a Jewess gracefully moves among the vines gathering fruits, or constantly lifts and lets down the hoe around the strawberry plant, murmuring a sweet popular Russian air. The boys and girls do not stay behind idly; they too, like busy bees, work the whole day, laughing, singing and cheering thus:

---

[*] By Charles D. Spivakovski, *The Jewish Exponent* (Philadelphia), August 19, 1887, 9–10.

Each morning sees some task begin,
Each evening sees it close.

"Thank God, we are happy—we have had a good crop; we have nothing to complain of"; this is the answer that you will receive from all sides to your question, "How goes it?" Oh, how significant these words are! What a change in affairs do they indicate! It is only he who knows the colony for a few years that can understand the full meaning of these words. I well remember the time when many families lived upon bread and water for months. I knew a family that had a "hermafrodite" pair of shoes, which was worn alternately by the head of the family and his spouse. I knew the time when milk was regarded as a rare article of diet, and no one dared even to think of butter. Now everything is changed. The bread is besmeared with butter, and the water is seasoned with sugar. The people are decently dressed and they have shoes "after its kind." Milk is a common article of food, and they not only dare, but positively enjoy every day a meal of meat.

The houses are painted, and show a different appearance from a year ago; the beautiful lawns and flowers before the dwellings indicate that the struggle for a bare existence is a thing of the past. Stables, farms, and additional rooms were built during the last two years. There are about twenty-five cows, and almost as many horses. Then, the colony itself has been increased. Four new houses I found on my last visit, and as many will be erected shortly, on a strip of land which joins the colony, and was bought for hard cash, I am glad to state, by those very men who left their farms once and have now returned.

This year's crop was the largest, as regards any very large quantity. Since last year the colonists are self-supporting, and they have made a comfortable living, which, thanks to Dr. M. Jastrow, Jr., and other gentlemen interested in the welfare of the colonists, through whom work was sent them from the city. There is no doubt, that with the small savings of this year's crop, and by working through the winter, the colonists will get along nicely, and the wolf will be kept at bay.

As I have not had sufficient time to gather all the information I wanted, I shall merely give an approximate idea of this year's income. About two hundred thousand quarts of berries have been shipped this season by the colonists, which brought fifteen thousand dollars, or on an average of three hundred dollars per family.

This is indeed the most prosperous and promising Jewish colony in the United States, and the only independent one in the world. This colony is a monument, not wrought of steel, or marble, but a living monument, which the American Jews have erected as an evidence of their generosity, and as a rebuke to the enemies of Israel. It would require more space than a newspaper article permits, to write the full history of the "Alliance" colony, and I will leave it to some other person who is more competent to treat this subject.

It is a well-known fact that the Immigrant Aid Society, now transformed into the Alliance Land Committee, of New York, conjointly with the Mansion House Committee, of London, are the original founders of the colony; but I cannot refrain from giving credit to those gentlemen who had a great share in, and largely contributed to, the building up of the settlement, and who completed the noble work. It will not be too much to say, that had they not come in good time to the aid of the colonists, we might have lost for a certain period, the opportunity of seeing Israel dwelling in their own tents. The two gentlemen whom I mean are Messrs. Alfred T. Jones and Simon Muhr, of Philadelphia. It was these who, two years ago, responded to the cries of the hungry, almost starving, colonists, and provided them with food and fuel. They were constantly communicating with the colonists, and went there and back almost twice a week. Had their generous hearts remained unaffected during that time, all the colonists would have left their farms forever, as a tendency towards it was then already afloat. Quite right were our Sages in saying, אין המצוה נקראת אלא על שם גומרה ("The merit of having performed a duty is attributed but to him who completes it.")

I was glad to learn from the settlers, that Messrs. Mayer Sulzberger and Simon Muhr accepted the invitation tendered them, and were present at the picnic given on August 7th. For the first time since the colony was founded the children had then a chance of listening to a band of music, and the young enjoyed it hugely, dancing the whole day and late into the night. Mr. F. Smith opened the picnic with a fine speech, and Mr. Lubaroff welcomed the guests from Philadelphia. Mr. Sulzberger responded with a short speech in English, and Mr. Muhr in German. In the peaceful and quiet life of the colonists a great event has taken place, and if you see two men talking, you may be sure that the subject is the recent picnic and the distinguished guests.

What is absolutely incomprehensible to me is the fact that those who took so much pains, and worked so hard for the welfare of the colonists; who saw so much misery and beheld such heart-rending scenes, do not come and enjoy the fruits of their labors. Where are Messrs. Henry, Gershel and Eppinger, of New York? Why do they keep aloof from the Colony? I vouch, they would not be "bothered" by a single "petition" from the colonists, but would meet beaming faces, contented hearts, souls overflowing with gratitude, and, above all, men who are conscious of their independence and dignity as free citizens. Unselfishness and devotion to good for good's sake is very laudable, and a charming philosophy is utilitarianism; but not to feel any pleasure in performing one's duty, to shun it even, must be a kind of self-mortification, a trait of asceticism which is not in accord with the teachings of the nineteenth century, and consequently contrary to reason, which is the basis of morality.

In conclusion, I want to say, that if any reader should happen to meet an "Alliance" colonist, let him say in the words of the poet:

Thanks for thee, my worthy friend
For the lesson thou hast taught.

And quite a new lesson it is, and a very hard one too; but the people who sat once under their own vine and fig tree will again experience the same pleasurable delights as of yore.

Three cheers for the "Alliance" Colony!

CHARLES D. SPIVAKOVSKI

The Jewish Colony at "Alliance"*

Editors of *The Jewish Exponent.*

While it is permissible for any one to discover beauties in common place surroundings, and experience joys at the sight of a Jew tilling his hard won ground, by the sweat of his brow; taking occasionally a draught of cold crystal (?) well-water, and having his wife around him gracefully (of course) moving among the vines (where she gets sometimes hopelessly entangled in the rough "stickers") gathering fruits, etc., etc.; and while there may be much truth in the report of your esteemed correspondent about the condition of the Jewish colony near Vineland, there is one thing at least which I cannot help correcting in the name of Truth, of Humanity, and for the sake of the colonists themselves.

The trouble with your correspondent, it seems to me, is that, like many other good-meaning men who write from insufficient information, he has thought himself fully prepared for his task, after having satisfied himself that certain persons, nearest and dearest to him, still take a warm interest in the welfare of that most remarkable experimental colony, established

about six years ago by the spontaneous aid of careful and experienced advisers, as Mr. M. Heilprin, and energetic philanthropists, as Messrs. Henry, Eppinger and Gershel, as well as the generous men of the *Alliance Israelite Universelle*. Your correspondent did not look at other facts, but gave full play to his imagination and brilliant style.

Now, it is true that certain Philadelphia gentlemen came in at the right time to the support of the wavering colonists. All honor to Messrs. Simon Muhr, Alfred T. Jones, and other like noblemen! But to say, referring to their services in this direction, that "the merit of having performed a duty is attributed but to him who completes it," is incorrect in principle as it is not true in fact. Who claims that it was right that he who braved the storms of a never-crossed ocean, and the unparalleled misfortunes of a real hero in affliction, should be refused the honor of having his name immortalized by giving it to the New World he discovered, while to him who first described or "completed" the discovery all merit be due? Truly says Tennyson:

The first discoverer starves—his followers, all
Flower into fortune—our world's way—

"Unselfish devotion to the good for good's sake is very laudable," says your good-natured correspondent in the same connection; but permit me to add that, in fact, the New York

---

* By Moses Bayuk, *The Jewish Exponent* (Philadelphia), September 2, 1887, 5. In reponse to Charles D. Spivakovski's article "The Jewish Colony at Vineland in 1887" in *The Jewish Exponent*, August 19, 1887.

philanthropists have done more for the foundation of the little colony than any body of men
who took some interest in the plan of colonization so admirably laid down and so nobly carried
out by such good servants of Humanity as Messrs.
Heilprin, Henry, Eppinger, and Gershel. And do
you believe that these gentlemen left the fruits of
their work for others to gather? Can you believe
that those who suffered so much and did so much
for the welfare of the colonists, will leave them
now when their advice and assistance are of the
utmost importance; now when their work seems
to be near completion? It is contrary to fact anyhow. The benevolent gentlemen who keep their
eyes, aye, and purses open, too, and watch the
life of the colonists with eager interest are still
ready to lend a helping hand to the needy; not
three full months have elapsed since a few families were gratified by receiving checks to purchase
horses, or additional room. And who is going
to place the crowning stone on the magnificent
edifice of human benevolence and solidarity, by
distributing the deeds which are to make the Jews
of this colony independent freeholders; rightful
owners of valuable property of which they will
have a right to dispose as they please? We had
only the other day an encouraging answer from
Mr. Henry that all of the colonists, except two,
notorious for their bad character, will soon get
their clear deeds, and the widow who suffered

badly by reason of a small crop this year will get
her deed free.

No, no, we would not let the names of those
who took a humane interest in the building up
of "Alliance" be buried in silence where praise
is pronounced for others. They may truly say,
in the words of the poet:

> Sir, in that flight of ages which are God's
> Own voice to justify the dead—perchance
> Spain once the most chivalric race on earth,
> Spain then the mightiest, wealthiest realm on earth,
> So made by me, *may seek to unbury me.*

The names of Heilprin, Eppinger, Henry,
Gershel, as well as those of Simon Muhr and
others are endeared to a large majority of the
colonists, and nothing can erase them from our
grateful memories.

In the same article of your issue of August
19th, my friend, Mr. Charles D. Spivakovski,
makes another mis-statement which I beg
space to correct; and that is the fact that, while
Messrs. Simon Muhr and Mayer Sulzberger
were present at the colonists' picnic, the New
York philanthropists were conspicuous by
their absence. Now, invitations were sent out
by the brethren of the Red Men's Lodge, the
occasion being the celebration of the first
anniversary of its existence. Mr. Henry as well

as others excused themselves for not being present; Messrs. Muhr and Sulzberger were there but on a different errand, though they attended the picnic and addressed our people.

Moses Bayuk
"Alliance," Vineland, N. J.,
August 29th, 1887

The Land Trust Committee at the Alliance Colony*

Editors of *The Jewish Exponent*:

The Jewish colony had a holiday appearance during the two first days of this week, the occasion being the eagerly looked-for visit of the Land Trust Fund Committee of New York, accompanied by the well-known philanthropists, Messrs. Schiff, M. S. Isaacs, and S. Lewison, of Hamburg. The Committee was represented by Messrs. Henry, President; Gershel, Vice-President; Dr. F. de Sola Mendes, Secretary; Eppinger; and Sternberg, Superintendent of the Colony. The distinguished guests occupied a large coach and first stopped at the synagogue, where they were met at the entrance by some farmers with peaches and other late products of their farms. As they rode along Alliance Avenue and Garden Road, they seemed highly gratified at the orderly appearance of the houses and lands. They stopped at every house, and sympathetically inquired into the condition of the inmates, and often halted at the signal of some farmer's wife, who held a petition in her hands explaining their condition. They listened attentively to all, happily chatting with some, encouraging others, and feeling

___

* By Moses Bayuk, *The Jewish Exponent* (Philadelphia), September 9, 1887, 8.

encouraged that their labors and moneys were not used in vain. "Look here, gentlemen," said a sturdy farmer, whose characteristic feature is to speak what his simple heart prompts him, "they were telling us, three years ago, there was little hope for Jews ever becoming farmers. Look at me; these strong arms wanted some kind of work and could not have it, and, of course, I had nothing then; but now my land brings me berries, which grow in orderly rows in the place of bushes and swamps; my ground gives all I want for myself and family; I feel happy and thank you all that helped me so far; and I tell you that hundreds of my brethren will soon become good farmers, like me, and better men, too. Oh, when they drove us out of Spain, there was a handful of us, but I tell you our *Mikva* made so many more Jews in a very short time." You can imagine that this impromptu speech, besides provoking merriment, must have produced a good effect on those who did so much to free the immigrants from their former habits of life.

Many things were there to cheer the hearts of the men who have the interests of their Jewish brethren so near at heart; they saw many new buildings—of which Dr. Mendes took photographic pictures,—as well as material for a few others. Besides the appearance, the manners of the colonists have improved considerably; their demands were modest and their general deportment more dignified. And those that acquired farms without the aid of the Committee, especially deserved the attention of the benevolent guests. Mr. Schiff, after hearing the petition of one of these farmers to cancel the $40 debt for trees, kindly offered $50, to which sum Mr. Lewison subsequently added $75, to be distributed among all the three "new" farmers. The same gentleman granted, furthermore, fifteen sewing machines, which were given mostly to the female members of the newly-arrived families living as yet with their fortunate relations, who succeeded at least in offering them a friendly shelter and an opportunity to work. Ex-Judge Isaacs, acting as a representative of the *Alliance Israelite Universelle*, gave promises to some farmers to get a few tickets for their nearest relations who are still suffering oppression in Russia; and when I spoke to him of my project to start a library for the building of which Mr. Schiff gave $250, he asked me to send him a catalogue of books and papers suitable for this library, promising to furnish what he could. This was not all. That learned gentleman seems to take especial interest in spreading knowledge wherever he finds opportunity for his generous activity. So, besides promising us the means to support a teacher of Hebrew for school children, he also granted our petition for organizing and maintaining a Night School for grown folks. There are many who are willing to spend two hours every evening to learn the language which must sooner or later supplant their mother tongue. I believe that a good man, who will have the respect and confidence of the colonists, can, besides teaching English and Hebrew, have a very salutary influence on their manners and thoughts.

The first day of the visit, the chief object of which was to arrange for the signing and distributing of the deeds, wound up with the $250 donation of Mr. Schiff, for the construction of a chartered synagogue, the cost of which the colonists place at $1,000. Before departing for a conference in Vineland, President Henry said that the deeds will be given the farmers by Lawyer Newcomb during the next month. The next morning, Mr. Mendes, Mr. Gershel and I took a ride to see some colonists and their farms. It was decided by the committee to allow the *shochet* six acres of land and a lodging in the rooms adjoining the synagogue, both the land and residence to be considered and used by him as public property as long as he performs his duties to the satisfaction of the community.

Now, Messrs. Editors, permit me to say that nothing could surpass the sight of the above party, paternally ministering to those who justly expected it. And I want to draw your attention to the fact that the new farmers were so generously considered by Messrs. Schiff and Lewison, the gentlemen who did so much for the older ones. Those who by their own industry, frugality and forethought saved a few dollars to buy a piece of land and, in many cases, build a house and barn on it, cleared the ground and held on to it as the anchor of their lives, must decidedly deserve the encouragement and aid of those who want to see the Jews take to agricultural pursuits more and more, instead of flooding the labor markets in the great cities, augment competition, and "starve" for a living, without decent comforts. I emphasize this fact because I know how hard it is for the newcomers to win ground without some sort of outside help. Only thus we can be in a position to regulate immigration. No committee in the world can help men so much and so well as they can help themselves. I hail this exhibition of thoughtful generosity and foresight toward the new settlers around us as a step—and a long one—in the right direction, which will not fail to bring its good fruits.

If Messrs. Schiff and Lewison broke ground by intimating a new departure in the way of disposing of the Land Trust Fund, Ex-Judge Isaacs did the same by opening new opportunities for the spreading of a much needed education and general enlightenment among our people. His

efforts towards the establishment of a library, and starting an evening school for the grown members of the colony, as well as the appointment of a teacher of Hebrew, must be very highly commended, and they will surely elicit general approval.

I believe that I express the sentiments of the whole colony when I say that the eminent gentlemen who honored the colony with their presence may rest assured that at this particular time of the existence of the colony, every little thing they do for it will not only be most gratefully received, but will serve it better than thousands of dollars misspent in former years.

Messrs. Henry, Eppinger, Gershel, as well as Messrs. Schiff, Isaacs, and others, will not be forgotten by the great bulk of the colonists, to whom they appear as good friends who take delight in the success and are interested in the future of "Alliance."

MOSES BAYUK
"Alliance," Vineland, N. J.,
September, 7th, 1887

Rosenhayn and Jewish Colonization[*]

Though a "Land of Flowers," yet almost without a single flower as yet! Such is Rosenhayn at the present moment. But such will not be the Rosenhayn of the future. All indications point the other way. Everywhere the signs of growth meet pleasantly the visitor's gaze. On all sides the work of building up this comparatively young settlement is pushed with apparent haste and hope. The central road of the colony, called Morton Avenue, is beaming with half-finished structures, and others just begun. The efforts of both the American and the Russian and Hungarian refugees who have recently arrived there are bent toward enlarging and beautifying the foundations laid for a prosperous settlement, one that is yet to justify the name given it by former colonists, the "Land of Flowers."

The history of the settlement lies all within the last two decades, and is contained, so far as its origin is concerned, in the subjoined clipping from a Vineland paper:

---

[*] By George Randorf, *The Jewish Exponent* (Philadelphia), May 30, 1890, 5.

Rosenhayn, which means in German, 'Land of Flowers' is located in Cumberland County, on the high, rolling land just midway between the large manufacturing town of Bridgeton and the model settlement of Vineland. It embraces a section of country about three miles square, and has long been known as a very desirable portion of the country, but until about fifteen years ago was covered with a heavy growth of timber, and held by a few old Bridgeton families, who are direct descendants of some of the original proprietors. The soil is a clay loam, capable of raising grain and grass, for which it seems well adapted, and is especially good for peach culture. The tract is well watered by two streams of water which are located in such a position as to be made useful both for water power and agricultural purposes and good drainage. About fifteen years ago Joseph W. Morton, a prominent Seven-day Baptist preacher, saw this tract, and conceived the idea of building up a settlement after the plan of Vineland, and to make it a Seventh-day Baptist town; but financial reverses overtook Mr. Morton before he had fairly got the place started, and what gave promise of a modern settlement returned to the wilderness.

It was after the appearance there of some twenty Jewish families eight years ago, that the place again attracted attention, and all sorts of people began to settle there, so that at the present moment there are over six hundred souls in place of thirty-six seven years ago, and more are coming weekly. Three-fourths of the population consists of Jews, says Mr. Purvis, the active land agent, in a letter to me:

They are contented and happy and are doing as well as can be expected of a people who come here with but little or no money. They are an earnest and industrious class of people, and though they did not receive help like those of the Carmel and Alliance colonies, they are trying to make a home for themselves by their own efforts. Many of them would be the better off for a little help, but so far they have done as the new American settlers: they commenced with what they had, and worked to help themselves. Out of the sixty families now at Rosenhayn we have no knowledge of one of them receiving aid. But they have not been able to make much headway yet, as most of them have bought the land within a year. Those few among them that had a little money made fine improvements, and one and all are desirable people and will make good farmers and succeed. There

are still about 3,000 acres of new land unsold, at from $12 to $15 per acre on five years' credit.

The children, the living hope of the colony, are thus described by Mr. Purvis:

The sixty children belonging to the seventeen Jewish families first settled here were taught by Miss Lily W. Cauvron, who in the period of nine months had them advanced so far that they could speak, read and write English. However, the temptation to keep these little ones at home to help the parents in their work is so great that only half of the above number regularly attend school, and when they do attend, they dress as the other children, and speak as well, so that it is hard to pick out the Jewish children from the rest. Even the teachers could not tell them except by their names.

As to the general prospects of the colony, Mr. Purvis writes as follows:

Rosenhayn lies in the township of Deerfield, which has some of the finest farms in America, and is known as the Hay Fields of Deerfield. They were settled before the American Revolution by Quakers, and are still owned by their descendants. The prospects of Rosenhayn are good. We expect to see one of the finest towns in the State in the next fifteen years.

This letter was written over a year ago, and since then great changes have taken place. The Jewish population has grown to an absolute and overwhelming majority; the "free" land is disappearing, and the uncertain settlement taking the form of a regular village. Nearly a hundred Jewish families, comprising some 400 souls, own over 2,100 acres of land, of which more than half is cultivated. And this seems to be only a beginning. The growing numbers defy the regular statistician. Statistics taken a few months ago are no guide at all for the present, and what of those taken as many years ago! I present here the tables of statistics, which I hope will be of interest as showing the growing possibilities of this promising locality:

I. The Ages of Jewish Farmers

From 22 to 30 years, 47
" 31 to 40 " 26
" 41 to 50 " 17
" 51 to 60 " 7
" 61 to 67 " 1
_____
Total, 98

II. Ages of the Children

From 1 to 10 years, 147
" 11 to 20 " 110
" 21 to 26 " 16

III. Vocations

Cigarmakers 3
Machine operators................................37
Painters 2
Pressers..4
Carpenters..4
Stocking Knitters..2
Laborers 9
Peddlers..4
Cutter 1
Tinsmiths..2
Shoemakers 2
Butcher 1
Smith 1
Grocer...1

IV. Properties

Houses 49
Stables...34
Horses...26
Cows..28
Wagons 21

V. Number of Acres Owned

Planted.......................................340
Newly broken up.........................250
Underbrush.............................1,536
                                      _____
Total.......................................2,126

How Planted

Corn .... 105 acres.
Sweet potatoes.........................55 "
Grapes....................................16 "
Blackberries...........................80 "
Strawberries...........................43 "
Fruit trees..............................46 "

But we must bear in mind that the farmers have only recently begun their labors, and consequently cannot expect any fruit as yet. Simon Gerson, one of the few who will gather their first crop this year, hopes to make out pretty well with his strawberries, especially as those in the vicinity were killed by the frost. The blackberries do not promise well so far. Mr. Gerson is considered the best informed Jewish farmer in Rosenhayn, he having been one in Russia, and studied here the conditions for good farming. He possesses over sixty acres, and is interested just now in experimenting upon a hot-bed for sweet potatoes, which will cost him $75, the seeds alone amounting to

$39. He constructed a special oven from which three pipes, laid beneath the board holding up the artificial "soil," convey the heat all over the "bed," which is sixty feet long and nine feet wide. He expects 100,000 plants, of which he will use 50,000 for his ten acres prepared for the purpose, and the rest he will sell. This is his second attempt this season, the first having failed on account of the high temperature, which he kept up out of ignorance. Mr. Gerson is a pronounced advocate of agricultural schools, and hopes to see one established at Rosenhayn, which he thinks will also benefit Alliance and Carmel. Though a practical farmer to some extent, he affirms that a farmer cannot exist from his farm alone, as he is likely always to be behind in something and get himself in debt; therefore he must work at something else. Of course he is of the opinion that after the land has been cleared, some profit may be expected. For instance, many of the products now bought by the poor farmer in the market can be raised, and thus expenses saved. The hay alone costs a farmer having a horse and other cattle, from $75 to $150 a year, which he can save by raising clover, but this requires well-manured land.

Mr. Gerson claims that Jewish farmers are on the increase, and that there are a number of them settled in a circle of about a mile and a half in diameter around Rosenhayn. On the other hand a nucleus of a Jewish colony forming at Malaga, N. J., which is twenty-seven miles from Camden, and where seven Jewish families resided for some time, recently received an addition of seven more that bought 250 acres of land, indicate that a very large area of unoccupied ground in the state of New Jersey will soon be made smiling by Jewish industry, perseverance and thrift.

As to Rosenhayn, there is one particular feature that strikes the visitor who has been in the other Jewish colonies, and that is the fact that alongside with the houses of the Russian or Hungarian refugees are those of the American born, and the impression is the better for it. The architecture is not monotonous, and represents the useful rather than the luxurious style. The houses are mostly two-story ones, and almost all painted. They are now being built rather close to each other, as the lots which sell for $150 to $250, contain only 1/4 of an acre. Very soon two important buildings will be distinguishable from the rest, the one a synagogue, and the other a four-story house which will contain a concert hall, meeting rooms, and a printing office. There are two more houses to be finished soon. They belong to a Jewish employer who transferred there his store from New York, having got tired of the city, with its high rent, its strikes, and the baneful influence of its streets on the children. He will do only custom tailor work for which he has engaged his old city hands.

Now I have been interested in finding out what could help the growth of the settlement and insure its members a permanent home. For it was evident that many may yet be compelled to wander away into the larger world trying to be a blessing. Most of the people there consider themselves owners of the land after they have paid their first installments, while this is sometimes only the beginning of the bitter end. Why and how does this happen is very plain, though at present it cannot be helped. For instance many came there with assurances from city manufacturers that they will be supplied with work for an indefinite period of years to come. But that happened in the year of the presidential election, which was followed by a year of dullness and then by another one of strikes and lockouts. Of course they learn thus a bitter lesson of politics, political economy and social science in general, and are only the worse for it, for they can foresee the same causes and effects after they have made the first wrong step. "What to do?" remains an open question, and there they are, without power to go either ahead or back. Those who have stipulated in their contracts to have houses built on their land are in danger of losing all their privileges, while those who have built houses and contracted debts in the building associations are thus *bound* to the ground. It is no wonder, therefore, to find such a universal demand for some local industry which would enable many to retain the newly established homes for which they have worked so hard, by placing them in a position to fulfill their contracts, and also by attracting the grown children, who would then not need to go to the city to help the parents in making a living. This brings us to what has been expressed by many prominent thinkers and philanthropists, the desirability of indirectly strengthening the existing Jewish colonies, for all are more or less similarly situated. The question only is how they should be further aided. There are at least three arguments in favor of developing agricultural colonies, which their critics are and ever will be unable to refute, and these are as follows:

First. While a large number of immigrants crowd into the large cities, cutting down the wages, and otherwise entering into competition with the native laborer, the settlers in New Jersey, for instance, are engaged in the work of building up a portion of the country which either none has yet attempted to do or failed in trying.

Second. While the people in large cities who have had the misfortune of becoming dependent on charities can show only a very small percentage of their number as having been raised by this means to a permanently independent position, the number of those who have been benefited by becoming farmers has never been less than that intended to be benefited. On the contrary it shows a tendency to increase. Besides, a *schnorrer* can only make a *schnorrer*, but one colony making another is quite different.

Third. The object of the charities in the large cities has never risen to the height of creating examples or ideals for others to follow; the charitable societies have rested satisfied when a single individual, perhaps one in a hundred, was made self-dependent through some usual vocation; while the money and energy spent on the colonies have served a high object of raising the spirit of those concerned to the consciousness of serving some high cause and their social position has been raised several steps, by their becoming owners of real estate and other property.

These are facts the virtue of which is recognized by many of the colonists themselves, and these very facts give their claim for a share of public attention a good deal of weight. They properly say you have enough peddlers, you make enough *schnorrers* in your cities, and there are but a handful of farmers. Why would you leave us to our fate, to contend with difficulties which are not of our making? Why don't you lend *us* a helping hand? Do you contemplate so easily the possibilities of our failure? While we are here we are in a position to help even those in the cities, by affording them opportunities for work, and otherwise attracting them to come out of the city slums and imitate our example. But should dire misfortune compel us to leave our farms, on which we have spent so much labor, money, energy and hope, where do you expect us to go but to the large cities, to swell the ranks of the overworked, underpaid masses; or still worse, of those who are unwillingly idle, discontented, wallowing in the dirty, unwholesome and demoralizing sections of the overcrowded districts of your large cities?

However, while the different "doctors" disagree as to whether the colonies are a success or failure, some even indulging in prophecies of all kinds as to their future, the common sense farmers of all the Jersey colonies do their utmost to gain a foothold on the soil, which they have cleared of the bushes and made fruitful by their hard labors.

It seems really strange that such a happy move as these colonies proved themselves to be, should be any longer misunderstood or even misinterpreted. Their critics would not admit that, in view of the new lever created for the natural diversion of the streams of immigrants bent on the overcrowded industrial centres, and the regenerative influence of the agricultural settlements themselves, the moneys were well spent on them so far. As to Rosenhayn, the concluding words of Mr. Moses Klein, the author of *Migdal Zophim*, illustrating the state of Jewish colonies here and in Palestine, seem to be well fitted:

As to the future, considering that the purchase of land was effected on very stringent stipulations, we must not be surprised to find the colonists rather embarrassed. Let us hope that the clouds, pierced by some bright star, will disperse, and that Rosenhayn will assume a distinct feature among her sister colonies.

Philadelphia

Will They Make Farmers?*

Russian Jews Trying A New Occupation in New Jersey

The Story of an Interesting Experiment—120 Jewish Families, Escaping from Persecution, Form a Farming Colony—Irksome at First, but Great Progress Made—They Live in Happy Anarchy and Have Only Once Invoked the Law—Will the Other Russian Jews do as Well?—Other Colonies Not so Successful.

I.

Cable despatches from apparently trustworthy sources indicate that thousands of Russian Jews will be on their way to this country shortly. Banished from the dominions of the Czar, and in many instances deprived of their property, these persecuted wanderers will be brought to America as the only country in which they will be received. Of course, the great majority will be assisted by the various Hebrew societies formed for the protection of the down-trodden race the world over. That means, to state the case frankly, that many of these immigrants will be assisted paupers. Their passage money, baggage, and means of

_____
* *The Sun* (New York), August 17, 1890, 15.

subsistence after landing must be provided by these societies.

Before the United States Government will allow these immigrants to enter its ports, the immigrants will have to furnish ample proof that they will not become burdens on the American people. The only way in which that can be satisfactorily done will be by securing from the New York Hebrew societies interested in this

ON THE ROAD TO VINELAND

immigration bonds that will be practical guarantees against pauperism. The Baron Hirsch Committee on the Relief of Russian Jews in New York, with its income of $10,000 a month, can do a great deal for such of the immigrants as get into the country; but it has frequently been asserted by officers of the committee that this fund is not intended to be used to assist immigration, but only to ameliorate the condition of Russian Jews in this city.

The only society that can be relied on to help the immigrants to land here is the Jewish Emigration Protective Society. The immigrants are likely to get their chief assistance from the Hebrews of Europe, especially the Paris Hebrew Alliance. It is the purpose of the prominent Hebrews here to prevent the immigrants, if they do get in, from settling in the large cities, especially in New York. The squalor and misery of the east side Jewish quarter is great enough now, and would be much increased if the population were added to by the green and helpless Russians.

The only hope of the latter is to become farmers, but it is no easy task to make them believe this. For centuries the Russian Jews have been compelled to devote themselves to trade. No other source of income was open to them. They have now an unholy idea of the power of money; they want to gather it in the quickest way, and they don't know how to do this better than in barter and trade. They haven't the faintest idea of farming, they are unused to manual labor, and last, they are averse to the discomforts of farm life.

Their own mode of living is not bound up with luxury, but yet it is not so rough and continuously toilsome as the average farmer's. Many attempts have been made to establish them on farms in this country, but very few have been successful. Many colonies have had to be abandoned altogether after much money had been expended in the attempt to establish them; of the others, only two or three can be considered real successes.

Of the latter, the settlement at Alliance, in New Jersey, is an excellent type. In its history are revealed much of the nature and the ideas of these Russian Jews, and in their present condition are manifested the results of a few years of freedom from persecution.

II.

Nestled among the rich fruit farms of southern New Jersey, about five miles from Vineland, and half that distance from Norma, on the Central Railroad of New Jersey, is the colony of Alliance, the most strange, curious, and yet quiet settlement in this part of the United States at least. It was founded in the spring, eight years ago, under circumstances very similar to those which now obtain among the brethren of the settlers in their native land. Then, as now,

THE BARRACKS

persecution had burst forth with great fury, and many scenes of violence were witnessed before its rigor had eased—families separated, property destroyed, women ravished, and men murdered by bigoted peasants and mechanics. Perhaps the Jews were not altogether blameless for the outburst, and perhaps the property destroyed was not altogether honorably won, but yet there was hardly excuse for the cruel and bitter methods adopted by their persecutors. Had it not been for the more honorable and enlightened Russian Christians, the numbers of the Jews would have been greatly depleted. These, however, did what the Government failed to do. They secreted and protected the Jews until the storm had blown over and then assisted them out of the country. The Government would not only not interfere in the violent actions of its people, but it attempted so far as it could to prevent the escape of the persecuted ones from the country. It threatened with the terrors of Siberia those who asked for assistance from persons outside of the country, and not a few were caught and transported for life.

The frightened Jews held secret meetings and established means of communication with the outside world, not unlike the underground railroads of the slaves of this country before the war. Subterfuge and disguises were adopted to enable messengers to reach London, Paris, and Berlin, and lay the facts before the prominent Hebrews there. Assistance was promised, but the problem arose as to what shape it should take. France, England, Germany, and in fact all Europe but Spain, were not desirous of opening their doors to thousands of beggared, ignorant Russians, whose traits and characteristics had gotten them into trouble in their own country.

The Spanish Government, through its Prime Minister, offered an asylum and assistance to any who chose to come, it being thought that these Jews might put new vigor into the dying commerce of the country. But the pride of the Jews of London and Paris would not brook the acceptance of this offer.

"We shall never forget," they said proudly, "the persecutions and cruelties to which our forefathers were subjected by the people of Spain. The horrors of the Inquisition of Ferdinand and Isabella will never fade from our memories. The land where the most precious blood of our race was spilled in idle persecution can never shelter us again."

The Russian Jews themselves wanted to go to Palestine and settle in the land to which their hearts fondly turned as the Land of Promise. But the Paris Jews again interfered. Previous attempts to colonize poor Jews in Palestine had proved disastrous failures. Neither the customs, the climate, nor the land were suitable to this class of Jews. The Paris Jews said flatly that they would not have anything to do with the Russians if they persisted in their determination, and would only help them if they would do as

THE PIONEER OF THE COLONISTS

they were directed. It was finally agreed that they should come to America.

They purchased 1,100 acres of wild brush land in Pittsgrove township, Salem county, removed from all the villages and towns and here the immigrants were taken. Of the 120 families that were led out into the wild tract of land on May 10, 1882, not one had ever handled a farm implement, and not one knew one berry from another. When they saw the spot selected for their new home they were greatly disappointed, and set up howls and lamentations similar to those described in various parts of the Old Testament. In fact, it would have required very little imagination to make one think he was back in those biblical times when the Jews were a stiff-necked race all by themselves, and when, as now, they looked to the leaders of their race to assist them out of difficulties. The faces and expressions were exactly like those handed down by portraits of the olden times, and some of the ideas and thoughts expressed bore a remarkable resemblance to the expostulations and objections offered by their ancestors when they were being led out of the wilderness.

Some of them had come from east and some from west Russia, but nearly all had lived in cities. The land to which they were now taken had been purchased for them from Leach Brothers, lumber merchants from Vineland, and they had also erected five long, low wooden structures, which they called barracks, which became the first homes of the settlers.

Each had fourteen little rooms, similar to stalls, and their appearance from the outside was decidedly unpleasant. They were unpainted then, but have since been coated with brownish yellow paint. When the settlers got into them they looked like five big hives filled to overflowing with noisy bees. The necessities of the occasion divided the settlers into five big family parties, and for some time jealousy cropped out in plenty. A committee of the Hebrew Emigrant Aid society saw them settled safely, gave them plenty of provisions for some time ahead, and provided such furniture as was absolutely necessary. They divided the land so that each settler had fifteen acres of ground for a farm and building site.

These were not given to them, but were sold at cost price and mortgages taken upon them at 3 per cent. The interest payments have ever since been counted against the principal. An expert German farmer named Fred Schmitt was employed the first year to instruct the settlers in the rudiments of practical farming. He had a good deal of difficulty with his pupils at first, because they were thoroughly dissatisfied and disgusted with their lot. Many had been well to do in Russia, and their new deprivations were disheartening.

Those were very unpleasant times for the settlers and all who had anything to do with them. The committee of the New York society frequently visited them, and invariably went away disgusted and discouraged. The people for whom they had done so much, and on whom they were wasting valuable time, for all the members of the committee were busy men, were anything but grateful. They threatened to develop into the most abject beggars, and they besieged the members of the committee with

IN THE VINEYARD

demands for assistance. Some went away and the others remained and grumbled. This state of affairs lasted several years. The first and second seasons showed no encouraging results, and it looked to even the most sanguine friends of the colony as though its history would be but a repetition of that of many other colonies started in a similar way and for similar purposes. But there came a change finally. The old hard question of "root, hog, or die," was brought home to the settlers with startling vividness. Their continued and ceaseless requests for aid were beginning to tire their patrons, and they were made to understand that they must look out for themselves. The result showed the value of not pampering this class of people.

Driven to hard work, they settled down to it with a vim that was astonishing. Once convinced that they must work for their living at the work laid before them, they accomplished astonishing results. The farms began to improve very rapidly. Luscious berries began to grow on every bush. The settlers left the barracks and put up individual houses. Vegetables were planted, and, with the proceeds of the first good season, horses and cows were purchased by the more frugal and industrious. Prospects began to brighten greatly, and, instead of certain ruin and degradation, the future began to appear bright and rosy.

But in those days there was a good deal of prejudice against the settlers among the farmers and villagers in the vicinity. This prejudice was only natural at that time, for the settlers were anything but pleasant persons to have around. They had not yet been able to drive out of their minds the fact that they were a hated and despised race. When they went into the villages of Vineland or Binghamton [sic] they never thought of walking on the sidewalk, but tramped through the middle of the dusty streets with their hats under their arms, bowing right and left in the most humble and abject manner.

It was almost impossible to get them out of this slavish habit. No matter who it was they met on the highway or in the villages, whether it was tramp or wealthy man, they always behaved the same, showing by their actions a desire to apologize for being alive. Of course, these things accentuated the prejudice against them in the eyes of the more ignorant Jerseymen. The children yelled after them in the streets, and the old farmers and residents of Vineland showed by their manners that they felt it a hardship that such an unprepossessing lot should be settled among them.

They expected confidently to have their yards filled with dirty peddlers and their poorhouses with paupers. The settlers knew no one outside of the colony in those days and made no attempt to become acquainted. When they went into a store to purchase something they always remained in the corner until everybody else had been waited upon, unmindful of their rights of succession. For a long time they could not understand how it was that they were not treated with a more open show of hostility.

They would probably have fulfilled the expectation of the farmers and villagers, and would have become settled inmates of the poorhouses, had not the New York committee stood by them so closely. The most important and vital principle which the committee persistently endeavored to drum into their heads was the fact that they could overcome any prejudice on the part of their Christian neighbors by becoming honest, straightforward, self-respecting American citizens.

"If you expect our assistance," said they, "if you expect to succeed, you must, like us, become American citizens; must learn to accommodate yourselves to the manners and customs of those around you; must live honorable lives and learn to speak the tongue of your adopted country. These things you can do by learning to respect yourselves."

Constant reiteration of these sentiments finally had effect. It grew upon the settlers very slowly that the prejudice against them was nothing very deep, and by degrees they became less obsequious and humble. They learned to walk on the sidewalk like other men, and to hold up their heads and to keep them covered unless occasion called for the contrary. They no longer cringed to anybody, and from that time on began the era of prosperity which has since marked their history.

Among the persons who assisted them were the two brothers from whom the land on which they settled had been purchased. The Leach brothers are known down in Vineland for kind-hearted and charitable dispositions, and from the first they felt that they must take an interest in the poor Russians. It was largely owing to their influence that intelligent persons were correctly informed as to the settlers, and that consequently prejudice died out to a large extent. Now only a small minority views the colony with anything like distrust, and many have positively friendly feelings for it.

III.

The New Yorker or average American who thinks only of the Russian Jew as a peddler, pawnbroker, or cheap merchant, would be both amazed and gratified if he could ride over the farms of the Alliance colony, as did a *Sun* reporter one day last week. To get there from New York it is usual to go to Philadelphia on the Pennsylvania Railroad and thence to Vineland on the Western Jersey Railroad. At Vineland it is easy enough to get a good horse and a driver who knows considerable about the settlement.

The Sun reporter started from Vineland early one hot, clear morning to drive over to the farm. On the way the driver regaled him with stories about the colony and the settlers. He was a Jerseyman, and had had, as he frankly owned, his prejudices against the colony when it was first formed. They had disappeared, though, he said, in the changes that had come over the colonists.

"Those Jews deserve a good deal of credit," he said, "for having got along in the way they have. I remember when I used to come over here with the committee from New York in the first years of the colony I used to think that I never saw such a lot of dirty, low-lived people in all my days. They used to crowd around the carriages begging, whining, and making everybody sick. 'Oh, Mr. Henry,' they would yell, or some other man, 'give me $5,' or perhaps they would say $10 or $25.

"That is all we would hear when we were over here. They used to live in the barracks then, like a lot of horses in a barn. They were huddled in together so that it seemed as if they couldn't turn around. Not one of them could talk a word of English, except what I have just said. They learned how to beg quick enough. I suppose they begged in their own language, too, because they used to jabber like talking machines. It is no wonder that nobody liked them then, and I guess the most of us would have been glad if they had picked up their duds and got out. It is different now, though. They have got a lot of good farms, and are putting up nice houses. They are building all the time, too. They know lots of people in the towns now, and they get along very well with them. No Christians can settle inside of the colony, which is reserved for these people, but they deal with Christians just the same as they do among themselves, and they deal fair, too."

The horse was getting out some distance from the village now, and presently a man came walking along the highway, whose cast of features clearly betrayed his origin. He was one of the settlers walking into Vineland. He was a sturdily built fellow, with massive shoulders, and a rapid, swinging gait that denoted considerable physical power. He had a bronzed face and short black hair, which was set off by a pair of sparkling black eyes. He looked the driver and the reporter squarely in the eyes and nodded to them in a free, off-hand manner, just as any other farmer might if he were of a friendly disposition.

BUILDING THEIR FIRST BRICK HOUSE

"He is going into Vineland," said the driver, "to get some provisions, I guess. He is one of the farmers."

A little further up the road there was a blacksmith shop, where there were three more of the farmers. Two of them had axes which they were having ground. They watched the driver, waving their hands in recognition.

"We are going over to the colony," the driver yelled to them. "We are going to look it over and take some pictures."

The men at once became interested, and came running over to the carriage. They watched the reporter and his camera very closely, and seemed to suspect that the latter possessed occult powers. They were very polite, but not obsequious.

"Who would be a good man to see in the colony?" asked the reporter. "Who could tell me all about the colony?"

"Mr. Bajuk, Mr. Lubiroff, or Mr. Steinberg," they said.

When the carriage started on they lifted their hats and went back to the blacksmith shop. A little further on a buggy came up the road, which the driver recognized as coming from the settlement. The horse was a sleek, well-fed animal, and the buggy would not have looked out of place in the streets of any small city. Two black-bearded and black-eyed Jews sat in it. They nodded to the driver as they drove past.

"They have got a number of good horses over there," said the driver, "and some of them are worth two or three hundred dollars apiece. They don't buy any poor horses."

The reporter now came across a curious sight. It was the railroad station at Norma. In a little square at this point were tethered a lot of horses attached to the carriages and teams of the Alliance colonists. Piled up on the platform of the station, so as to impede the progress even of foot passengers, were crates upon crates of blackberries. The men were working like beavers getting them up into piles that could be easily put on to the trains, and there was a confusion and bustle which seemed strangely out of place in that lonely strip of country. The men had no time to indulge in curiosity, and, therefore, paid no attention to the driver or his companion.

Some of the crates, which were open, revealed berries as fine as any that ever came into the New York market. Although the platform was so jammed, and the road was filled with teams and horses, the driver said that this was a faint picture of the scene during the busy season.

"It is getting very near toward the end of the berry season," he said, "and farmers have almost got through shipping. In the height of the season it is almost impossible to drive a team through. There isn't a place anywhere around here then, not even in Vineland, that looks as lively as this. They ship all their things from here because it is nearer to their farms than the Pennsylvania road. The Jews do more shipping than any of the other farmers around here. Most of their produce is sent to New York, but some of it goes to Philadelphia.

From the station out, the main road goes directly into the colony. The latter is a collection of scattered houses, most of them being at least half an acre apart. The country is not very much diversified, the hills being very low. The houses are spread out over the whole tract of land, each house being on a separate farm.

Along the road in the direction in which the reporter was going a number of buildings were being erected. They were all of modern architecture and some of them were exceptionally well built for farmhouses. One large brick house was in course of erection, and the workmen stopped to look at the carriage as it came

THE SORT OF HOUSES NOW BUILDING

up. The reporter, who had never seen a Jewish mechanic before, although he had been around a good deal in the Jewish quarter in New York, was surprised to see that all the men engaged on this building were Jews. There were carpenters, bricklayers, masons, plasterers, and glaziers, all with their implements and all industriously at work. The reporter stopped to observe them for a time and noticed that each one worked independently, there being no boss. Each man seemed to have his own idea of how his work should be done and worked according to that. Nevertheless, there was no confusion of ideas presented in the result, and the building looked solid and substantial in every part of it.

Alongside were several wooden houses just being finished. They were modifications of the Queen Anne style. The owners or builders had evidently desired to make them ornate, but apparently the expense of the paint had deterred them when they were half finished. There was a light blue and a Pompeiian red paint under the eaves on two sides of the houses, but the others were plain.

From this point the farms began to stretch out in every direction. They were all under cultivation and every foot of space had been put to some good purpose. Grape vines, peach trees, berry bushes, and sweet-potato fields stretched out one after the other as far as the reporter could see. All the farms appeared to be flourishing, but some were in better condition than

others. Several of the farms looked as though somebody had gone over them every morning to pick up stray stones, pull off dead leaves, and clear up the place generally. All the rows were as regular as could be wished.

The vines were loaded down with green grapes, but the peach trees and the berry bushes were nearly all bare. The berrying season was practically all over and the peach crop in southern New Jersey has been a failure this year. While looking over the farms, a man came up the road who was pointed out to the reporter as Moses Bajuk, one of the leading colonists. Mr. Bajuk was a rather kindly faced man of medium stature and a lighter complexion than most of the colonists. He had brown hair and brown beard and brown eyes. He was about 40 years old. The reporter had a letter of introduction to him from Judge Isaacs of New York, one of the members of the Hebrew Emigrant Aid Society.

Mr. Bajuk greeted the reporter cordially, and invited him up to his house. On the way a number of farmhouses were passed, and the reporter left Mr. Bajuk to look at these before going further. Here he came across the first settlers at work in the field. Two young Jews were weeding in a sweet-potato field. There were a number of weeds, but none of them escaped their attention. They looked up as the reporter came along and gave him a chance to get a snap shot at them with his camera. When he told them that he had taken their portraits they looked amused, but didn't seem to have any curiosity to see them. Possibly they doubted the statement.

Mr. Bajuk's house stood back some distance from the road, and there was quite a patch of ground, covered with berry bushes and trees, in front of it. It was a small house, not unlike the ordinary farm house, and contained six rooms. A carriage stood at the door waiting for one of Mr. Bajuk's visitors. The reporter was shown into the parlor, which reminded him very much, in some respects, of the same room in a New England farm house.

Mr. Bajuk had evidently obtained his ideas of furnishing from his Christian neighbors. He had the cheap lace curtains, white as snow; the bright patterned carpet, the black walnut chairs, the prints in gilt frames, and the little glass vases to be found in nearly every farm house parlor.

In other parts of the house, however, there were certain distinctive and characteristic features. On the door posts of every room were nailed little tin shells containing Hebrew proverbs to ward off bad spirits, and the cheap wood cut portraits of Moses and Aaron occupied places of honor in the dining room.

Mr. Bajuk came in immediately to receive the reporter, and toddling in after him came three infantile bearers of the same name, the difference in their years being difficult to discover. Mr. Bajuk had come from Grodno, in Russia, and his family consisted of six persons.

He had altogether 17 acres of land, 12 of which were laid out in fruit and 5 in sweet potatoes and other vegetables. He was the first of the colonists to reach the haven. He had been sent ahead to investigate and see whether the land was desirable or not.

Since then some of the farmers have increased the size of their holdings, having purchased in some instances more than double their original number of acres. When the colonists first settled, some of them were sent over to Philadelphia, where they learned to become skilled mechanics. It was these men who have since become the carpenters, bricklayers, and so on of the colony. Mr. Bajuk explained in very clear English the progress of the colony.

None of the colonists could speak English when they first came there, and as they did not come in contact with their neighbors for a long time they had to rely on their own ingenuity to acquire the native tongue. He himself and many others learned to speak English through books. Russian and English readers, and the like. Mr. Bajuk spoke it almost without accent and with surprising purity. His expressions were idiomatic, and he appeared to understand the words that he used.

The early times of the colony had been very unpleasant, he said, but those who stuck through were beginning to reap the reward of their labors, and there was a general feeling of satisfaction in the colony. The reporter was surprised to learn that the 612 persons comprising the colony looked up to no one as a leader. The colony is entirely without government, and the settlers live in the purest and most ideal state of anarchy. No one person has any authority over the other.

Although there is a Justice of the Peace over at Centretown and another one at Elmer who could be called in in case of necessity, there never yet has been occasion to do this. In the eight years in which the colony has existed there never has been a brawl or a row of any kind which would call for police interference. They have no liquor and no drunkenness.

The men meet regularly once every two weeks in the meeting rooms of one of the synagogues and there talk over the affairs of the colony. There is no presiding officer, but each man has his say. The majority vote decides upon every measure proposed. Each one has the right to state his views and the others must listen, but this, too, is an unwritten law and merely the result of the general idea of fair play. The reporter asked Mr. Bajuk if he did not think the colony would get along better if there was one head to direct its affairs, but he said he did not.

All were on a footing of equality as it was, and there was a spirit of fraternity which could not be improved. Each man looked out for his own affairs, did as his own conscience prompted him, and stood by the results. If a man did not act honorably, he was generally shunned, and no severer punishment could be imagined, he thought, than that a man should be avoided by those upon whom he must rely for companionship and friendship. There had been no fixed idea when the colony was started of having it thus free and independent of all law, but that had been the natural development. Very few, and possibly none, of the colonists had heard of such a thing as anarchy, or understood it, if they had, to mean the style of non-government which prevailed here. To be sure, the committee of the New York Society still took some interest in the affairs of the colony, but it had no governing power and could only recommend to the individual settlers such changes as it thought wise. They remained at liberty to accept or reject them.

THE BELLE OF ALLIANCE

The farms have not all been paid for—in fact, very few have paid off all that was originally expended on them, but large payments have been made and the mortgages are constantly growing less. The past two seasons have been very successful, and some of the farmers cleared as much as $1,100 apiece on their berries alone. Considering their small holdings, this was a very substantial return. Although a good many of the farmers have learned to speak English, the majority are still unable to converse with their neighbors.

Four different languages are used in the colony. These are Hebrew, English, German, and a jargon composed of Hebrew, German, and Russian mixed. The jargon is used much more than any of the others. The children are taught both in Hebrew and English. Only three stores exist in the colony, and these are small groceries, one of which also sells dry goods. A shoe store will soon be opened.

One of the first things that was done after the colony was established was to name the various roads cut through it. They were named after the leading members of the New York Hebrew Emigrant Aid Society in gratitude for their assistance. They are all avenues, and it seems very odd to hear down in Jersey such names as Isaacs, Henry, Gerschel, Eppinger, Mendez, Mendel, Schiff, Reichendorfer, and Rosenfeld. The roads were all cut through by the settlers themselves and made to connect with the regular roads that had been established previously. Mr. Bajuk thought that the settlers could get along much better if they had larger farms. At present they have to buy all their corn and hay, and keep only a limited number of cows and horses. With farms of thirty and forty acres they would be able to do much better. The only objection to buying up land around there is the prejudice of the settlers against getting too far from the centre of the settlement. They all feel clannish in the sense that they want to have their farms near enough together so they could get from one to another. Even as it is now the farms are getting pretty widely scattered, and the boys who are growing up have to take farms very far from the centre.

The question as to what is to be done with the children is getting to be a serious one. Most of the boys are willing to stay in the colonies and become farmers, while others are going into the city to join the army of paid workers. Some have already gone and are making cigars in the tenements, or working over machines.

The great advantage about these farms is that when the season is over the work is done for the year. There is no aftermath, and the farmer is at liberty to turn his attention to other things, as soon as he has sold his produce. As a result, a good many of the more industrious settlers have been doing other work in the winter. They have received contracts for making clothes which have enabled them to make the long winter nights pay them very well. Men and women both work at these and add to the net income. Some of the settlers, however, are averse to doing this sort of work, and think that if they are farmers they should stick to farming and do nothing else.

The progress of reform ideas in Judaism has been noticed down even in this far out-of-the-way little colony. There are two synagogues, and the colonists are about equally divided between them. One is known as Ashkenasy and the other as Safardy. Really names mean nothing in the way in which they have been applied, but they serve to distinguish the reform and the orthodox. The latter maintain to the letter all the old customs and forms of religious worship, and still look upon every act of labor on the Sabbath as extremely sinful. They were all this way when they came to the colony eight years ago, but now the so-called reformers ride into town on the sabbath, light matches, do their cooking, and some of the men even smoke cigars. There does not, however, appear to be any bitterness in this difference in sentiment as there is elsewhere, and the division in religious ideas does not appear to affect in any way the everyday dealings of the settlers.

All of them cling strictly to the Mosaic laws, and no meat is eaten except that of animals slaughtered by the official butcher, or shochet, as he is called. In fact, the settlers eat very little meat, anyhow. They have not many cattle or

THE ORTHODOX SYNAGOGUE

fowl, and it is too expensive to purchase them for the mere purposes of killing them. The result is that meat is rarely eaten in any house more than once or twice a week. Mr. Bajuk said that the settlers have outgrown their liking for meat, and have become practical vegetarians. Eggs, however, still furnish them with a part of their food, and the rest of it consists of berries and vegetables. Their mode of life is simplicity itself, and yet they have more amusement and society than most farmers have.

A number of the colonists who had pretty hard experiences before they got away from Russia still remember them and congratulate themselves upon their present comparatively prosperous condition. Among these the most prominent in the colony is Solomon Lubiroff. He, with the other colonists who were the greatest suffers by the persecution, came from

Elisawetgrad. The persecutions there had been worse than in any other part of Russia. Mr. Lubiroff had barely escaped with his life, together with Elias Stavitsky and Jacob Rosinsky.

After leaving Mr. Bajuk's place the reporter walked over to Lubiroff's farm. Mr. Lubiroff

LUBIROFF, ONE OF THE LEADING CITIZENS

is a man about 40 years of age. He has a great deal of push and energy in his composition. Like the other colonists, he came over practically penniless. He had seen prosperous times in Russia and had been agent of a large Virchow farm at the time when the persecutions began. His property was all stolen or destroyed, and he and his family had to take refuge with a Christian friend. Altogether 186 families had been driven from their homes. None of them was able to take along any property, and had to rely upon such assistance as was furnished by their co-religionists in other countries. Mr.

Lubiroff himself barely escaped being killed by an infuriated mob, and was glad to get out of the country alive. The families went first to a town in Austria, which was made a headquarters for all of the immigrants, and from there they went to London, where they embarked for America. Only about one-third got to the New Jersey colony, the others being scattered throughout the country.

Mr. Lubiroff has recently put up a new frame house which is one of the most pretentious on any farm in that part of Jersey. It stands in front of the house which was put up some years ago. Part of his new house is used as a factory, for he has gone into the manufacture of shirts, boys' waists, and summer clothing, and employs, when busy, 120 hands. He has contracts from Baltimore, Philadelphia, and New York. When the reporter came over, Mr. Lubiroff at once conducted him into the parlor of his new house and called in a half dozen members of his family. The parlor was very neatly furnished and looked bright and cheerful. There were screens in the windows and a wide plaza in front. The farm looked very well with its berry bushes, grape vines, and peach and pear trees.

Mr. Lubiroff soon showed that he was a hustler and that he was ambitious to increase his success. He thought that it would assist the colony greatly if one or two factories were put up. Mr. Lubiroff thought also that, inasmuch as the main business done at Bradway station was done through the colonists, it would be only fair to change the name to Alliance. There is another station called Broadway, with which Bradway, he said, was often confounded, and therefore it would be of advantage to prevent confusion to have the one known as Alliance.

Mr. Lubiroff's father and mother, recent arrivals in the colony, are among the oldest people in the colony. The oldest of all is a man named Lubaskow, who lives in Schiff avenue in a handsome new house. He is 75 years old. Most of the colonists, however, are around 40. Those who are older are parents who have been brought over since the colony became successful, while those who are younger are the children who have been born there or who were born some short time previous to the settlement of the colony. When the reporter started to go away Lubiroff pressed him very hard to remain and take dinner with his family.

"We have nothing but eggs and berries," he said, "and good milk, but you are most welcome to what we have."

From Lubiroff's the reporter went over to one of the barracks, which is still standing at the top of the hill on the main road. He found it an ugly building, every inch of its interior space occupied by families. The rooms were very small and cheaply finished. A horde of infants of varying ages and a lot of curious women came out to gaze at the reporter and the driver.

A TYPICAL HOUSE OF THE EARLY KIND

They talked together in jargon, and watched them all the time they were there. In one room in which the reporter looked the shochet was seated at a table with about a dozen little children around him. He had a Hebrew book, of which they had copies, and was teaching them Hebrew prayers. As the reporter looked in the old man was reading off:

"Boruch arto adonai (Blessed be Thou, oh Lord.)"

The children repeated each word after him in chorus. Some of them could not have been over six years old, and the oldest was probably not twelve. The old man was a typical east side Polish Jew in appearance. He had a long gray beard, unkempt hair, and slovenly dress. His house, a little bit of a frame structure, was a short distance from the barracks. He could not talk English, but understood and spoke German fairly well. He was the first person that the reporter had met in the settlement who had that air of suspicion which is characteristic of the east side New York Jew.

He wanted to know what the reporter was there for, and when he was told, he wanted to know whether that was going to do the colony any good. He consented very readily to have his portrait taken when he was assured that it wouldn't cost him anything, but was disappointed at not getting a copy right away. He insisted upon posing and could not be induced to get into a natural position. He eyed the camera as though it was some infernal machine that might go off at any moment.

A short distance below the old teacher's house is a frame house occupied by a man named Behrman. It is some little distance from the other houses, and the reporter learned that Behrman was generally avoided by the other colonists. Behrman, in fact, appears to be the only one of the colony who has strayed very noticeably from the path of rectitude. He was well thought of at first by the other colonists, and married a young Jewish woman after he had secured his farm. One day a middle-aged Jewess walked into the settlement from Vineland and announced herself as Behrman's wife. He had married her in Russia, and had left her behind when he came to this country. Of course, there was a row when she learned that there was a wife No. 2, and the latter was also somewhat indignant; but Behrman stuck to the second wife, and she also remained with him.

Some of the colonists sympathized with wife No. 1, and for the first and last time the law of the county was invoked against one of the settlers. Before any criminal action was instituted, however, friends of both parties secured a compromise whereby wife No. 1 abandoned her claim upon Behrman in return for certain payments of money. After she received her money, however, she pushed her claim more vigorously than ever. This act lost for her some of the friends she had gained, but she was enabled to annoy her husband, and that was apparently her chief object. The colonists have not approved of the methods of either party, and Behrman has had to get along as best he could without their friendship. He is said to be a very shrewd sort of fellow, and has done some dabbling in real estate. His wife does not live in the colony. When the reporter came down to his house, Behrman thought he had struck a victim, and immediately offered to secure a nice farm for him at a very low price.

The two synagogues of the colony are very much alike in outward appearance. They are simple wooden structures, containing a place for religious worship up stairs and two meeting rooms down stairs. The one occupied by the orthodox is at the corner of Gershel and Schiff avenues. The other is on Isaacs avenue. Both are located on little hills, so that they can be seen from any part of the colony. Besides the regular bi-weekly meetings held in the meeting rooms, there are special meetings on special occasions, and hitherto the children have been taught in one of them. One hundred and twenty-five children attend the school, which is taught by George S. Seldes, who is also the Postmaster.

Seldes is a young man of more than average intelligence, and instructs the children in English and the ordinary studies of the public schools. A library of all sorts of books, including those printed in jargon and Hebrew, has been given to the colony, and is in one of the meeting rooms. The school season had closed before the reporter got there, but Mr. Seldes said that the school had been a great success, and a number of children had received prizes before the close of the term. Some of the children used to go to the public school at Lower Neck, but recently the State determined to erect a school in the colony, which will be known as Alliance Pioneer School, District No. 71. The foundations were being laid at the corner of Isaacs and Henry avenues at this time. The Post Office is a very unique affair. It is a rough, unpainted wooden

THE HOUSE OF THE PATRIARCH

structure, with a shingle out over the entrance and a United States mail box also on the outside. Mr. Seldes, besides being the Postmaster, is district clerk of the school funds and has charge of the money loaned from the State for school purposes. There are two religious teachers in the colony, the shochet, Wolf Levinsky, and N. Chipliacoff. There used to be another one, a man named Randolph, who had a reputation for considerable learning, but he wasn't one of the settlers, and had been in the country a long time before he came here. He lives in Philadelphia and only goes to the colony occasionally. During the regular school term the children are taught their Hebrew and catechism in the evenings at the houses of the teachers.

The cemetery of the colony is one of its most neglected features. There have only been about a dozen deaths in the eight years that the colony has been founded, and there is only one tombstone erected. It is said that there has not been a single child born alive that did not live, and as the population of the colony has increased very steadily, this is a marvelous fact. There is no doctor in the colony, and when one is needed he is sent for from Vineland or some other town. The cemetery is back of one of the farms, and is a very small bit of land, enclosed by a picket fence. Bushes and shrubbery grow at will, and the few graves are almost hidden.

Strange to say, in this Jewish community there is no rabbi or cantor. As was explained to the reporter, there are about a dozen of the colonists who are competent to lead the services at any time, and these take turn at acting rabbi. Every one of the colonists, when he gets up in the morning, binds a black strap around his arm, and, turning to the east, bows repeatedly in the direction of Jerusalem and says his morning prayers. The strap is wound and unwound a good many times, each winding having its own significance. Every day some of the colonists go into town, and they can be met in almost any of the villages around the colony. Most of them, however, go to Vineland, and here is where they buy their supplies. All through the farms may be seen little places where arbors have been built, under the shade of which the berries and other fruit are packed in crates before they are taken to the station. When the reporter got back to Vineland he was told by the Leach brothers that the children who have been attending the public schools at Lower Neck have stood very high in all the classes, almost invariably higher than children of the same ages from the other villages. There has been a good deal of prejudice on this account, it having been averred that the Jewish children were not so neat and clean as the others, but the trustees, who were not partial, put the objectors to the test, and there was no evidence adduced to show that the children of the colonists were not as well behaved and as cleanly as the others. The Messrs. Leach said that while some prejudice still existed, it was only in the minds of those who would not be convinced under any circumstances. The industry of the colonists was the marvel of the whole country side.

"It is wonderful," said one of the brothers, "to observe the change that has been wrought in

A FEDERAL INSTITUTION

them since they came here. It is almost impossible for us to believe that they are the same persons who went shuffling through our streets, more abject than any tramps, eight years ago. They are prospering and rapidly paying off the mortgages on their farms, and are all eager to acquire more land. In fact I never saw a set of men so land hungry as these are. The last time the committee of the New York society was down here, the settlers crowded around them very anxious to get some more land from them.

Several of the settlers produced fat wallets, and one offered to put up a forfeit of $50 at once. In my opinion the colony is a great success."

IV.

There are two other colonies not far from that of Alliance also settled by Russian Jews. Neither one, however, is so flourishing or so typical. Carmel, which is nearer to Binghamton [sic] than it is to Vineland, was originally settled by a Jersey hotel keeper, who, having made his pile in the city, and being tired of its noise and bustle, retired to this spot and put up an immensely big house containing eighteen rooms, which was the wonder of the whole country side for years. Nevertheless, he did not attract many people there, and about six years ago Michael Heilprin, one of the editors of the *Nation*, and a distinguished philanthropist, concluded to found a colony there on the principle of the one at Alliance. He gathered together some two or three hundred Russian Jews and bought land for them at Carmel. It was his original intention to make this, like Alliance, a farming colony, but for some reason the colonists didn't take to farming and settled down to the same class of work that they do in the city. This colony is not what could be called a success. Mr. Miller, the hotel keeper referred to, is the only Christian living in the colony now, but there are sixty families of Russian Jews. Nearly all the land occupied by them was purchased by Mr. Miller. The colonists here work on sewing machines the year around, and except that they have more room, more air, and less squalor, they are not much different from the same class of persons in New York. Mr. Heilprin used to visit the colony very frequently during his lifetime, and did much toward establishing it on a firm basis. He devoted time and money and much patience to this project, but when he died a few years ago the colony was still in a very unsatisfactory condition. Most of the clothing manufactured there is of the light summer grades, such as seersuckers and similar kinds.

Last January an attempt was made under the leadership of Joseph Parvin of Carmel to revive the farming idea on a cooperative plan. The produce was to be sold directly to consumers instead of the marketmen, and the consumers would become shareholders in the society by purchasing shares at $10 apiece. The individual holdings of land were to be given to the society, which would give shares of interest in return. Mr. Parvin's ideas were on a grand scale, and included sales depots in New York and Philadelphia, and dairies, wine factories, canning factories, cider mills, and jelly factories in Carmel. A number of officers with long titles were to supervise the affairs of the society which, unlike the government of Alliance, came near being ideal Socialism. Schools, physicians, and entertainments were embraced in the scope of the society. Printed circulars have been sent out, together with blank subscription lists for consumers. The fate of this scheme has not yet been decided.

The third colony is at Rosenhayn. This was also intended to be a farming colony, and was settled four years ago. The settlers here, however, were not aided by anybody. There had been some Christian families living there, and the Jews came there and bought land through the building and loan associations. These still hold mortgages on their farms, which are very small. In fact, there is not land enough on any of these farms to make it profitable to cultivate them. The houses are prettier than those at Alliance, but they were all built by workmen from other places. None of the settlers here is skilled in a trade as are those at Alliance. There is very little farming attempted and, as at Carmel, the settlers rely upon their work on the sewing machine for their livelihood. The incomes from these, however, are by no means

large, and there is no prospect of these settlers becoming as independent as those at Alliance.

They have practically no future before them, while every year sees material progress in the condition of the Alliance farmers. It would not be at all surprising if both Rosenhayn and Carmel were abandoned altogether in the not remote future, but Alliance seems to be permanently and solidly established. If all the Russian Jews who come to this country could follow in the footsteps of the Alliance farmers, there is no likelihood that American citizens would object to their presence. But the difficulty that has attended the establishment of even this colony, and the lack of success that has accompanied other efforts, would make it clear to the student of this social problem that no evidence has yet been adduced to warrant the presumption that the coming immigrants will make successful farmers.

Russian Jews as Colonists In America[*]

A Thorough Investigation of the Hebrew Settlements about Vineland, N. J., Goes to Show That the Much Reviled Refugee Possesses All the Qualifications for Good Citizenship.

FROM KIEF TO ALLIANCE, ODESSA TO ROSENHAYN.

Fruit Gardens Thrive Where a Wilderness Prevailed, Profits Accrue Where All Was Barren Waste, Shopkeepers and Mechanics Till the Soil Without Previous Experience.

Facts for Baron Hirsch

Is Baron Hirsch to be a modern Moses to lead the sorely pressed children of Israel away from contumely, persecution and extermination?

Is the continent of America to be another promised land flowing with milk and honey to which his benevolence shall direct them?

These are questions which begin to stir the sympathies of the philanthropist and command the scrutiny of the political economist.

---

[*] *The New York Herald*, July 16, 1891, 8.

The Hebrews of Western and Southern Russia are a proscribed people in the land of their birth. Their homes, shops, schools and synagogues are regarded as plague spots, breeding and disseminating foul miasmas. Deprived of civil rights, shunned in society, boycotted in trade, these unhappy outcasts are at last reduced to an alternative between isolated degradation at home or hopeless banishment abroad.

At Kief, Odessa and Elizabethbund the first faint wails of distress were so sternly rebuked and suppressed by the utterance of that one dread word "Siberia" that it was years before the sob broke through the environments of iron rule to reach the ear of compassion beyond. Once freed it grew to such an angry, passionate howl of complaint that the civilized world first stood aghast and then hastened to frame measures of relief.

This was obviously a case for private interference and benevolence. There was no appeal possible to the Russian government. Charity, not diplomacy, must be invoked. The people of the United States became the more deeply interested in the fate of these wretched refugees, because the tide of exiles sets naturally toward the shores of the free. It is in the nature of our institutions and precepts to share with all who are worthy the blessed haven which we found and built upon so well.

The beginnings of relief were small. In 1882 the Jewish Immigrant Society of New York found that refugees from Russia were arriving in larger numbers than could be provided for in the city. A tract of land, comprising about 3,000 acres of shrub oak land, was acquired five miles from Vineland, a thriving town in the southwestern corner of New Jersey. As fast as practicable the land was cleared, divided into small farms, a wooden shanty was run up on each, the easiest kind of terms were made for immediate possession, and the long, hopeless journey from Russia was thus made to end in shelter that at least bore some semblance of a home.

Such was the first start made in America toward the colonization of the Russian Jew. The first 3,000 acres have long since been disposed of at premiums to eager buyers. The original settlement has served as a model for many others that have sprung up round about it. The plan of operation has taken the fancy and provoked the munificence of so generous a promoter as Baron Hirsch.

It is because of Baron Hirsch's magnificent intentions, it is in view of the vast sum of money he puts aside for the foreign colonization of the Russian Jew, that the *Herald* has been at pains to investigate fully and fairly the deserts of these people, their capabilities as colonists, their desirability as citizens, and their use and appreciation of the chances that have already been given to them of beginning a new life in a new land.

The following facts are laid before the public, not because there is a probability that Baron Hirsch will select New Jersey or any other of the States for the development of his great scheme, but because the only way of determining what can be done is by sifting what has been done, because the character, the steadiness, the industry, the tenacity of purpose of the colonist will not differ materially whether he be placed in North or South America, in Australia or Alaska, and because it is grateful to the *Herald* to bear witness to the complete success which has followed the modest attempt of our countrymen to domesticate the much reviled Russian Hebrew on the arid soil of New Jersey.

Life with the Exiles

"They are found to be a peaceable, prudent, patient, painstaking people." [By telegraph to the *Herald*] Vineland, N. J., July 25, 1891

There is nothing in the approach to Vineland that suggests the promised land. The milk and honey are kept in the background until the last moment and for that reason, perhaps, are all the sweeter when tasted.

The Southern Railroad of New Jersey is the main avenue to our El Dorado, although Vineland is also easy of access from Philadelphia.

After leaving Lakewood the train discards all the airs of civilization and schedule time and plunges through a wilderness of shrub oak and stunted pines, stopping incidentally here and there at little hamlets to take on and put off sundry crates of fruit, but primarily to give the train hands a few minutes' gossip with pretty girls, who must come from the backwoods, but don't look it.

At Winslow Junction there is such a great hub-bub of four trains meeting like friends in a desert that a general stop of half an hour is made while notes are compared from Philadelphia, New York, Cape May and Atlantic City.

From Winslow on the aspect improves rapidly. We are now running through peach orchards, grapevines and berry patches, all improving in quantity until the train pulls up with a flourish at the very imposing brown stone station at Vineland, five hours from New York.

Vineland must be the creation of an artist or a greater boss than Tweed. It is one of those few places with pretty names that are not abject in appearance. It is laid out in broad streets shaded with double rows of trees under which one may drive for miles over hard, well kept, clay roads; it is built mainly of brick, is blessed with a brass band which practises nightly, eighteen ice cream "parlors" also in full running order, and a cast iron temperance law, which, being a total stranger, I was immediately invited to violate.

It is, perhaps, to the highly imposing respectability of Vineland that the neighboring settlements of Russian Jews owe their temperate and thrifty habits. I prefer to believe, however, that such conduct is innate and not instilled.

First Acquaintances

It was on the train that I received first intimations of the kind of people I was going to investigate. Vineland is imposing apparently because her people stop at home and dispense their dignity within their own borders. There were no other passengers for Vineland besides

TYPES OF COLONISTS

myself, my faithful artist and a family of Russian Hebrews bound for the promised land.

There was the old grandfather with the pathetic, pleading, frightened face of a suspect framed in a thick gray beard; the grandmother, a heavy featured, coarse grained old virago, who wore a quilted hood through all the heat; the father and mother, more sprightly and hopeful; and three pretty little girls as jolly and careless as youngsters should be the world over. They all sat in the smoking car, of course, and fairly littered it with their household effects, contained in bundles (there was no sign of a trunk or box of any kind) which ranged in size from the huge bag of bedding to the little brown paper package of Penates.

Only the son could speak a little broken English. I learned from him that they were from Kief. His father had been well to do, a shopkeeper, until oppression began to press too heavily upon his patience and profits and he was forced to emigrate. The son was a machinist. They had friends at Alliance (the first Jewish colony out of Vineland) and two or three hundred roubles between them. They would buy land if they could, but had been warned it was scarce and high priced. They knew where they could board with friends.

NEW ARRIVALS

As the train arrived and their friends met them and, sturdily shouldering their bundles, bade them welcome in familiar tongue to their strange home, our artist made a hurried sketch of a group which seemed so outlandish in prosaic bluenosed New Jersey.

I didn't meet this interesting family again, although I subsequently made many friends and acquaintances among their compatriots. I hope that some fairy godmother, if they have such things in Jersey, will take special charge of little Olga—she of the shining locks and dazzling orbs who kept a stick of lemon candy in her mouth and her eyes on me during the entire period of our acquaintance.

On to Alliance

The finest avenue that runs out of Vineland leads directly to Alliance, about five miles distant, the first of the Jewish settlements referred to above as established in 1882 by the Jewish Immigration Society.

I was astonished when informed by our guide that this land ten years ago was the same sort of wilderness of shrub oak and pine as we had passed through on the railroad.

It is certainly not a Garden of Eden today, but there are those signs of cultivation and thrift on every hand that betoken the prosperous and industrious community. Of the three thousand acres comprising the colony of Alliance I may say that there is not a square yard of land unoccupied by dwelling houses that is not devoted to some branch of tillage. Indeed land is so highly prized that there are scarcely any roads or paths. The crops are planted squarely up to the little front porch, and if your wagon doesn't happen to "wheel" with the harrows and furrows of the field, your visit of inspection may do as much damage as if you were chasing the anise bag, regardless of cost.

The Imaginary Line

It is an imaginary line on the road where the Jerseyman, proud ruler of the roost, leaves off, and the Jew, meek supplicant for space, begins. But the line is only geographically imaginary. Within a hundred feet you pass from the commonplace to the weird, from comedy to tragedy, from Jersey to Russia. Can you imagine a more sudden plunge?

As we pass this line which is in reality as obtrusive as a Chinese wall, we leave a native sitting complacently on his piazza and overtake an old man trudging along the road. Over his bent shoulders is slung a United States mail bag. He walks slowly but steadily, with the aid of a curious old gnarled stick. He looks neither to the right nor left. A long, reddish beard tinged with gray droops low from his thrust out chin. His clothes are of curious cut and make. Nowhere but in Russia, Siberia or

New Jersey will you find such a type. The admirable illustrations in the *Century* magazine of Kennan's Russian articles are full of just such images. This pedestrian has been selected by the colony to act as mail carrier. Every day in the year he makes his long tramp of eighteen or twenty miles before the contents of his bag are distributed among his neighbors, and perhaps his coming is not anxiously, fearfully awaited! What news from home does he bring? What new imposition or indignation must be suffered by those left behind?

In Medias Res

But we are now *in medias res*—in the middle of Russia, as it were. We have come into this region without letters of introduction from the White Czar or Baron Hirsch. We are already looked upon with suspicion. It behooves us to put ourselves in communication with the colonists to explain that our mission is conciliatory and peaceful.

The opportunity occurs. On the porch of a small shanty to the right an entire family is taking dinner (it is ten a.m.). They are the most Russian looking people I have ever seen in or out of a picture book. The head of the house occupies the usual head of the table, the wife the tail, with a liberal assortment of children between. My approach is most respectfully received and recognized by many salaams and a jargon of speech that reminded me of Billy Birch's stage French. We bowed and grinned, but not a word passed that was intelligible.

This would never do. The potatoes, berries, milk and bread and butter, which formed the meal and were offered in pantomime, were declined with pantomimic thanks, and we passed on to the next house.

As in most communities, so at Alliance prosperity is fringed with poverty. I learned afterward that the outskirts of Alliance, through which we were now passing, were the home of the very poorest of the immigrants. Indeed, this was self-evident, for the next building on the road was a long, low, rambling shed, infested with at least twenty families, the men and women to be seen making cheap cigars within, the children running wild about the premises.

There was no international code of signals to be exchanged here either. So, contenting ourselves with a look at the barracks and passing one or two prosperous looking little inclosures on either side, we pushed on to a very neat brick house which was just receiving its finishing touches from two or three Russian artisans.

The owner, Mr. M. Bayuk, I found to have been one of the original settlers of Alliance in 1882. To my delight I found he not only spoke English with some fluency, but was a man of education and discernment, who had been a lawyer in his native town and, as he described it himself, was never more surprised in his life when he found himself set down in an unknown land thousands of miles from home and was told that he was now to become a farmer! It was in conversation with Mr. Bayuk and a neighbor of his, of whom more anon, that I received the most valuable information about the hopes, the prospects, the character and capabilities of the Russian colonists in America.

Mr. Bayuk, his energetic little wife, his two pretty children, his workmen and the faithful old dog that followed them into exile were all duly photographed in front of the fine new house which the owner proudly informed me had cost $2,000, which sum, he naïvely explained, he didn't care to trust to a bank, so he had put it into a house of his own.

They are witty as well as shrewd, some of these high cheek boned, Tartar looking fellows.

Synagogue and Graveyard

Directly opposite the Bayuk homestead is the synagogue, an unpretentious frame structure, in which the community religiously gathers every Sabbath (Saturday). When I asked who conducted the services M. Bayuk shrugged his big shoulders and said:—

"We have no need for rabbis here. Every man and woman may speak or exhort from the fullness of their own souls. There are always many of us who have words to say—words born

THE SYNAGOGUE

of bitter, biting experience. Let me show you the graveyard."

We stepped carefully across the Bayuk sweet potato vines and entered a little enclosure with a wooden shed at one end which served as a mortuary chapel and receiving vault. There were not more than ten or a dozen graves, for, as my cicerone apologetically explained, the Russian Jew dies hard and the colony was exceptionally healthy. A box or rough boards nailed together covered the top of every mound, but there was a general air of neglect about the place which suggested that death found no favored place in the new scheme of life under the blessedness of freedom.

I was loath to leave Mr. Bayuk, for there was a manliness and honesty about the fellow's manner and talk and his way of putting things and absorbing things, combined with a hopefulness for his countrymen and a certainty that they would triumph over the slight difficulty

THE GRAVEYARD

of beginning life over again in a new world, which made him positively captivating. But I was anxious to meet one Senior Baly, of whom I had heard much and from whom I expected much valued advice.

Some Odd Characters

I had not got far from my adieux with Bayuk and on the road to Baly's when a group of men, women and children, old, young and infantile, suggested material for a sketch. But our wagon was no sooner halted for the purpose than the entire group of tillers of the blackberry bush forsook their vocation and surrounded the wagon with plaints and appeals.

It was evident that we were taken for representatives of the Hebrew society which founded the colony. With a hurried suggestion to the artist to catch all the types he could, I encouraged the people to talk.

It seemed that the agents of this same society had not been making their rounds much of late. In fact, there was nothing for them to do. Affairs at Alliance were marching forward as fast as prudence and economy permitted. There was no Baron Hirsch back of this enterprise. It was sweet Charity alone, robed in her usual threadbare garments.

So the mistaken opportunity was seized upon to ply me with all sorts of questions and to rip my heart wide open with compassion had I understood one-tenth of what was said.

While the artist was getting in his fine work I expostulated vigorously against the clamor, with the result that the mere babblers were thrust aside and two spokesmen who used fair English laid their own and their compatriots' ideas and grievances before me. There was much more sense than nonsense in their talk. The wheat separated from the chaff you shall have later. The chaff will not keep so long. Here is some of it:—

Some Chaff

"Oh! Shentlemen, gif me a farm!" besought the long bearded old gent in the skull cap and frock coat, whom our artist has caught capitally. "I bromises to pay so much each veek."

I had to assure this land grabber that I was positively all out of farms, might not have any more in till next week, and even those might be only job lots, &c.

The other man staggered me even more. He evidently knew what he was talking about, had been reading the *Herald*, knew all about Baron Hirsch's splendid projects, and wanted to get in with that nobleman on the ground floor plan.

"Please, sir, to gif me Baron Hirsch's address. I vill write him von letter myself."

"I think simply 'Paris' will reach him," I replied, confidently.

"No? Ees it not Wien?" and I saw him actually make a note, "Baron Hirsch, Paris." If the philanthropic Baron ever receives such a missive, signed by one Lewinsky—I think he so called himself—he will perhaps pardon the innocent part played in the correspondence by a newspaper man rattled in the performance of his duty.

While all this was going on a funny looking little old chap, with the face of a child, who had been dancing up and down on the outskirts of the crowd, sputtering unintelligibly, pressed up to the wheel and got a spokesman to explain that he wanted to write his name in my notebook. What for no one will ever know, except it was an application for one of my job lot farms.

I have forgotten to say that the driver of our vehicle was a Jerseyman, with a suspicious taint of Irish brogue lurking round the wag of his tongue.

As the little Russian spat on the pencil and began in the right hand lower corner of a page to write Hebraic hieroglyphics backward and upward from right to left the ill mannered driver gave such a loud guffaw that our lazy horse started on, and, barely missing running down some women and children, dragged us out of the crowd and rescued me from a position that was becoming falser and more false every moment.

Thence on to Mr. Baly's it was plain sailing, and so let us throw aside the ludicrous in our experience and come down to the plain, unvarnished truth about this foreign colonization of Russian Jews.

The Baly Homestead

The Baly house is one of the simplest in the settlement—in fact it is nothing more than the cheapest and most ordinary kind of frame cottage—two rooms, a kitchen-dining room and a sitting room, on the first floor and three living rooms above. There is not a vestige of carpet on any of the floors. A few little pictures and photographs, evidently treasured relics of other days, adorn the white walls. The rooms were scrupulously neat and clean.

It is not pleasant to go into details of a gentleman's home in which you have been cordially received and given the best the house affords, but I am sure that Mr. Baly himself will be the first to admit that any description of the capabilities, the possibilities, of the Russian colonist would be incomplete and impaired without a truthful description of the sacrifices which he and his devoted wife have made and the example they are setting.

Baly (now Americanized into Bailey) was in the field when we drove up, but a call fetched him at once. He strode into the little sitting room, and, looking me straight in the eye, said in English, in an extremely well modulated voice:—"Will you be pleased, sir, to tell me your name and business?"

Baly is a good looking fellow of not much more than thirty. There is not a trace in his physiognomy of the typical caricature of the Jew. He would rather remind one of half a dozen of our young New York dandies of the day, if any one of them had quite completed his intellectual and physical education. He has only been in this country and in this colony for five years, but is already recognized as the head and front of the community—the representative prize colonist.

Baly told me that he was in the midst of a successful university career at Odessa when a government ban closed any of the higher mediums of education to his race. He bears the mark of that insult to his intelligence and manhood on his brow. He is a man with a grievance, who will bear its ineffaceable trace to his grave, not in bitterness or passion, except when reference is made to the persistent attacks against the character and capability of his brethren, but with the calm of a strong mind that realizes what it has lost by being deprived of culture. He had intended to enter one of the learned professions.

"You see what I am now," he said, glancing from his cowhide boots round the humble little room. "I read and write articles for the Hebrew papers whenever I have the time, but my work on the farm leaves me little time for any intellectual pursuit. Allow me to present my wife."

Mrs. Baly had come into the room—a bright looking little woman with golden hair, who had also received a university education and showed me, with much pride, her diploma and a photograph of her class, most of whom are now scattered in exile like herself. Mr. and Mrs. Baly both converse fluently in Russian, French, German and English.

Our talk lasted so long that Mrs. Baly insisted upon serving refreshments, preserved fruits, black bread and milk, a feast over which she presided with as much grace as though at home in the old drawing room in Odessa. Baly's brother-in-law, a young medical student, also joined the party.

It was not difficult in such company to reach a proper understanding of the condition and prospects of the colonists.

Taking up the Farms

Alliance was started in 1882 with six families, who each took up and received title for fourteen acres of land valued at $15 an acre and a shanty valued at $150. In payment for this the Jewish Immigrant Society, now known as the Alliance Land Trust, accepted a first mortgage of $180 at three per cent. It was on this same basis that nearly all of the 3,000 acres were eventually disposed of, until there are only a few acres left, held as building lots, three lots to the acre, at $150 the lot.

A number of the mortgages have been paid off, no interest has ever been defaulted and no mortgage has ever been foreclosed. There are now over two hundred farms in operation, with a population of about six hundred and sixty—200 men and 460 women and children.

The farms are all laid out alike, in the following proportions:—

4 acres of blackberries.
3 acres of strawberries.
1 acre of black caps.
1 acre of raspberries.
2 acres of grass.
3 acres of sweet potatoes.

————

14 acres.

The soil is too light to produce anything else to advantage; indeed, the grass is so thin that those who keep a horse and a cow, as most of the colonists do, are obliged to buy feed.

The Crops

The average crop from such a farm, with the use of a little stable manure and phosphate, is:—

100 crates of blackberries.
100 crates of strawberries.

10 crates of black caps.
10 crates of raspberries.
100 barrels of sweet potatoes.

The average gross proceeds from such a farm are from $500 to $600. When the price of berries is high—from six to ten cents a quart—the profits are over fifty per cent; when berries are cheap, as this year at four cents a quart, the profits are extremely small.

The general complaint is that the farms are too small. It would cost little more to till twice as much land, and the profits would be four times as great. Some of the more thrifty and industrious settlers have added piecemeal to their holdings as fast as they could save enough purchase money. Baly now has twenty-one acres; Bayuk, twenty-eight; Moed, Opochinsky, Groodsky, Persky, Silberman, Lewison and many others are slowly increasing their farms, but are obliged to go to a distance to obtain land. They now value their original holdings at $100 an acre, and would scarcely sell at that price.

BERRY PICKERS

The Houses

This craving for land and the laying out of money for its acquisition has militated against the improvement of the farmhouses and buildings. There is no profit in fine houses, say these shrewd observers; wait until we have farms of thirty and forty acres and you will see the fine brick homes. The houses, therefore, are shabby in the extreme, being for the most part the original shanties patched up and repaired, while the roughest kinds of sheds serve as stables and cow houses. Bayuk is looked upon as a reckless spendthrift to have put up a $2000 house. Even Mrs. Baly seemed contented in her modest surroundings, so general is the preference for thrift over display.

The People

The people are intelligent, peaceable and orderly in the extreme, nothing approaching a crime having been committed during the ten years of association, except the suicide of one poor fellow who lost his reason. No liquor or beer is used, milk and an excellent quality of well water being the staple beverages. The climate is equable and disease and death are practically unknown. The families are sufficiently prolific without being unduly so, three children to a household being the usual average. The men and women are rather undersized,

A PICKER AND HIS FAMILY

but I never saw a lustier and better grown lot of youngsters than the children who have been born under the Western Star.

The women and grown children are of material assistance to the men on the farms, particularly when the berries are picked, but it is not at all unusual to see women handling the plough, harrow and hoe.

There are two synagogues in the community, a library, two schools, several stores, two benevolent societies, which assist the very poor; a free system of burial, a branch of the Jewish Alliance, and twenty-four of the better class of farmers already belong to the Farmers' Alliance.

There is a large hall which is used for lectures and meetings, and several times during the winter a company of Polish players comes down from Philadelphia and treads the boards.

The universal language is of course Russian, but many of the colonists already speak very good English and the children who attend school are making such famous progress that a number of them are to enter the high school at Vineland in September. Their teachers report that they are exceptionally bright and capable, rather out stripping in capacity and application the children to the manor born.

One Great Need

The dark side of this picture which I could not see but heard of on all sides is the winter—there is nothing for the people to do there—little to earn and many to keep.

The great need at Alliance and in all similar colonies is factories, in which all hands may work while the land lies fallow. There is a certain amount of sewing done on men's clothes and shirts sent from Philadelphia and New York, but the wages are on the starvation scale, twenty-five cents a day being the very utmost that a man and a machine can average.

Baly hopes to be able to establish a co-operative berry canning factory before long. The berries often ripen on the vine faster than they can be picked, and such a factory would be economic both in saving loss and adding to gain. Capital, however, is very scarce. The first mortgages on the farms preclude the lending of more money on them, and the land trust apparently either does not recognize such a need or has no funds available for such a purpose.

Other Settlements

I have devoted the whole of my space to Alliance, because this is the original settlement, the best developed, the most thoroughly tested and the fairest criterion of what has been accomplished to colonize the Russian Jew.

But Alliance is only the centre of a whole circle of similar communities which have grown up around it and ramify through Cumberland, Salem and Atlantic Counties.

There are Malaga and Estelville and Newport and Port Elizabeth and Bridgeton and Rosenhayn and Carmel, all merging one into the other, with a total population of some two thousand five hundred Russian Jews.

Each and every one of these is modeled after the mother colony. From all come the same reports of thrift, industry, sobriety and perseverance. In one or two, hat factories have been established to the great advantage of the general weal, proving, as I am persuaded, that winter employment and an increased acreage of farms are the only two things needed to make out a perfect case for the success of this enterprise and for the triumph of that greater one which Baron Hirsch has under consideration.

Cases in Point

But Baron Hirsch is not all, not the only one to whom this subject appeals with pity and reason. The Jewish Alliance of America has just issued a pronunciamento from their headquarters in Philadelphia inviting the attention of philanthropists and economists to the cause of the exiled Russian and urging their colonization away from seaboard cities, as outlined above.

A despatch just comes from Boston stating that forty Russian Jews are refused admission at that port of princes because they seem to have no visible means of support and have been "assisted" to leave their native homes.

A story in the *Herald* a day or two ago related the heartrending experience of a man from the class of whom I write, which is typical of the cases of thousands who are ground down into absolute poverty and then given the imperial Russian boot toe as a parting salute.

This question is in its infancy. If men of this character, education and adaptability are at loose seeking a foothold, a *pied à terre*, we must in view of the above facts think twice, think twenty times before we slam our doors in their faces.

To put it on the most sordid, inhuman grounds, "Can we not make money out of them?"

The Southern Railroad of New Jersey does, for instance.

**ONE OF THE LEADERS
OF THE COLONY**

The Wonder of It

And I must conclude this little story with the greatest surprise of all, a fact which is incontrovertible, and would have been apology enough in itself if the whole scheme of colonization had been a dismal failure instead of a great benefit.

Not two per cent of the men who have within ten years transformed this arid region from a wilderness into a lovely fruit garden had had any previous experience of farming or agriculture in any shape. Indeed, a vast majority of them had never seen the country at all. They were all city bred and city reared, and with but few exceptions had been small shopkeepers, artisans and mechanics at home.

Would Englishmen or Scotchmen or Irishmen or Frenchmen or Germans or Italians have done better under the circumstances than these harried and hounded Russian Jews?

It seems to rest entirely with the gentlemen in Wall street who have control of Baron Hirsch's and other benevolent funds whether by a moderate outlay of money and an intelligent exercise of supervision the Russian Hebrew refugee should not be made over into one of the most useful and respectable type of our foreign born citizen.

He evidently has the proper stuff in him.

A Decade in Colonization. What Jews Have Done in the New Jersey Settlements*

Two years ago the Governor of Virginia, in addressing a distinguished assembly of Jews that had assembled in Richmond, invited them to send their newly arriving co-religionists to his state, "to build up its waste places."

Inwardly I scoffed at the suggestion. Jews clear the forests, level the ground, sow seed in desert places, that they flourish and give forth abundantly? Impossible! It was well enough to make speeches about, but as for hoping to make such dreams realities, you might as well search for the philosopher's stone that would transmute all metals to gold.

Yet when I visited the Jewish colonies in New Jersey, a few days ago, I found that what Governor Kenney had hoped for had come to pass; that the Jews had "built up the waste places," had made the desert to bloom like a garden, had established settlements that, while

------

* *The Jewish Exponent* (Philadelphia), April 22, 1892, 1–2. The author of this article has not been identified, although it does not appear to be Moses Klein. Charles Hoffman, editor of *The Jewish Exponent* at this time, colleague and friend of Klein's, is a candidate. The article opens with a reproduction of the photo of Castle Garden at Alliance which illustrated the original edition of *Migdal Zophim*. See p. 46.

not abundant in wealth, were yet permanent and successful. I felt like bowing in reverence before those wise men who, ten years ago, were far-sighted enough to lay the foundations of this colonization enterprise, and to those who, in the dark days of storm, disaster and despair, saved the colonies from disruption.

Alliance

The Landis road, leading from Vineland to Alliance, is one of the finest in the land: smooth, hard and free from dust. The landscape, even in the early spring, before the fields put on their best attire, is attractive. For a distance trees line both sides of the road which as my friend remarked to me, was equal to any that led into Paris. The country has no longer the appearance of wilderness and desolation, but is cleared and cultivated.

As you approach Alliance, the comely houses on the roadside become more numerous. A sturdy Jewish farmer, with an axe, is cleaving wood; another workman is painting the outside of a newly constructed house, not yet completed. When you arrive at the colony itself, and inspect the work done, you find vineyards arranged with the precision of an artist. Rows upon rows of stout supports are ranged alongside of each other with mechanical precision, upon which the vines will soon cling, and the grapes appear in plenteous clusters.

The peach orchards are just beginning to blossom. Raspberries and strawberries are already planted, and begin to show their green leaves above the surface of the ground.

The first place that we stopped at was at the house of one of the original settlers. His wife and chubby young ones greeted us with a friendly welcome. His seventeen acres of land, already planted, gave an air of sturdy prosperity to the surroundings. Nothing could better demonstrate the change that ten years had produced than the difference between the small new brick house which he had recently erected and the mean-looking wooden structures at some distance removed, which he had first occupied, but which he now rented to another more recent arrival.

Not far from this place is "Castle Garden," which played such an important part in the early history of the colony. It is a long, low, wooden structure, in which the first settlers were received, and in which they dwelled for some time, until better arrangements could be made. Then it was turned into a cigar factory, and now it is partitioned off, and serves as the dwelling-place for a number of poorer colonists. "Castle Garden" should be preserved as a reminder of the early and bitter struggles that were encountered, and to mark the advance that, from year to year, the colony makes.

We passed a comely structure which was pointed out as the Synagogue Tifereth Yisrael.

This is the smaller of the two religious edifices that Alliance contains. Why there should be more than one is not easy for an outsider to understand. It is not due to a difference in ritual, as might be supposed, but rather to a difference among the colonists as to the proper situation of the structure. The first and larger Synagogue Eben Ha Ezer is a large wooden structure, which is firmly put together and adorned on the inside by the gilded fixtures for giving light. On the ground floor is a large room fitted up for meetings and supplied with a stage or platform for entertainments of various kinds.

Here is contained also the nucleus of a library. In this we were particularly interested, and it was one of the objects of our visit. We found a collection of books and papers in jargon and in English. The English books were few in number, and while there were a number of good novels of George Eliot and Dickens and the *Robert Elsmere* of Mrs. Humphry Ward, they seemed to have been picked up at random. The library is supported by about thirty members, who each contribute ten cents a month. It contains all told about one hundred and fifty books. Here was a chance for some real good work to be done. If a proper supply of books could be procured at reasonable prices, if current periodical literature, both Jewish and non-sectarian, could be furnished, the colonists would be provided with mental and moral nutriment they would eagerly consume, and the results of which would tell in the development of character and the speedy growth of refinement and culture among the people. The Jewish Publication Society should send its books there at once. Nowhere would they find more grateful and more appreciative readers. An encyclopedia would be a great assistance, and so a number of useful works could be mentioned which would help in this truly beneficial educational work. A movement is now on foot in this direction for all the three colonies, and will unquestionably receive the support of all those who take delight in the betterment of their fellow-men, especially in those engaged in a work such as is here seen.

The colonists are ripe for this step. The men are not only sturdy in body, but vigorous in mind. The younger generation talk English like the natives; scarcely a perceptible accent is noticeable in their speech. The agencies for entertainment and study are exceedingly limited and a library and reading room would be a centre whence the best influences would emanate.

The public school is not far distant from the synagogue. Here about one hundred children receive daily instruction from two teachers in the ordinary rudimentary branches of an English education. There is no distinctively Jewish school, but each family has private instructors in Hebrew for the children.

The whole colony now numbers about six hundred souls. The colonists are healthy, strong of limb and contented. Last year the profits were reduced because of over-production. This year the prospects are bright. One of the most successful colonists declined to sell his summer's crop for five hundred dollars. What the colony needs is some industry with which the people can supplement their work in the fields. A canning factory would be directly in conjunction with their other work; but any industry would be of great advantage and would be a great stimulus to the colony. What pleased me most about Alliance was the fact that it was genuinely devoted to agriculture. All else was subordinate, almost to annihilation. We have here the fact demonstrated, as far as a single settlement can, of the success of Jews as farmers. When I remember how near disruption this colony was only a few years ago, and that but for the timely assistance of a few Philadelphians the thousands of dollars expended in is foundation would have been wasted, and now contemplate the evidence of success and permanence everywhere manifest, I cannot but think that those who at that moment of danger came to the front and assisted in overcoming the difficulties must find this act among the crowning achievements of their lives.[*]

---

[*] Above this paragraph, the article reproduces the photograph of children standing in front of the school house at Carmel. See p. 74.

Rosenhayn

As we passed through the broad avenue that lends beauty to Rosenhayn, and marked the numerous stores that lined the thoroughfare, with here and there a house, in which people could be seen at work on machines, the fact was impressed upon us that, while the fertile lands round about gave evidences of cultivation, yet that this place bore the marks rather of an industrial than of an agricultural settlement.

The colony has grown somewhat since Mr. Moses Klein, in 1889, fixed its Jewish population at 294. It has also Christian inhabitants, and I am informed that, unfortunately, the best of feeling does not prevail between the two classes. Rosenhayn has the advantage of being on the line of the railroad, but has not made the progress that can be noted in Alliance and Carmel. It has, like others, its school-house, library and post-office. The land is possibly even more fertile than at Alliance. Yet all the land thereabouts is good land; rich in its composition, and yielding plentifully to cultivation. Its selection is amply justified, not only because of the proximity to the large cities, without which the colonies would have utterly failed, but also because of its inherent value. "There is nothing the matter with the land," remarked one of the colonists to me.

Our time did not permit us to stop long in Rosenhayn, and we pressed forward to Carmel.

The three colonies are each not an hour's drive from each other.

Carmel

In Carmel there was abundant evidence of life. The avenue was lined with houses, and with people going to and fro. This settlement has already the appearance of a regular village. Miller's factory is the largest structure in the place, but the houses along Heilprin Avenue are also large, well built, of good appearance, and altogether the best that I noted anywhere in the colonies, although Rosenhayn approaches them very nearly. In Carmel agriculture is made subordinate to manufacturing industry. The organization calling itself "Co-operation" is the most important in the place. It is simply a combination of work-people, who appoint their own superintendent, and thus do away with middle men and the sweating system. The work-people, about eighty in number, work on shirts and clothing of various kinds, mostly received from New York. They are paid in orders, which circulate as cash in the colony, but are, of course, of no commercial value elsewhere. When the payments are received for the manufactured goods, these orders may be cashed, but by that time they are rarely found in the hands of the original workers. The grocer and the butcher and the baker, the coal dealer, and the various other dealers, have taken them in exchange for their various commodities.

During the latter part of last year some fear was felt in Carmel because of the springing up of numerous settlements on all sides, notably that established by the Baron de Hirsch trustees; but now there is plenty of work and the people are cheerful and contented. Weisman, whose farm is one of the best in all the settlements, has made arrangements for receiving visitors for a more or less prolonged stay, and not a very long time will pass before this will grow into a regular inn for travelers, constituting a much-needed addition to the place. We examined the library here also, and found a small collection of books, all of which had been much used. There is here a synagogue, a *Mickve* (for ritual baths), a school, and a cemetery (which will soon be provided with a suitable railing). The population is gradually increasing, and while the speculation in land has decreased, the settlement has settled down to a steady and certain development. A second street has been laid out, and houses are located thereon, and the fields back of them are cultivated. One most important piece of pleasing information that I received was that a corporation had been formed in Bridgeton for the establishment of an electric railway connecting that town with Millville, and which will pass through Carmel, thus making the latter place much more easily reached.

The drive back in pure, bracing air over the firm roads was a healthful exercise, and the pleasing impressions carried away from the colonies gave additional zest to our day of outing, investigation and observation. Carmel, too, had passed through its critical stage. The five thousand dollars which Baron de Hirsch loaned have born bountiful fruit in this place. His beneficence would be indeed blessed if it could everywhere bring about such notable and noble results.

I cannot too strongly emphasize the benefits which the Jewish settlers are conferring upon New Jersey. Its land is now found to give abundant returns, but it is to the hard work of the settlers that it owes its productiveness. Jewish colonies are spreading in various directions, many the result of private speculation, but where a fair return is given for the money invested this enterprise is not to be condemned.

There are many things yet needed in these three original settlements in order to secure their proper development. Varied industries, a good library, a night school, increased population, will do much for their success. It is my firm belief that these settlements should receive the attention and support of the philanthropic, since they have now been stripped of their drones, and those who remain are earnest, sincere and in the main independent and worthy of encouragement. They need no pecuniary support, but every community needs public-spirited help to carry it forward in a proper direction. It is better to forward their growth than to start new settlements, although these latter must in the nature of things spring up and tend finally to the good of all.

The colonizing experiment in New Jersey is a success. With this conviction we concluded our journey.

The Progress of Jewish Immigration*

The Colonies in New Jersey

The agricultural communities of the immigrants to this country, located as they are in New Jersey within a few miles of our borders, are of special interest to our association by reason of the gradually increasing numbers of the new arrivals whom we find occasion to forward to them. In connection with this matter, I had recently to direct our agent, Mr. Ehrlieb, to visit the colonies and report concerning the existing conditions there, and Mr. Moses Klein kindly volunteered his experienced services for the same purpose. From their several statements I glean that, notwithstanding the marked failure of berry and peach crops which this year greatly disappointed the colonists, the majority of the farmers were in a condition of compar-

* *The Jewish Exponent* (Philadelphia), November 24, 1893, 6. An excerpt from "The Progress of Jewish Immigration," by Louis E. Levy, the President's Report of the Association of Jewish Immigrants, presented at the annual meeting on November 12, 1893. The first half of the report, published in the November 17, 1893, issue of the *Exponent,* details numbers of arriving immigrants into Philadelphia during the preceeding years as well as current conditions in Russia.

ative independence. Vines and potatoes of both varieties have yielded satisfactorily, the former having been unusually prolific in the past season. One farmer obtained from seven acres of land 3000 gallons of wine, selling it at fifty cents per gallon, and twenty other vine-planters were likewise more or less successful.

Alliance Colony

Of the three principal communities, Alliance is chiefly devoted to agriculture, while Rosenhayn and Carmel are mainly dependent on the products of the sewing-machine. As a consequence the two last-named colonies are suffering severely from the prevailing business depression, while Alliance is, at least comparatively, in a prosperous condition. There are 180 families settled at Alliance, comprising about 1100 souls. One hundred and thirty-six (136) of the families are dependent on agriculture, while the remaining fifty earn a living at tailoring. Ten families who had recently gone from New York to Alliance to work at the sewing-machine had been unable to maintain themselves, and were compelled to return to the city, the several shirt factories maintained in the colony by New York and Philadelphia manufacturers being at present idle. Those who remain must necessarily endure serious privation should the stagnation continue; but it is satisfactory to consider that even the poorest of the farmers are finding the poultry, truck and sweet potatoes which they have raised a means of tiding over the coming winter. It is not to be overlooked, however, that the maintenance of the factories is of great importance to the community generally, as many members of the agricultural families who would otherwise be insufficiently employed are thereby enabled to earn a livelihood. In point of fact it is highly desirable that other industries be established there, a canning factory being apparently a great desideratum.

The public school, which is situated next to the larger of the two synagogues, employs two teachers, who give instruction to 150 children. Religious instruction is afforded the children by two teachers after the public-school hours, from 4 to 7 o'clock. Mr. Steinberg, the president of the congregation, deplored the inefficiency of this instruction, but, such as it is, there is a likelihood that the children may be deprived of even this through lack of means to maintain the teachers. If the principle that charity begins at home is at all applicable, it could not well serve a better purpose than by dictating the use of at least part of the fund of our local branch of the Alliance Universelle Israélite to sustain the school at the colony which bears the name of that great organization.

Rosenhayn Colony

The colony of Rosenhayn includes a population of about 1000 souls. There are settled at this point some sixty (60) families of farmers and thirty (30) others, chiefly shirtmakers. Rosenhayn covers about 4000 acres, of which 2500 acres are tilled by Jews. The shirtmakers obtain their work from local contractors or "bosses," but all are now out of employment. Last year this element comprised fully one hundred families, but two-thirds of these have had to leave the place for lack of work. Rosenhayn has an attractive little synagogue and a public school wherein 60 children are taught.

Carmel Colony

At Carmel about 200 Jewish families are settled, including 20 farmers, who cultivate some 550 acres of land. Over 2600 acres are held by Jewish owners, but much of it on speculation, and the colony is mainly dependent on the various branches of tailoring. As a consequence many of the settlers there have recently suffered greatly through lack of employment, and 32 families had latterly to call for assistance. Relief was afforded through the instrumentality of Messrs. Simon Muhr and David Sulzberger, of this city, but the distress will necessarily continue until the tailoring industry revives. There is here a co-operative company of sewing-machine operatives, which has recently bought a factory building, but the members are too poor to acquire the much-needed outfit of power and other labor-saving appliances, and such work as they obtain is being done by foot power.

Carmel is situated at the junction of three townships—Cumberland, Millville and Deerfield—each of which maintains a public school in its section of the settlement. These schools contain 26, 80 and 98 Jewish pupils respectively. The village contains about 150 houses, including 2 factories, a number of general stores, a synagogue and a bath-house.

The present depression is causing many of the settlers to turn their attention to agriculture, with the purpose of making the industrial pursuits auxiliary to farming, and in this respect it may eventually prove a blessing in disguise.

Woodbine Colony

Woodbine, the new colony founded by the trustees of the De Hirsch Fund, near Cape May, was also visited. At that point there are now settled 71 families, comprising about 500 individuals. Of these, 51 families are farmers, the remaining 20 being tailors and artisans. There had been some 25 other families of the latter class, but lack of employment compelled them to return to New York. Efforts are being made to introduce the manufacture of willow ware, and latterly a kindling-wood mill was started into operation, which affords employment to about 25 hands.

Two schools, with one teacher in each, afford excellent instruction to about 150 pupils. Another teacher is employed for religious instruction, and altogether the colony is thoroughly organized. The entire settlement is under the direction of a scientific agriculturist, Prof. H. L. Sabsovitch, and although the farms are not as yet under effective cultivation, there is no doubt whatever, from experimental results obtained, that the colony will become successfully established.

How to Help the New Jersey Colonies[*]

Special attention should be directed to the communication of "Hazopheh" in the House of Israel Department, which graphically describes the present condition of the three Jewish colonies in New Jersey. His account, it is true, is gloomy with regard to the future of these settlements. All of them seem to have declined in numbers, and several of them are staggering under the weight of the mortgages upon their lands. Yet at the same time we find that many of their farms are well cultivated, that the lives of the colonists are wholesome and healthy, and expert medical testimony is given that shows that under all their disadvantages their condition is far better and happier than that of their fellows in the crowded tenements and alleys of our great cities.

What can be done to help these remaining colonists out of their distressful condition and to tide them over their difficulties? The curious may ask how it was that they became so heavily involved; and the skeptical may inquire if these embarrassments will not recur. These questions are proper in their season, but the

immediate and practical problem is what to do under existing circumstances. We all know that Jewish farmers are not the only ones whose lands are encumbered with mortgages, and the experience with other Jewish settlements has been that they have all passed through a protracted period of hardship and difficulty and required at intervals more or less frequent outside assistance.

This has been given to these very colonies in the past, and we believe it ought to be done again in the present; so that the large amounts of human effort and of money may not be entirely lost. When nearly a decade ago Alliance colony was in dire distress, Philadelphia came to the rescue, and under the leadership of the late Alfred T. Jones and Simon Muhr, and our present active fellow-townsman, Louis E. Levy, gave adequate relief. When Carmel suffered, Baron de Hirsch advanced the means at the instance of Rev. Dr. S. Morais, and through his agency, joined with that of Judge Mayer Sulzberger and Messrs. Moses Klein and Oscar B. Teller, the colony was again restored to a prosperous condition.

Something of this kind must now again be done. The affairs of the colonists ought to be investigated and re-established upon a firm foundation. It may be that but a comparatively small amount would be required to set them on their feet again. Perhaps the payment of the interest on the mortgages of some of them

* Author unnamed, presumably Charles Hoffman, the editor of *The Jewish Exponent* (Philadelphia), August 13, 1897, 4. The opening references the article that follows.

would be all the relief absolutely required. There ought to be in Philadelphia, as in former years, men public-spirited and strong enough to step into the breach; thereby saving the colonies for the future, bringing comfort to those who have worked long and faithfully at their most arduous task; and bringing honor and undying blessings upon themselves.

The Land-Tillers of Israel in America*

A reader, prominently identified with the "Jewish Chatauqua" meetings of Atlantic City, would not forgive me the sin of diverting the people's attention from those grand assemblies to such old and worn-out subjects as "The Lamentations of Jeremiah and the Zionist's dream of re-inhabiting the Holy Land," which formed the subjects of this department last week. "Have we not enough to do here that we should waste our time and energy on things foreign to our American spirit?" concluded my friendly critic.

I agree that we have enough to do here, and venture to say, even a great deal more than my friend thinks of, or than the Chautauqua or any other society can ever accomplish. The polishing of Judaism and systematizing of its teachings, while, perhaps, good in themselves, cannot supply the cravings of our multitudes for bread, air and shelter; a problem which has already assumed alarming dimensions in all our large communities. My friend may be an opponent to Zionism, and may yet contribute his share to the salvation of a vast number of our suffering people in this country. But such

---

* By Moses Klein, "Hazopheh," under the weekly column "The House of Israel." *The Jewish Exponent* (Philadelphia), August 13, 1897, 5–6.

a "salvation" lies, to my mind, pre-eminently in colonization and kindred industries.

A Visit to the Jewish Colonies

A few days ago it was my privilege to pay one of my customary annual visits of 14 years to the three Jewish settlements, Alliance, Rosenhayn and Carmel, which are situated in a triangular shape between the cities of Vineland, Bridgeton and Millville in South Jersey. This time I was fortunate to be accompanied by Dr. B. L. Gordon, one of the physicians of the Society of the "United Hebrew Charities," whose object was to analyze the nature of the climate and water.

The city of Vineland and its beautiful boulevard along Landis Avenue, through which we drove to Alliance, seemed to have emerged from the recent heavy rainfalls in glorious attire. With the bright sun above us, salubrious air about us, and the beautiful scenery before us, we thought ourselves in the "Land of Israel," where heaven and earth used to kiss each other. The name of Alliance sounded to us like Judea; Rosenhayn—like Chavazeleth Ha'Sharon: but Carmel retained its Oriental name. While so thinking, our team approached the colony.

Alliance

As one who has always taken a deep interest in the welfare of Alliance, I felt very much depressed at seeing the same smiling gardens of two years ago neglected this summer, a considerable number of the houses deserted, and the population declining rapidly. What in the world could have caused such a desolation? Was it persecution that expelled many good people from this soil which they have improved with the "sweat of their brow" for sixteen years? No! True, that there was, some years ago, a slight attack upon Jewish glassworkers by strikers in Millville; but, so far, I have never heard of any attack upon Jewish farmers in this country, and I hope I never will. What, then, could have produced this remarkable decline of that pioneer of American Jewish colonies? Was it the drought of insects that ruined their fruit for several years in succession? These have undoubtedly contributed considerably towards discouraging the farmers, but not to wipe many of them out of existence. But there was a combination of causes which turned portions of this American Judea into desert land. In the first place, the division of Alliance into lots of fifteen-acre farms was inadequate to sustain goodly-sized families. Then, the increase of the families demanded the erection of new and large houses, which were erected by building associations at the average rate of $1200 per house, on security of first or second mortgages for heavy interest. The absence of any substantial industry in the place, the poor crops and their low prices in recent years, rendered it impossible for many of the farmers to meet their obligations to the building associations, who took possession of the farms. Hence the decline of the once prosperous and proud Alliance. Yet, there are a large number of farmers so dearly attached to the cultivation of their berries, orchards and vineyards, that nothing except death can tear them off from their soil. It is in them that I rest my hope for the future of Alliance and Jewish farming in this country.

Rosenhayn

The condition of Rosenhayn is similar to that of Alliance. Empty houses and desolated gardens are met in the centre of the town. Since my last visit, many a rose has turned into a thorn; many a farmer into a tailor; and many tailors have girded their loins and assumed their former Russian nomadic life. There was a pathetic ring in the narrative of one of these ex-farmers who four years ago invested the sum of $400 in a small farm, and after spending on it three years of labor, was obliged to leave it altogether to the building association to cover the mortgage. But he made a vow never to leave his beloved Rosenhayn. So he and his family of five concluded to work on other farms. Thus they sustain themselves and the rest of their family of one cow, one calf and about fifty-five chickens—the relics of their past. Notwithstanding these reverses the party seemed to be happy, robust and contented.

Another family that never had money enough even to invest in a farm, has rented a house and twelve acres of land deep in the woods of Rosenhayn. Twice a day, from 3 to 6 o'clock in the morning, and from 6.30 to 8.30 in the evening, the father attends to his land, while the main part of the day he devotes to the shirt factory, where he earns five dollars per week. His rented farm supplies his family of wife and four small children with all the vegetables, poultry, milk, butter and eggs. All are evidently contented.

In Rosenhayn, like in Alliance, there are a great number of genuine Jewish farms in the far outskirts of the colony. They live in houses of primitive construction, yet they are as happy as Adam in the Garden of Eden, as the serpents of the building associations could not suck out their life-blood through mortgages.

To Carmel

While departing from Rosenhayn, a crowd of co-religionists, headed by a noble-looking old man, evidently the Schochet, or the Patriarch of the town, approached us to take a *Jerusalmit* in our carriage for Carmel. What irony of history!

A messenger from *Jeruschalayim* to Carmel of New Jersey! Could he be any one else than *Elijahu*—the Messenger of Peace? "We welcome him to our carriage!" I said, believing that he was sent from on high to announce the salvation of the colonists and the redemption of this, their Holy Land, from the cruel building associations. Alas! to our great disappointment, we learned that the gentleman was simply an envoy of the *chalukah* to distribute boxes for the collection of charity for the poor of the Holy Land.

"*Gam zu le' tobah*—This, too, is a good sign!" said my friend Dr. Gordon. "It is a pleasure to see people struggling for their own existence, as these Jewish settlers do, entertain ideals of casting their bread to their poor brethren across the Atlantic Ocean and the Mediterranean!" The Doctor finished his sentence and we arrived at Carmel.

This, the most industrious little town of the three colonies—in shirt-making, seemed to have suffered less from the leeches of building associations than its two sister colonies, Rosenhayn and Alliance. Was it Providence that prevented them from tilling the ground for building associations, or was it their preference for the sewing machines in the huge Miller factory that saved their blood and marrow from feeding the land of mortgagees? It is difficult to tell. This much, however, is fact, that while Carmelites did not escape altogether the fate of

Chavazeleth Ha' Sharon and Judea, it presents, nevertheless, a more cheering appearance than either Rosenhayn or Alliance. *Carmel* having been the main object of our visit, afforded us a better opportunity to make closer inquiries into the condition of its inhabitants in particular and her sister colonies in general. The following summary will tell the story:—

Carmel's present population consists of 98 families. Most of these will soon resume work at the shirt factories, and only twenty families cultivate their farms. These farmers produce enough milk, butter, eggs and vegetables to supply the whole settlement. Two of these farms are among the best in South Jersey. There are several butchers, groceries and shoe stores competing with each other and selling their articles at reduced prices.

The population of Carmel formerly was much larger, but a great many left for lack of work; others left their properties to cover mortgages. The shirt factory, with hundreds of hands clustering around it, has been idle for several months. Regardless of these facts, the building associations and the State demand interest and taxes. But so far, there is no visible sign that either Carmel, Rosenhayn or Alliance will be in a position to comply with these demands. I was told that some time ago, two representatives of the Baron de Hirsch Fund visited these settlements and were so favorably impressed with the colonies and people that they promised that the Fund would relieve all of them from their present dilemma. In fact, we ourselves were asked everywhere, "whether we had not been entrusted by the 'Baron de Hirsch Fund' with the mission of settling all the mortgages of the three colonies," of which, of course, we had not the slightest knowledge. Especially were we deeply touched when a genuine farmer, after conducting us for 20 minutes through the several parts of his excellent farm of 23 cultivated acres, exclaimed "O! my friends! *Ovar Kuzir, Kalah Kajitz, v' Anachnu lo Nashanu!*" ("The berry harvest is over, the summer is nearing its end; the grapes will shortly be ripe; yet, we are not helped!") as all our produce can not settle the heavy mortgages.

Dr. B. L. Gordon's Sanitary Statement

The first thing that struck me when I visited, the other day, the Jewish colonies of Western New Jersey, was the marked difference in the countenance of the people there from the same class of people living in the large cities. While in the latter we see a large proportion of our co-religionists careworn and emaciated, nervous and debilitated; people with pale faces, sunken eyes, hollow cheeks, going from one public dispensary to the other, and from a private physician to the physician of the United Hebrew Charities, when they are out of work, endeavoring to remove the trouble afflicted on them during their busy times in the suffocating factories and sweating shops, in the former, I noticed the exact contrast. I have met in the colonies faces that express contentment and happiness. I have seen men in the fields that present the perfect type of health, women around the houses that possess a healthy and natural color not influenced by the peculiar appearance caused by the overcrowded tenement houses, happy children playing in the open air and enjoying sufficient supply of oxygen. I have also seen parents sitting on the porches in half-reclining position, the children playing in front and the dog lying around them, and a beautiful landscape in the distance. I could hardly believe when my friend 'Hazopheh' told me that these land owners were Russian fugitives of 1892, now sitting under the protection of the outstretched wings of the emblem of the great republic.

The dwellings in which the colonists live are neat-looking two-story frame houses, nicely painted outside, and consist of a cellar and seven rooms (in the most of the structures). The houses, especially in Alliance and the farming parts of Rosenhayn, are considerably apart from one another. The sun reaches through every side of the house, and although many of these structures are occupied by two families, the people in general are not overcrowded, and

can be even comfortable if they would have the inclination to do so.

The sanitary condition of the houses, while it could be better if a board of health would force them to carry out sanitary regulations, yet it is not bad.

Their water supply, which is mostly derived from wells situated in the rear yard, is potable in the true sense of the word. It is cold, clear and refreshing.

The fact that the houses are far apart from one another, and the colonists follow the healthful pursuit of farming, the fact that they get the proper amount of oxygen in the air they breathe, and the absence of contaminated matter in the water they drink, one must certainly expect that the average farmer's health is good. Diseases due to overcrowding, as smallpox and diphtheria, I was told are very rare. Scarlet fever does make its appearance, but not as frequent as in the big cities. Dyspeptics in soil operators are not as often seen as in cloth operators. Cholera infantum, which carries away thousands of children in largely populated centres, is merciful there. Diseases due to polluted air are foreign. Venereal diseases among the colonists are almost unknown; this is partly due to the model chastity and purity of Jewish home life, and partly to their early marriages.

Alcohol, which is the cause of a large proportion of human misery, including diseases,

poverty, and crimes, is harmless in the Jewish colonies, as the men are very temperate,
and drunkenness of any kind is absolutely
unknown; an intoxicated person would be a
curiosity.

      Benj. L. Gordon

Can Jews Be Farmers?*

The mere association of the word Jew with that of farming is of such vital importance to me that I am bound to postpone for the present my weekly reviews of Jewish events abroad, and devote the columns of the "House of Israel" for the discussion of the above question.

Even *The Jewish Exponent* in its last week's important editorial evades giving a definite answer by concluding that "there are some who can be farmers, others that cannot." We do not doubt for a moment the correctness of this assertion. Jews as a class, like all other classes of society, dare not concentrate their whole activity in one particular line of work. Jews, like all other classes, must have their various occupations of labor. Yet, there is no reason why Jews could not carry on agriculture on a large and centralized scale in proportion to the number of farmers of other classes. It is this phase that has to be borne in mind when the question, "Can Jews be farmers?" is raised, as it was this particular phase of the question that became a weapon in the hands of Anti-Semites in Europe, who charged the

---

* By Moses Klein, "Hazopheh," under the weekly column "The House of Israel." *The Jewish Exponent* (Philadelphia), November 3, 1899, 6. This is the first in a series answering the question "Can Jews Be Farmers?"

mercantile Jews with being "consumers and non-producers."

The mere name of "Anti-Semitism" is the strongest refutation of their charge. In the face of Anti-Semite exceptional-laws, which for many centuries deprived the Jews of the right to own real estate or even to hire land, Jews, thus torn from the breast of Mother Earth, had to seek various other occupations for gaining their livelihood. For Jews, like Christian mortals, have a tendency to seek all possible means for self-preservation. But can Jews be farmers in a time like this, when they have access to real estate in different civilized countries? Let experience answer.

Jewish Farmers

I. Abroad

As the time since Jews were admitted to own real estate is comparatively short, even in countries like Austria and Hungary, it is surprising to me to recall the numberless Jewish farms that I have seen in my early travelings through Hungary, Transylvania and Galicia tilled by Jewish hands and by the sweat of their brow. Even in Russia, where the privilege of real estate ownership is still denied to Jews outside of the pale, even there government reports are full of praise of the excellent state of cultivation in which the Jewish colonies were found by the State Inspectors of Southern Russia. Based upon favorable reports, the Minister of the interior proposed to grant to the Jewish colonists additional government land on their adjoining districts. Furthermore, had the government experiment of colonizing Jews as farmers been a failure, the Russian Holy Synod could not have advocated the free establishment of great masses of Jews, who might embrace the Greek Orthodox Church, on government soil. Surely the sacred drop of water sprinkled upon the converted Jew could not transform him all of a sudden from a merchant into a farmer; from a saloon-keeper into a wine-grower, and from "a consumer into a producer!" The Palestinian agricultural exhibitions at Hamburg and Frankford; the Vine de "Rishon L'Zion"; the geranium juice of Ekron and the oranges of "Pettrach Tikvah" [sic] which find markets in every European centre. All these tell the tale of what 6000 Jews have accomplished in a body on the for-centuries-desolated soil of the Holy Land. Indeed, were it possible to draw a map of all the Jewish farms of Europe and Palestine, the world would be astonished to see a Jewish agricultural territory almost as large as a good-sized State! But in their scattered condition and regions they are lost to the public eye which sees in the Jew anything but a farmer. Hence the question: "Can Jews by farmers?"

II. At Home

What is true of the Jews of Europe and Asia Minor is true to a much lesser degree of the Jews in America. Of the two dozen Jewish colonies that passed away like phantoms from the face of American soil, within the past two decades, there are still some remnants left, bearing the imprint of Jewish farming life. Let Alliance Colony speak out whether Jews can be farmers? I shall not dwell here upon the early history of this settlement and the hardships it had to endure during the first decade, "hardships" strong enough to exhaust the patience of many an American farmer; these having been amply demonstrated in the book *Migdal Zophim*, Philadelphia, 1889. I shall merely recall its state of two years ago, as published then in this department and carried by the secular press across the Atlantic, and contrast the same with its condition at present, by which the readers may judge for themselves whether Jews can be farmers or not?

Condition of Alliance in 1897

"The city of Vineland and its beautiful boulevard along Landis Avenue, through which we drove to Alliance, seemed to have emerged from the recent heavy rainfalls in glorious attire. With the bright sun above us, salubrious air about us, and the beautiful scenery before us, we thought ourselves in the 'Land of Israel,' where heaven and earth used to kiss each other. The name of Alliance sounded to us like Judea; Rosenhayn—like Chavazeleth Ha' Sharon: but Carmel retained its Oriental name. While so thinking, our team approached the colony.

Alliance

"As one who has always taken a deep interest in the welfare of Alliance, I felt very much depressed at seeing the same smiling gardens of two years ago neglected this summer, a considerable number of the houses deserted, and the population declining rapidly. What in the world could have caused such a desolation? Was it persecution that expelled many good people from this soil which they have improved with the 'sweat of their brow' for sixteen years? No! True, that there was, some years ago, a slight attack upon Jewish glassworkers by strikers in Millville; but, so far, I have never heard of any attack upon Jewish farmers in this country, and I hope I never will. What, then, could have produced this remarkable decline of that pioneer of American Jewish colonies? Was it the drought of insects that ruined their fruit for several years in succession? These have undoubtedly contributed towards discouraging the farmers, but not to wipe many of them out of existence. But there was a combination of causes which turned portions of this American Judea into desert land. In the first place, the division of Alliance into lots of fifteen-acre farms was inadequate to sustain goodly-sized families. Then, the increase of the families demanded the erection of new and large houses, which were erected by building associations at the average rate of $1200 per house, on security of first or second mortgages for heavy interest. The absence of any substantial industry in the place, the poor crops and their low prices in recent years, rendered it impossible for many of the farmers to meet their obligations to the building associations, who took possession of the farms. Hence the decline of the once prosperous and proud Alliance. Yet, there are a large number of farmers so dearly attached to the cultivation of their berries, orchards and vineyards, that nothing except death can tear them off from their soil. It is in them that I rest my hope for the future of Alliance and Jewish farming in this country."

Farming Life in America Judea

Dear Hazopheh: Being a constant reader of your valuable weekly contributions in *The Jewish Exponent*, I have often wondered at the omission of interesting news in the "Land of Israel," as you was fond of calling this Jewish "agricultural" colony. Has your interest in Jewish farming cooled down? Or, are your sympathies all taken up by our great national

Zion movement? and therefore you have simply overlooked us during the last two years? I am more inclined towards the latter reason, because as a Zionist and builder on the House of Israel you could not intentionally disregard or neglect agriculture and Jewish farming life, one of the foundation stones—in my opinion the most important one—in this house, our future home.

Therefore I would like to see your attention again directed to this miniature "Land of Israel," an appropriate name on account of the predominant agricultural occupation of its inhabitants. An occupation by which our ancestors, during centuries long gone by, and in the then real Land of Israel, have lived and prospered until they were rudely torn from the bosom of their beloved country by an unmerciful and cruel foe. There has been a marked improvement of late noticeable in Alliance and surroundings owing partly to the wave of general industrial and business activity, which wave is beginning to strike our shores also, and partly to the efforts of the Baron de Hirsch Fund in encouraging tailoring manufactories that are giving employment to a portion of our brethren, who are not fit for farmers, and, on the other hand, creating a market for part of the farmers' products. With Zion's greetings,

I am, yours respectively,

ONE OF THE JEWISH FARMERS

In this brief communication our friend has demonstrated, unconsciously perhaps, that "Jews can be farmers."

HAZOPHEH

Can Jews Be Farmers?[*]

III. Let Alliance Answer

ALLIANCE, N. J., Nov. 12, 1899.

Dear Hazopheh: I was delighted to see your very able exposition of the question, "Can Jews be farmers?" in your department of *The Jewish Exponent* of November 3. Oh, what a question! Of course they can. Let any unprejudiced observer come down to Alliance and surroundings and see for himself how the Jewish farmers have transformed a tract of rough brush land into a blooming garden covered with grapevines, fruit trees and vegetables of all descriptions that are suitable for this locality. We must remember against what odds the Jewish farmer had to work. Starting on his experimental farm career with inadequate means, with a constitution enfeebled by cruel persecution in a barbarous—their native—country, without experience or knowledge in the principles of agriculture (most of them were merchants in Europe), and in addition to all these drawbacks started on a virgin soil, covered with dense forests and bush. Still, by their perseverance, they succeeded in becoming what they are now—as good farmers as their Christian neighbors who were brought up from their childhood upon the farm, and, in most cases, such "clear and productive" farms were inherited from their fathers; whereas the Jewish farmer had, so to say, to make the farm out of a wilderness and, at the same time, make a farmer out of himself.

It will give you satisfaction to know that although we are working very hard, and our struggles to gain a comfortable existence are not over yet, we still keep in touch and heartily sympathize with our great Zion movement, and meet from time to time to discuss the problems that are confronting our poor, scattered race.

With Zion's greetings, I am
Yours respectfully,

ONE OF THE JEWISH FARMERS

---

[*] *The Jewish Exponent* (Philadelphia), November 17, 1899, 7.

Klein's second weekly essay on Jewish farming, found in *The Jewish Exponent* (Philadelphia), November 10, 1899, 9, discusses the increased competition in Trieste among Greek, Italian, and Jewish farmers selling citrons from Palestine for Sukkot, the Feast of the Tabernacles. It has not been reproduced.

Can Jews Be Farmers?*

IV. A Voice from American Judea

Whether the designation of America as Zion will be sanctioned or not by Israel at large, this much is certain, that the farming settlement Alliance fully deserves the name of American Judea. We are not afraid to proclaim this since the ancient sages of Israel predicted: "*Athidah Eretz Jisrael shetithpashet beehall h' Aratzoth!*"—"The Land of Israel is destined to extend into all countries!" and where and when has the ancient mode of Jewish farming life been realized in this country, as it has been in Alliance? Are there many other places in America whose inhabitants can demonstrate by their very life and occupation the fact that Jews can be farmers? "Let any unprejudiced observer come down to Alliance and surroundings and see for himself how the Jewish farmers have transformed a tract of rough and bush land into fertile fields covered with grape vines, fruit trees and vegetables of every description suitable for this locality." For this demonstration alone is Alliance entitled to bear the name of American Judea. What an

_____

* By Moses Klein, "Hazopheh," under the weekly column "The House of Israel." *The Jewish Exponent* (Philadelphia), November 24, 1899, 8.

honorable distinction this, to be able to refute the old, old charge that "Jews are only consumers and non-producers." The question is no longer, "Can Jews be Farmers?" but rather,

Can Jews Subsist on Farming?

In compliance with the above call, as well as with a written invitation to address the society "Agudath Zion," of Alliance, on last Saturday night, Charles Hoffman, Esq., president of the "B'ne B'rith" Grand Lodge, of District No. 3, and Moses Klein, an old friend of the farmers, paid a visit to the place, and as a result of their twenty-four hours' inquiries and observations all doubts as to the ability of Jews to pursue farming vanished forever. The enthusiastic reception of the audience given to the visitors at the beautifully illuminated Synagogue Eben H'Ezer; the heartfelt greetings with the melodious password, "*Shalom A'lechem*"; the cheerful and joyous applauds that frequently interrupted the English, Hebrew and German speakers; and the kind hospitality of the farmers in general and that of Mr. J. C. Reis in particular all remind one of Israel's patriarchal life of yore, when Judah lived under his fig tree and vine. So deep and sweet are these impressions to me that it would be cruel to interrupt them with any questions. Let this week be a jubilee Sabbath for our noble and real Zionists

of Alliance—the Amerian Judea! and let the question, "Can Jews subsist on farming?" be postponed for treatment until the next issue of *The Jewish Exponent.*
   HAZOPHEH

Alliance Colony[*]

Editor *Jewish Exponent*: It will interest the readers of your valuable paper, I think, to learn of the visit of two distinguished coreligionists from your city to our place—the Alliance Colony. They were Mr. Charles Hoffman and Mr. Moses Klein.

They addressed a large audience of our people at a meeting held on Saturday evening, November 18, in the Emanuel Synagogue, with the writer of these lines in the chair.

Mr. Hoffman delivered his eloquent address in English. He laid special stress upon the importance of relying upon one's own capacities and resources—trying everything in one's power to make a success of his undertakings without relying upon outside (human) assistance, thereby assuring in advance the partial success of the undertaking. In glowing terms he mentioned the names of the real friends and benefactors of the Jewish colonies, now deceased: Simon Muhr and Alfred T. Jones. As president of the B'nai B'rith, Mr. Hoffman set forth the benefits that would ensue if our people would join that order. His appeal found a sympathetic echo in our breasts, and a number of our people expressed their willingness to follow his advice.

Mr. Moses Klein was introduced by the chairman "as a special friend of the Jewish farmers." He proved himself as such during the entire evening, as every feature of his very able address—which he delivered in our sacred Hebrew tongue (elucidating and explaining in German)—breathed sincere love and admiration for Jewish farming life. It was balsam to our heart to hear him speak thus! Mr. Klein cited Berthold Auerbach, and laid great stress upon the necessity of having a principle or ideal in connection with one's undertakings. He illustrated this with facts: how such colonies that were guided by a higher principle, and not by material considerations alone, have managed to maintain themselves so far, and are on their way to complete success, whereas, such as were guided by the "bread and butter question alone" had failed.

The meeting closed at a late hour amidst great applause for the lecturers.

J. C. REIS
Alliance, N. J.,
Nov. 21, 1899

---

[*] Letter written by J. C. Reis to *The Jewish Exponent* (Philadelphia), November 24, 1899, 11.

Can Jews Be Farmers?*

V. A Voice from American Judea

Dear Hazopheh: In your department of *The Jewish Exponent* of November 24 you ask "Can Jews subsist on farming?" Being a farmer myself (and the good condition of my farm you have seen at the occasion of your recent visit to this place), I would answer this question in the affirmative. Of course, there are some among us that find it hard to subsist on farming alone, but this is not the fault of farming in general. It is the fault of "their" farms being either too small for the size of the family, or unproductive. This latter reason is more cause for failure, according to my judgment, than the small number of acres. Further, there are, as among Christian farmers, a vast difference in the farmers themselves. I mean the physical and mental capacities of an individual which account greatly for the success or failure in farming. For the purpose of being able to answer the above question, "Can Jews subsist on farming?" more correctly, I made a little visit yesterday afternoon to some of my friends and neighbors, the Jewish farmers. As it may interest your readers to get a glimpse of Jewish farming life in "American Judea," I will

_____
* Letter written by J. C. Reis to *The Jewish Exponent* (Philadelphia), December 1, 1899, 4.

describe a few of our farmers and give in concise form their opinions and ideas:

Israel Opachinsky, twelve in family, farm 18 acres, well cultivated and in high state of production; one of the original settlers. He is proud of his homestead, having started to work on his farm about eighteen years ago. I say "farm," it was then a regular wilderness, but it is now a nice and good farm. He and his wife take great care of their children, having them educated in Hebrew and some German, in addition to their regular public school education. He would not change his for city life by any means, and he pointed out the healthy condition of his children, the two oldest girls, growing into promising womanhood, being 18 and 16 years respectively. Right here I would remark that we have the Schleiermachers and Schoppenhauers with us (in very small number, thank God), who always look upon the dark side of life, and they point to this very farmer "how hard the farmer's life is, that he (Opachinsky) is compelled to let his two oldest children go to work in the factory here." I questioned him upon this subject, and he is far from taking the gloomy views of those pessimists. He simply explained to me (and I find it fully correct), that although his farm is in a good, productive state, still his family is large (*unbeschrien*), and they are growing up to be young ladies and need decent clothes; and it would be wrong to expect everything from such a small farm.

Another good farmer is Hirsh Levin, ten in family; owns 41 acres, good farm in productive state; is eighteen years on the place and likes farming by far better than city life. His children, mostly boys (the oldest of whom is secretary in our library), are industrious and promising young farmers.

Mr. Levin said to me: "They (his sons) all like farming; if I only could give them each a farm, but my farm is not large enough to parcel up in this way. You know," he continued, "I had a new barn built, and one of my daughters got married recently, which expenses were quite a drain upon my resources. Still I am all right and will work up again." He is of the opinion that we need here more industries and more people, so that the farmer will have a home market for his products and dairy stuffs. My time being limited at present, I am compelled to postpone my further description of farming life in "American Judea" for a future number of your valuable paper, when I shall continue to present types of our farmers and descriptions of their farms. With greetings, I am, yours respectfully,

J. C. Reis
Alliance, Nov. 27, 1899

In giving preference to the above description to my own observations of Jewish farming life, I am merely performing pleasant duty towards the cause so dear and essential to our people at large. Let our "man of the plough" wield his own pen, as his simple words are bound to supply food for contemplation to those who have the cause of Israel at heart.

Can Jews Be Farmers?[*]

VI. A Voice from American Judea

Dear Hazopheh: In accordance with my promise, I will take up the thread of describing Jewish farming life in "American Judea." Eli Stavitsky has three in his family at present, his two sons having married and left his house some years ago. His farm consists of fifteen acres, and he has good reason to be proud of his achievements during the past eighteen years, as his farm is in a high state of cultivation and is one of the best little farms around here. He is generally of a cheerful disposition (his wife and children are the same way), and I was, therefore, surprised to find him somewhat dejected in spirit when I visited him that afternoon. He said to me: "How can I be cheerful seeing my oldest son, Fish, having a wife and two children to support, without a farm and compelled to work as day laborer (chopping wood and the like) to make a scant living? The great pleasure of parents is," he continued, "to have their children provided for and settled around them: and I, although making a living of the farm myself—as you well know that I do nothing but farming—have not been able to provide a farm for my son also, from which he could draw subsistence for himself and family. As a friend of my family, I have told you some time ago," he further continued, "how my son had a chance to buy a farm in Carmel on very favorable terms. Fish had a little money saved up of his own, and I was going to help him with all I could towards buying the farm implements and live stock that are necessary to make a beginning, and you know what a good farmer my Fish is, and that he would have made a success of it just as well as I do upon my farm. Well, we have applied to the Baron De Hirsch Fund for a small loan (I think he told me three hundred dollars) so as to be enabled to purchase that farm, and offering them full security. It did not as much as answer us even. How, then, can I be joyous, seeing my son going down from worry? My younger son, Jake, fared better. He married the only daughter of a farmer, and went right into the family, took hold of the farm and works it successfully." He told me some more interesting—although sad—things, but, for the sake of brevity, I will not repeat them. Mr. Stavitsky is an honest, straightforward man, and impresses everybody that speaks to him as such. Besides, I have been intimately acquainted with the family for several years past, and can vouch for the full truth of his statements. The above picture of a Jewish farming family will prove to you, therefore, the correctness of my assertion in your last week's paper: that not only can Jews be farmers, and like to be farmers, but can also subsist on farming, provided they have

---

[*] Letter written by J. C. Reis to *The Jewish Exponent* (Philadelphia), December 8, 1899, 6.

a farm and the necessary tools to work it. Only our great Creator could create something out of nothing: Jewish farmers, however, like other mortals, must have something to work with and a place upon which to work. I have pointed out to you upon the occasion of your recent visit to this place, how he (Stavitsky) keeps order upon his farm—everything in its place, and a place for everything. What pride he took in his beautiful, full-blooded heifer calf, which he intends to raise up to a cow—how the little creature looked at you and all around with its kind, large, bovine eyes, seemingly more happy, alas, than its human surroundings. Mr. Stavitsky has shown you then, the big stumps (some larger and heavier than himself) which he took out from the ground, and gave you an adequate idea of what his "farm" was when he settled upon it about eighteen years ago—nothing but a piece of forest land. This piece of land, with the assistance of his brave and industrious sons, and sometimes his wife also, he worked out to be a good and productive farm. "The Jews learn fast," said a Christian farmer to me some time ago, when conversing with him about Jewish farmers, as compared with their Christian neighbors. "It was fun to see them," he continued, "carting their sweet potatoes to the railroad depot for shipment in former years; in what an awkward way they used to pack them and handle things connected with farming. Now, they farm as good as anybody" (meaning Christian farmers).

Now, dear Hazopheh, this testimony as to Jewish farming comes from the lips of a successful and so-called "crack" farmer, who is on the spot here and comes in frequent contact with Jewish farmers. In further support of the truth as to the ability of Jews to learn quickly and become good farmers, I would also quote what a large shipper of sweet potatoes in Vineland (our nearest trading town) told me two years ago, when he returned from a business trip to the city, to the effect that he had seen Heilig's (a Jewish farmer here) "sweets" bring the highest price at that time in the New York and Brooklyn markets. You understand what this means—stuff to be called "fancy," and, therefore, bring a high price—has not only to be good in quality and appearance, but "must" also be put up right and neat. I am glad to say that we have here quite a number of Jewish farmers as good as Stavitsky or Heilig.

My time being again limited, I must defer further description of Jewish farming life in "American Judea," as well as my own remarks thereon for a future stage of this article in your valuable paper. With greetings, I am,

Yours respectfully,

J. C. REIS

Alliance, N. J., Dec. 4, 1899

Can Jews Be Farmers?*

VII. A Voice from American Judea

Dear Hazopheh: Having demonstrated in my former communications in your department of *The Jewish Exponent* that Jews can subsist on farming, under favorable conditions, of course, I will now conclude my article by describing a few more of our farmers: David Steinberg bought his place about fourteen years ago, entirely with his own means. His farm consists of 20 acres, and he worked it out of bush land. His married son, Harry, an intelligent young farmer, lives with him, and they both farm the place. Mr. Steinberg, senior, is quite an authority upon grape culture. His place always looks neat and attractive.

Joseph Kleinfeld, two in family, and his son, Samuel Kleinfeld, with five in family, farm together 60 acres; and good farmers they are, as everybody can tell at a glance by looking upon their fields. Kleinfeld, senior, started originally 18 years ago with 13 acres. In speaking to young Kleinfeld about Jewish farmers, he told me that it depends mostly upon "the man" to make a success, and that a Jew can make a successful farmer if he so chooses. Father and son

are perfectly pleased with farming life, principally on account of being independent of any bosses. They favor manufacturing establishments to afford home markets for the farmers' products. Young Kleinfeld believes in diversified farming (they have plenty of land and can do so). They raise, in addition to their own hay and corn for their stock, large quantities of sweet potatoes. Several acres of their farm are devoted to grape culture. I questioned young Kleinfeld (knowing him to be an authority on all matters pertaining to farming): "Why is it that our Jewish farmers do not fare better in making a 'comfortable living?'"

"It is because," he said, "they had started with nothing, and had to exhaust their lands by the continual draughts made upon it, in contrast to most Christian farmers, who get, or inherit, their farms from their parents."

Hirsch Coltun's little farm is one of the very best around here. He uses great judgment in keeping up the fertility and productiveness of the soil of his little place. His farm has only 14 acres, but by his skillful management of the same he makes a fair living for his family, consisting of 5 or 6 persons at present, as some of his children have married and left him.

His son, Aaron Coltun (three in family), is also a good farmer. His principal crops are sweet potatoes, strawberries and blackberries.

Joseph Zeiger is another good farmer. His family consists of eleven persons, eight boys,

---

* Letter written by J. C. Reis to *The Jewish Exponent* (Philadelphia), December 15, 1899, 6.

and the ninth is a girl. His farm contains 30 acres. His original farm was of 15 acres, and he purchased the other 15 acres just lately. Nearly all of his land is in fine, productive condition. I did not find Mr. Zeiger home upon the afternoon when I made my round to the farmers. But what a beautiful picture met my eyes! The mother—she looks very youthful and by no means like a mother to nine children—surrounded by her healthy looking boys with forks and rakes cleaning up the yard and raking together the fallen autumn leaves. She remarked to me, jokingly: "We have to do something so as to revive our appetites, the work upon the fields being meager now." The mother as well as her boys did not look, however, as if they would suffer very much from loss of appetite. The phrase of our great poet occurred to my mind at that time: "*Em Habinim Smechah*" (the happy mother of children).

I could describe a good many more Jewish farmers, and good ones, at that, but I am afraid that I may trespass upon the patience of your readers on the one hand, and, secondly, I am really too busy with my own work. There is always something to do for one man upon a farm, even in the winter time.

In conclusion, I will gladden your heart, dear Hazopheh, by announcing that our farmers have here a Zion Society, called "Agudath Zion," and we do heartily sympathize with our great leaders that are trying to find a resting place and a permanent home in our ancient Fatherland, now under the Turkish Sultan, for our persecuted brethren in foreign countries. May the Almighty crown their efforts with success, and the prophecy of Isaiah for the people of Israel be at last fulfilled: "then shall thy light break forth like the dawn! And thy healing shall speedily flourish!"

With Zion greetings, I am yours, respectfully,

J. C. Reis

Alliance, N. J., Dec. 11, 1899

The "House of Israel" is thankful to Mr. Reis for his graphic and truthful descriptions of "Farming Life in America Judea." His words will strike deeply into Jewish hearts and will awaken them towards their duty to themselves as well as to new exiles who may find a refuge in the farming district instead of in the sweat-shops.

Hazopheh

Attention to Jewish Farming Life Demanded*

Editor of *The Jewish Exponent*:

Being a constant reader of your House of Israel department, I notice that "Hazopheh" has discontinued the discussions under the head of "Can Jews Be Farmers?" and has headed his articles with the title "Some Jewish Phases of the Nineteenth Century."

Now, I do not take umbrage at the change of the heading, but I am wondering at the sudden discontinuance of the discussion of Jewish farming life. Is not this also "a Jewish phase" worthy of your and all good men's consideration and serious attention? To my mind this is the more important and concerns the Jewish people more vitally than the generalities of "Jews embracing Christianity" in the *Exponent* of January 12, and of "Revival of the Martial Spirit of the Jews" contained in your edition of January 19.

I know well that a good many (it may be the majority) do not look upon this subject in the light I see it, but I have taken "Hazopheh" to possess some of the spirit of our great seers

_____

* Letter written by J. C. Reis to *The Jewish Exponent* (Philadelphia), January 26, 1900, 6. The original text is signed "L. C. Reis," which I presume is an error in typesetting.

and sages (as indicated by his nom de plume), and therefore had expected him to face boldly and discuss fearlessly the great problem: How to make the existing Jewish colonies self-supporting permanently and on a sound basis, which colonies will then serve as models and beacon lights for future similar enterprises.

The anti-Semetic outbursts in several European countries lead me to think that these are the forerunners to serious persecutions and bloodshed that will bring a flood of our unfortunate and destitute brethren to the hospitable American shores.

I ask you therefore very seriously if it is not your duty to "cry and cry aloud," like the Prophets of old, and warn the better-off portion of our people, reminding them of their duty "to provide shelter in time for their kin," and not wait until the storm breaks out or when it is in full force, as in 1882. Dispel their delusions that "Such barbarous persecutions will not happen any more." In my opinion, based upon the study of history, they can happen at any time in one or the other of even the so-called civilized countries of Europe.

Apart from the necessity of fostering and encouraging agricultural occupations among our brethren, it is well to consider it from a Zionistic stand-point; as it was rightly observed by a writer in *The Jewish Exponent* several weeks ago, "that we cannot form a nation out of such material as merchants and peddlers." I fully agree with that writer—that when we succeed, please God, and establish a commonwealth with a number of our people, and form a State in our ancient fatherland, even under the suzerainty of the Turkish Sultan, we can only expect ultimate success by reverting (even if it is only by a portion of our brethren) to agricultural pursuits, by which pursuits our ancestors have lived "contentedly" and prospered for many centuries during our glorious past.

L. C. REIS
Alliance, N. J.
January 22, 1900

Baron De Hirsch's Colossal Colonization Plans*

Jewish Farmers in the Argentine

According to the sixth annual report of the Jewish Colonization Association there are 7015 Jewish souls in the twenty-three colonies of the Argentine Republic.

In North America

The same report refers to five colonies in North America, viz: Hirsch Colony in Canada, Woodbine, Alliance, Rosenhayn and Carmel in New Jersey. One hundred and fifty farmers out of the three hundred families living at the three last named colonies, Alliance, Rosenhayn and Carmel, are reported as having received grants advanced by the council.

Isolated Farmers in New England

According to a recent article in a prominent Boston journal, together with the pictures of J. N. Hecht and M. Mitchell, representatives of the Boston Jewish Charities, it seems that great success has accompanied those Jews who settle on isolated farms. Here is what the journal says:

"In New England the Hirsch fund has enabled more than 600 Jewish farmers to settle on as many homesteads. More than $1,100,000 of the money of immigrants is invested in these farms. And there is invested $1,250,000 of loans on mortgages other than those held by the Baron de Hirsch fund.

"These investments have been made safe and productive by the loans and advances made by the fund.

"The fund is aiming all the time to remove to the vicinity of these farms the industries, such as the tailoring trades, in which many of the immigrants are employed. Thus is created a constant market for Jewish farm products, at the same time relieving the so-called ghettos from the congestion that obtains in large cities."

In Palestine

Five of the Palestinian colonies have been assisted by the Jewish Colonization Association, according to its Sixth Report.

In Cypress

One colony was established in Cyprus by the above colonization association.

---

* By Moses Klein, "Hazopheh," under the weekly column "The House of Israel." *The Jewish Exponent* (Philadelphia), February 2, 1900, 6.

Farming in American Judea[*]

The yearning to restore Jews to their ancestral occupation of farming, which alone amongst all the other industries and professions is capable of restoring the equilibrium between Israel's mind and body; the anxiety to see my brethren—whom centuries of persecution have reduced to a peculiar creature of "skin, bone and brain"—revitalized and invigorated by their close reunion with Mother Earth, the fountain head of physical existence; the longing to see our people attached to the soil, like all other sons of earth under God's heaven. This yearning, anxiety and longing, which run like golden threads throughout the modest writings contributed by me during the past two decades to Jewish literature in the Hebrew, English and German languages, are no longer an "idle dream," as some of the so-called wise and great were apt to term them. No. The dream, the notion, the yearning and the anxiety during so many cheerless years, countries, people and environments, are assuming the shape of stern facts and realities. Journey from Dan to B'er Shabah in Palestine, and your eyes will be charmed by thirty-four Jewish farming settlements, flourishing like the Rose of Sharon.

Traverse the triangular vista extending between Vineland, Bridgeton and Millville, and behold American Judea—Alliance, Rosenhayn and Carmel, in their emerald garb of nature. Take a trip to Doylestown, in our own State, and you will be confronted by a bewildering paradise of our National Farm School, the dream-land of Dr. Joseph Krauskopf. Do you need stronger proofs than these facts illustrating the force of clear visions and of the yearning souls for a free spot on earth under God's heavenly dome?

Yet I fear that the facts enunciated are incapable of convincing indifferent minds of the existence of permanent Jewish farming settlements. Watch the hosts of wealthy sons and daughters of Israel who will soon sail like summer birds to every centre of Europe and to the various seashore resorts of America. They will soon fly to Buffalo, Atlantic City, Newport, San Francisco, London, Paris, Zurich, Berlin, Vienna, Budapest, Rome and Venice; but how many of them will find time to grace with their presence such wonderful farming centres as Rishon L'Zion, Pesach-Tikvah, Zichran Jacob and Rosh Pinah, in Palestine, or the colonies of Alliance, Rosenhayn and Carmel in American Judea? Jewish farming settlements are, however, so important that if our wealthy co-religionists turn their eyes away from them they must be brought near to their sight. If Mohammed declines to go to the mountain, the mountain is bound to come to Mohammed!

---

[*] By Moses Klein, "Hazopheh," under the weekly column "The House of Israel." *The Jewish Exponent* (Philadelphia), May 17, 1901, 6.

The Jewish Colonies in South Jersey
(By the Chief of the New Jersey Bureau of Statistics)

In the narrow-confines of the columns of the "House of Israel" it is impossible for me to describe the present condition of the Jewish farming settlement in Palestine. This will be done in the forthcoming souvenir of the Fourth Annual Convention of American Zionists. This article is to be confined merely to a review of the recently published pamphlet under the title, "The Jewish Colonies of South Jersey," which was prepared and issued by William Stainsby, Esq., Chief of the New Jersey Bureau of Statistics. This historical sketch of Jewish farming settlements, coming as it does from such high authority, may perhaps have a stronger effect upon those Jewish minds who are still indifferent towards Jewish farming, than all the cries, pleadings and descriptions of dreamers, visioners and observers. The first chapter of the profusely illustrated booklet deals with the oldest Jewish settlements.

Alliance

The history of this, as well as of the other colonies of South Jersey, has been described time and again in these and other columns of *The Jewish Exponent*, a repetition of same would be superfluous, as it is well known that the settlers of Alliance "had been cast out as paupers; their humble homes in Russia had been taken from them, and they fled, as did the Pilgrim fathers, from tyranny and relentless persecution to a land they knew not, but with the promise of such assistance as would enable them to make homes for themselves and children, and where they would be free to worship God in their own way, assured of liberty and the protection of the law."

What was done for these farmers during their critical period in 1884 is equally well known to those Philadelphians who, at the instance of the late Simon Muhr, Alfred T. Jones and others still living, contributed the $7000, which sum is perhaps credited erroneously by the author of the new pamphlet, to the Alliance Land Trust of New York.[*]

The very important statements of the pamphlets that deserve universal attention are the following paragraphs:

Jews Successful Farmers

"In the spring[†] active farming and trucking operations begun, and from that day to the present time the result has been a steady uplift and improvement in the moral, social and financial condition of the people. Can a Jew become a

---

[*] See *Migdal Zophim*, pp. 47–79. Published in Philadelphia, 1889. Hazopheh

[†] Apparently, of 1884 or 1885. Hazopheh

successful farmer? is a question frequently asked, and almost invariably answered in the negative; but a careful and impartial investigation of the work accomplished by these colonies will justify a more hopeful conclusion. A visitor will observe good houses, improved and thoroughly up-to-date outbuildings, healthy and well-conditioned stock, and crops growing that are admirably adapted to the character of the soil. These and other details of management open to observation, which show a high degree of intelligently directed industry, will justify the assertion that the Jew not only can, but has become a successful farmer, at least in these settlements."

Condition of the Farms, Products, Stock, Markets and Manufacturing

The Statistical Bureau, in its description of the farms, products, stock, markets and manufacturing, says:

"The farms have a very neat appearance and give evidence of great care in cultivation, no rubbish being permitted to accumulate. The vineyards have been carefully laid out, the vines are healthy and strong and the yield is very large. But little attention is given to wine making, as shipments of the grapes in fresh and sound condition to New York markets is found to yield more satisfactory results.

"In the shipment of strawberries, raspberries, blackberries, etc., great care is exercised in selecting and packing, and they have thus secured a good reputation in the markets.

"The sweet potatoes raised at Alliance have attained such high repute in New York that they command from twenty-five to fifty cents per barrel more than can be obtained from those raised elsewhere.

"The farmers of Alliance have good stock, the cows especially being of the very best; the poultry also will compare favorably with any in this section of the State. As cows and poultry are prime factors in solving the problem of family subsistence, they receive a vast amount of care and attention. The Jew farmer will give the stock the best to be obtained and the strictest attention to its comforts and health to the verge of his own self-denial. Special details of items of crops could not be obtained, but the berry and fruit crop of 1899 amounted to $40,000. The sweet potato crop realized for these thrifty farmers $18,000.

"Manufacturing in Alliance has not advanced as rapidly as in the later colony at Woodbine. There is one large factory, which is operated by the Alliance Cloak and Suit Company, of which Mr. Abraham Brotman, a thoroughly wide-awake and progressive man, is the head. The factory is located on the northern portion of the tract, which is known as Brotmanville.

"This factory, occupied by three parties—Brotman, Eskin and Brod—furnishes employment to 55, 30 and 15 hands respectively."

This sketch of Alliance, which contains one illustration of the Brotmanville factory encompassed by the tailoring settlement, one Woodbine farm, one school, and a section containing the houses of tailors in the latter place, closes with the following paragraph:

"The colony at Alliance has had a hard struggle, but has passed the experimental stage, and is now fairly on the road to success. It has recently passed from the control of the Alliance Land Trust to the Board of Trustees of the Baron de Hirsch Fund: these trustees propose to extend immediately material aid to the colony. They will spend $10,000 in public improvements and build twenty fine dwellings. This, the first colony establishment in South Jersey, has not had the success which has crowned the colony at Woodbine, but it must be remembered that Alliance has not had hitherto the benefit of large appropriations from the Baron de Hirsch Fund as have been given to the people of Woodbine."

If the author had in mind in his term "the first colony establishment in South Jersey," a tailoring settlement or an agricultural school, then he is right in stating that it has not had the success which has crowned the colony of Woodbine; but if his term applies to farm colonists, then it is safe to say that the Alliance farming families have achieved infinitely better results as farmers on the 1100 acres of the Alliance tract than have the Woodbiners shown on their larger tract of 5300 acres. Tailoring and farming are each beneficial for the material advancement of a community while confined to their individual spheres, but each must stand on its own merits.

HAZOPHEH

Farming in American Judea*
The Jewish Colonies in South Jersey

II.
Rosenhayn

The Bureau of Statistics of New Jersey traces the origin of what it terms "the prosperous Jewish colony Rosenhayn" to the same red-lettered year of 1882, which gave birth to the Alliance colony. Here, as in Alliance, the "Hebrew Emigrant Aid Society" of New York City is credited as being the founder of the settlement. This society located six Jewish families in a wilderness of pine and bushlands in 1882, which tract has now grown to be a village of some note, with a population of 800.

The general progress of the settlement is indicated in the report by the following facts:

Rosenhayn is located on the New Jersey Central Railroad, midway between Bridgeton and Vineland. It has a broad, well-shaded avenue, over one mile in length, with excellent sidewalks. It has a thriving community of about 250 families, consisting almost exclusively of Russian and Polish Jews.

_____

* By Moses Klein, "Hazopheh," under the weekly column "The House of Israel." *The Jewish Exponent* (Philadelphia), May 24, 1901, 6.

Industrial Pursuits

The population is equally divided in followers of industrial and agricultural pursuits, the industries being clothing, hosiery, foundry work, tinware and brick. The following is the number of hands employed in the various factories:

Clothing...160
Brickyard...17
Hosiery 5
Foundry 4
Tinware...2

The average wages of these operatives is given as $10 per week. Fifty per cent of the employees own their own houses and these houses are described as being in good condition. Such is not the case in the factories, where little attention is paid to ventilation and sanitary rules.

Agricultural Pursuits

Now I come to the part of the report which describes the farming element of Rosenhayn, which is the main feature of this extensive review.

"The farming portion of the community," says the report, "appears to be fairly prosperous. Of the 1900 acres comprising the tract, about one-fourth is under cultivation; the farms are in excellent order and exhibit evidences of skillful manipulation in clearing the soil of stumps, roots and noxious weeds. The soil, as in other colonies, is not well adapted to the raising of cereals, and the attention of the farmers is given to the culture of fruit and vegetables. The shipment of berries, sweet and white potatoes and other vegetables to the New York market is very large, and the railroad station presents an animated scene as the farmers bring in their produce on shipping days; large quantities of grapes are also raised for shipment; wine-making is largely carried on, and the vineyards, being carefully cultivated, present a thrifty and strong appearance. The great source of profit, however, is the sweet potato crop; the yield is enormous and of such fine quality as to command the very highest prices in the New York market. The farmers here are planning for the construction of a canning factory, to avoid the shipment of berries and tomatoes. The farmers of Rosenhayn are hard workers and do not count the hours of labor; from the earliest dawn until sundown they are hard at it, and their untiring industry is winning its reward in ownership of the fine farms and the feeling of independence that emancipation from oppression and poverty brings."

When I recall the melancholy appearance of the Rosenhayn farmers four year ago, when most of them were in a despondent condition,

I can realize the importance of the following statement: "About fifty per cent. of the farmers have their farms clear of incumbrance; it was a hard struggle and uphill work for years, but their perseverance and economy have at last brought them to a fair degree of success."

Jews Can Make a Success of Farming

Although the chief of the Jersey "Bureau of Statistics," the author of this book, has already rendered his verdict in the case of the Alliance colonists, that "Jews not only can be, but are, good farmers," yet this question is so important that no experiment of a single colony should determine its final solution.

I am therefore happy to quote the following conclusion of the author:

"The farmers of Rosenhayn have good stock and keep it in excellent condition. A Jew may be trusted to take the best possible care of his horses and cows.* He regards them as very potent factors in winning his way upwards, and they are treated as well as the family. Considerable attention is paid to poultry raising, and, as in the case of the other colonists, these people seem to have the knack of doing it well. The

---

* This extraordinary care and protection of animals is to Jews a Biblical injunction. "Thou shalt give to thy cattle and thou shall eat and be satisfied." First comes the mute, helpless cattle, then—yourself!

                                                          Hazopheh

farm dwellings are small, but with their surroundings neatly kept, and the outbuildings are also in reasonably fair condition. The annual value of crops raised is between $10,000 and $12,000. There is no question but that the Jews can make a success of farming. These colonies located in South Jersey have demonstrated that fact beyond controversy."

Two photo-engravings, one of the Forcing House, Agricultural School, the other the Apiary Department of the School of Woodbine, accompany the article on Rosenhayn.

Rosenhayn, despite its name, has but few and isolated roses. But the wreath presented by the author of the booklet is one of the finest and most tender decorations ever tendered by a Gentile hand to the Jewish people. Such a recognition by State authority of Jewish activity in the domain of agriculture is especially welcome to the "House of Israel" on the eve of the approaching Feast of Bikurim!

HAZOPHEH

History of the Alliance Colony[*]

By J. C. Reis

Following upon the cruel persecutions in Russia during the years 1880, 1881 and 1882, this pioneer of the American Jewish colonies saw the light on the 10th day of May, 1882, when it was settled by the first contingent of expatriated Jews of the "Holy Muscovite Empire."

There were twenty-five families, mostly small traders and store-keepers from home. The spot upon which these colonists were settled is situated in Salem County, State of New Jersey, five miles from Vineland, ten miles from Bridgeton, ten miles from Millville and about 35 miles southeast from the city of Philadelphia.

The soil was then covered with dense forests. The Jewish settlers set out right away to clear the land, so that by the end of the same month of their settlement they had corn planted already. They worked together upon a certain tract of land, about thirty acres, and they fully proved the truth of the adage "In union is strength."

Plantings of potatoes and other vegetables followed as soon as more land was cleared.

_____

[*] *The Jewish Exponent* (Philadelphia), April 12, 1907, 1–2.

Soon after their settlement the Hebrew Emigrant Aid Society of New York city had several large buildings erected and in each of these buildings were housed a number of families, and all were fed from a common kitchen, the provisions being furnished by the above-named society. This state of affairs continued for about six months, during which time the colonists worked diligently and with good spirits upon the land. Mr. Sternberg was the superintendent and Mr. Schmidt was the instructor in farming. Several of the Jewish colonists worked out part of the time for the neighboring Christian farmers.

In the meantime the Hebrew Emigrant Aid Society (at a later stage of the history of Alliance this society developed into the "Alliance Land Trust," when it co-operated in this noble undertaking with the Mansion House Relief Committee of London, Eng., with such prominent gentlemen at the head of it as Henry S. Henry, Isaac Eppinger. L. Gerschel and Dr. F. de Sola Mendes, all of New York city), purchased about 80 acres of land, including the tract upon which the colonists worked and divided the same into small farms of fifteen acres each. Upon these farms (so-called, as there was not as yet any resemblance to a present well cultivated Alliance farm then; there was nothing but thick woods everywhere) the society had small houses erected and wells dug. The houses were 12 x 14 feet, one and one-half stories high. In the fall of the same year the colonists drew lots for their "farms" and each family was settled upon their allotment.

The Hebrew Emigrant Aid Society furnished stoves, furniture and household goods to each family.

During the ensuing winter and spring, 1882–83, a period of 9 months, each family received from eight to twelve dollars per month, their living expenses, during which time they were busily engaged in clearing as much of their land as they could. Each family also received "the value of $100" during that spring for tools, plants and farm utensils.

To save the expense of horses and farm tools, the colonists tried to work four neighbors together, allotting to each the work he was mostly adapted to. This plan, nice in theory, did not work right in practice, and the settlers soon discontinued this system. They disposed of their partnership horses and each family worked its own farm separately, hiring the horsework done from the neighboring Christian farmers.

They planted trees, grape vines, blackberries, strawberries and some truck for their own use.

During the summer and early fall of 1883 the colonists worked out for the Christian farmers; they were picking berries, digging potatoes, husking corn, etc. Most of them had to walk several miles to and from their work as there were not many farmers in the immediate neighborhood. During the same fall a cigar factory was started in one of the large buildings formerly occupied by the colonists; part of the same building was also used as a shirt factory; and so the colonists were kept up during the ensuing winter of 1883–84, some making a living by sewing and some by cigarmaking. (About 40 worked at sewing, and 26 at cigars.)

I would remark right here that there were a good many families sent to the colony who were not intended, and they themselves did not intend to be farmers, and the New York Committee had to look after and provide for them too. The cigar manufacturing was called into existence, I understand, upon the suggestion of Mr. M. Mendel, of New York city.

This same generous gentleman erected a large brick building (several years after the happenings just recorded), which is now used as a tailoring establishment, employing quite a number of people.

The shirt and cigar industries came to an end because the building where these industries were carried on burned down. This was in the spring of 1884. At this juncture the more capable Jewish farmers bought horses and the necessary farm tools and began to work their farms themselves, thereby dispensing with the horse hire from the Christian farmers. They not only worked their own farms, but also helped their Jewish fellow-farmers thereby earning the money which went out from the colony previously.

Every family received fifty dollars this spring (1884) from the committee. With this money they planted more trees, grape vines and berries. The farmers had a good deal to replant, owing to the inexperience of the farmers themselves, and to the inexperience of the management, in not furnishing the right kind of plants and not in the right time for planting during 1882 and '83. In the fall, 1884, the Jewish settlers worked for the neighboring farmers, helping to gather in the crops (their own crops being light as yet and not occupying all of their time).

During the winter of 1884–85 some of the farmers went to the cities of Philadelphia and New York and brought out tailoring work for their own and other Jewish families at the same time they worked upon their land also, chopping wood, clearing away brush and stumps, etc.

The philanthropist, Mr. Leonard Lewisohn, of New York city, donated a fine sewing machine "to each family."

Notwithstanding all these auxiliaries for making a living quite a number of families were in great distress. They appealed to the Association of Jewish Emigrants of the city of Philadelphia, whereupon Mr. Alfred T. Jones and Mr. Simon Muhr, president and treasurer, respectively, of said association, came out often during that winter and supplied the needy families with all the necessities of life: food, clothing and household goods; also tools and farm implements. Mrs. Reckendorf, of New York city, furnished one thousand dollars to re-establish a cigar factory in the colony. The factory was run for some time by Mr. Jacobson, who gave it up upon the death of his wife.

In the spring of 1885 the Jewish farmers were very enthusiastic and worked their farms with great energy, stimulated to it by having secured some profit from the fruits of their labor during the previous years. Fall and winter passed as before; partly working their own farms, partly for others, and partly tailoring.

Spring and summer of 1886 gave a fresh impetus to Jewish farming in the Alliance Colony. Some farmers took off their lands products to the value of from 200 to 400 dollars. They felt proud of their achievements and began to improve their farms, erecting the necessary dwelling houses (the original houses were not fit to live in for a fair-sized family), barns and other outbuildings.

The winter of 1886–87 passed as usual, the settlers occupying themselves with tailoring and farming. During the spring and summer of 1887 the farmers were in high spirits, enjoying the blessings of a free government in contrast to the despotic and galling tyranny from which they escaped, and at the same time partaking of the bountiful blessings upon the table of Mother Earth, "the fruits of their own exertions and labor."

The income of some of the Jewish farmers during this summer was from 400 to 700 dollars. Winter of 1887–88 was spent in the colony as usual; tailoring and farming.

Now Alliance began to experience a "little boom." Attracted by the success of the old settlers, newcomers from the cities and green immigrants came over and settled in Alliance. They were employed as tailors during the winter, and as farm laborers and berrypickers during the summer. Some of the best farmers in Rosenhayn and in Carmel worked, previous to their settlement in those places, for Jewish farmers in the Alliance Colony. Summer of 1888 was also good and the Jewish farmers prospered.

Having reached the summit of prosperity (as compared with the seasons of privation at the commencement of the settlement) in the history of Alliance, it is now meet to diverge from the prosaic narration as to its material course and to turn our attention briefly to the mental and spiritual attainments and achievements during the few years of Alliance's existence.

For this purpose I quote from the Philadelphia Sunday Mercury, in its issue of October 20, and 27, 1889 (copy of Migdal Zophim, by Moses Klein, pages 87 and 97).

"Away back in the days of the prophet Jeremiah, the precursors of the barbarians that afterward extinguished the civilization of Rome and plunged Europe into the darkness of the Middle Ages had already begun their encroachments on their more civilized neighbors. At that time the empire of Media was suffering from the incursions of predatory tribes of Scythians, and when Jeremiah threatened Israel with the wrathful visitation of those savage hordes, he little dreamed that 2500 years later the descendants of his people would be fleeing from the oppression of the same barbarous power to find a refuge in a land of promise beyond the seas. So far as the Jews are concerned, they come in large part for much the same reason as that which impelled the Pilgrim Fathers to Plymouth Rock, and they bring with them today the same indomitable spirit of enterprise and industry as that through which, two hundred years ago, the Puritans made the New England forests to blossom as a rose. . . . On last Tuesday, 22d inst., about seventy of the Alliance colonists, who had completed the probationary term of five or more years' residence in this Republic, applied for their final naturalization papers to the Court of Salem, N. J. They will thus become 'full-fledged citizens' of the United States and will presently be accounted as factors in State and local politics. As might be supposed, their party preferences are by no means uniform; differences of opinion are more than ordinarily pronounced among these people, and these differences have manifested themselves even in their religious observances. With regard to the latter, the majority are of the most orthodox school, but a strong minority have already introduced innovations upon their customs, and have arrayed themselves as 'Reformers.'"

As the observations of the *Mercury* seem to me correct, I think they ought to be given space in the history of the Alliance Colony.

Of greater importance, however, seem to me the remarks of the colonists themselves, which I find recorded in one of their congregation books. The original is in the Hebrew language, and this is its translation:

"On the first day of Mar-Cheshvan, 5,648 (about November, 1888), in the congregation of Sheerith Israel (the remnant of Israel), of Alliance, there was resolved to record in a book what has befallen us ever since we were in the land of our birth, Russia, and our arrival and salvation in America, upon our lands, where we now live in tranquility, so that these incidents may be a remembrance to us, our children and to future generations." . . . Here follows a detailed description of the barbarities practiced upon them and thousands of their brethren by the Russian rabble, with the connivance of the authorities, such as robbery, murder, desecrating the houses of worship and the holy books, and dishonoring women in the presence of their husbands and fathers. The account goes on to tell: "How the Alliance Israelite Universelle helped thousands of their brethren to get out of Russia and settle in other countries."

It closes with these words: "Many came to this land of freedom, and among them we, too, came here impoverished and destitute. But thanks are due to the Hebrew Emigrant Aid Society, who helped us in everything that we asked of them. They also gave us a tract of land in the State of New Jersey, upon which we now live and work, and we draw our subsistence from the blessings of Mother Earth 'and by our own handiwork.' We call this colony 'Alliance' after the name of that great Alliance that came to our succor. The streets and avenues we called after our noble brethren who helped us with their kind generosity and whose names are 'engraved upon our hearts': from New York, H. S. Henry, Leopold Gerschel, Isaac Eppinger, Jacob H. Schiff, Lazer Rosenfeld, Joseph Rickendorfer, Leonard Lewisohn, M. H. Mendel, Gottheil, Dr. Huebsch, Dr. de Sola Mendes. From Philadelphia, A. T. Jones, Simon Muhr, Dr. Morais, Dr. Jastrow. Jehova, the God of Israel, shall bless all this holy congregation and their names shall not be forgotten forever. Amen!"

Upon another page of the same book I find the following, also in Hebrew:

"The fifteenth day of Mar-Cheshvan, 5648, at a meeting of the Congregation Sheerith Israel, it was resolved to record the following: After all the many troubles and sufferings that passed over us, we live now, thanks to God, tranquilly upon our lands, 'everyone under his vine.' Therefore, we have resolved to erect a house to our God, the Rock of our salvation, a nice building, as much as we can afford it. The house shall be called 'Tiphereth Israel' (Decoration of Israel), so that it may be an ornament and decoration to us before the nations among whom we live. We, the undersigned, pledge ourselves each to give his share towards the expenses of this building. The corner-stone will be laid on the first day of Chanucah in this year, upon the spot which the Land Trust of the colony gave us as a present, upon the hill, corner of Gerschel and Schiff avenues." Here follows a list of names, founders of the Synagogue Tiphereth Israel.

I have quoted from these two sources so as to show in the first place, to what degree of respect and consideration the colonists worked themselves up from their low and impoverished condition (put there by their cruel enemies), so as to bring forth favorable comment from the public press; which comment was fully deserved. One of the *Sunday Mercury*'s staff spent three days in Alliance, so as to get at the true state of affairs in the colony.

Secondly, and of far greater importance, I want to show to what degree of "independence and liberty of mind," as well as to material welfare, they have grown during their few years of residence in a free country under the benign government of the "Stars and Stripes."

In their own touching words we notice their truly religious gratitude to the God of their fathers, who has again—as often before—not forsaken them, but delivered them out of the house of "modern" bondage, and has set them up in a free country to form a nucleus—maybe—for the now persecuted and expatriated sons of Israel in another barbarous country.

We notice, further, their sincere gratitude to those really noble and generous gentlemen, who came to their rescue in this great land of "the Brave and the Free," as is expressed in the simple, but meaningful words I have just translated.

With what persistency they clung to their ideal (agriculture) the appended statistics will show, which goes to show that, after many years of reverses, when their star seemed to go under, they still hung on to their farms, and their numbers have not diminished to any extent, although the state of their prosperity in 1897 (when these statistics were collected) was much below that of 1889 (when the reporter of the *Mercury* visited them).

The statistics of 1897, taken by myself, show a population of 96 families with 512 persons, possessing 1502 acres of land, for Norma and Alliance. The railroad station to Alliance is now called Norma, instead of Bradway.

From the year 1889 the fortune of the colony was on the wane for several years. The colonists were compelled to go into debt, to buy lumber to repair and improve their buildings, for farm tools, horses and cows (at one time the farmers were cheated by a company from Bridgeton, selling them worthless horses for big prices).

In the course of the following few years most of the farmers were compelled to borrow money of the building and loan associations of Bridgeton and Salem, N. J., and mortgaged their farms. With the money they paid off the debts they had previously contracted, to recover which the creditors were pressing them—and made the necessary improvements upon their farms.

The farmers paid their dues to the building association as long as they could; but the reduction of the proceeds of their farms, due to causes above described, and principally, to the stagnation of business and the low prices of farm products during the several years of the nineties caused them to fall behind in their payments. The Building and Loan Association of Salem, N. J., threatened to foreclose the mortgages and eject the Jewish farmers.

By the timely intervention of the Baron de Hirsch Fund, in 1897–98, this great calamity was averted. The Baron de Hirsch Fund bought out the mortgages of the Jewish farmers from the building association and arranged a plan for the partial and gradual paying of their debts by the Jewish farmers. The Baron de Hirsch Fund is now encouraging tailoring industry in the Alliance Colony.

I am indebted to my fellow farmers: Messrs. Israel Opachinsky, Moses Bayuk, Joseph Diamond, for much of the history just narrated, as they were eye-witnesses of the proceedings during the first years of the settlement of the Alliance Colony. I compared their statements with those I found in print, and questioned them closely, so as to get at the true historical facts. My own residence in this locality (Norma, N. J.) dates only from 1892, when I bought a small farm of thirteen and a half acres, which I improved, and have lived upon it ever since.

Since the year 1900, the farming industry among the Jewish farmers began to improve considerably. A considerable share of credit in this improvement is due to the brothers Maurice and Joseph Fels, of the Fels-Naptha Soap manufacturing firm of the city of Philadelphia. These two brothers began to take an interest in this colony some time around the years 1898–1900, and have ever since kept up their interest. Their plan is to give the farmers a chance to help themselves, and they adhere to this plan strictly. They repudiate the "charity idea" altogether, and want the farmers to help themselves.

They have established a large canning factory where the farmers' products are canned; thereby making them independent, to a great extent, of the commission houses in the large cities.

Previous to the establishment of the cannery the farmers were "compelled" to send their products to the commission houses of the large cities (the local markets are limited around here), and when the market in the city was glutted—and often it was so—the farmers lost heavily.

Mr. Maurice Fels is the president of the said "Alliance Canning Factory" at Norma Station, N. J., and he takes a lively and "personal" interest in the management of the same.

City stable manure and commercial fertilizers are advanced to the farmers for which they pay with the products that they are bringing to the canning factory. A census, compiled by myself in November, 1905, shows 165 Jewish families with 891 persons. Their possessions have considerably increased, and their material condition has greatly improved. It may be interesting to note that the whole of Pittsgrove Township, in which Alliance is situated, contained in 1905, according to the official State Census of New Jersey, 2154 souls.

The history of Alliance, with its railroad station of Norma at the one end, and its tailoring industrial corner of Brotmanville at the other, has taken quite a new swing since the year 1900; the details which I reserve for a future date.

Addendum Images

Cow pasture, Carmel, c. 1907. *Image courtesy of Mickey Smith.*

Bathing place, Carmel, c. 1907. *Image courtesy of Mickey Smith.*

Irving Avenue, Carmel, c. 1907. While the building on the right looks like a schoolhouse, it is actually one of the settlement's garment factories. *Image courtesy of Mickey Smith.*

Columbia Hall, Carmel.
Postcard correspondence (written on front of card): "Carmel Jan 22nd 1907. I guess you think I have forgotten you but I have not I have been sick that is the reason I did not write and soon and I will return[.] From your Friend M. Miller." [Beneath photograph] "This is Carmel Hall." Addressed to: Miss Jessie McColum, Belleville, Mifflin Co., Penn. Postmark: January 22, 1907, p.m. *Image courtesy of Mickey Smith.*

Carmel Public School.
Postcard correspondence: "Here is a picture of my school. We have four large rooms and have lots of fun. Wish you could step in sometime. I have two music scholars now. Gave a lesson to-night. We certainly have some dandy rooms to live in this year. Much nicer than last. Lovingly – Mildred." Written on front of card: "Come out and see me in my new home. Mildred." Addressed to: Mrs. Emily J Sheppard, Cedarville, New Jersey. Postmark: Carmel, N. J., September 24, 1908, a.m. *Image courtesy of Mickey Smith*.

Franklin Hall, Rosenhayn. Note the remarkable similarity in construction to Columbia Hall, Carmel, c. 1907. *Image courtesy of Mickey Smith.*

Mortin Avenue, Rosenhayn, c. 1907. *Image courtesy of Mickey Smith.*

Rosenhayn Station, c. 1907. *Image courtesy of Mickey Smith.*

M. Alper's Rosenhayn Hotel, c.1907. Note the small dwellings to the left and the young man with the snare drum on the hotel steps. The image is replete with the community's second and third generation. *Image courtesy of Mickey Smith.*

Cedar St. looking west, Rosenhayn, c. 1907. *Image courtesy of Mickey Smith.*

Lemuel Parvin's Mill Pond and mill dam looking east along Parvin Mill Road, Pittsgrove Township, Salem County, New Jersey, c.1907. The timber posts projecting above the guardrail behind the man on the left, are the rails for the gates that control the volume of water flow over the dam. *Image courtesy of Mickey Smith*.

Looking west along Landis Avenue past Frank Parvin's gristmill, c.1907. The mill obtained its power from what, today, is known as Rainbow Lake. Rowboats await summer revelers along the shore. A carriage clatters over the boards bridging the mill dam as some ladies gather to watch it pass. *Image courtesy of Mickey Smith*.

Duck pond, Rosenhayn, c. 1907. *Image courtesy of Mickey Smith.*

Farm house, Rosenhayn, c. 1907. *Image courtesy of Mickey Smith.*

View of M. E. Barnhart's general store containing the Rosenhayn Post Office, c.1907. Many of the settlement's children can be seen in this view. The dairy cow standing with the youngsters represents the agrarian, bucolic nature of Rosenhayn. A mail delivery wagon waits outside the rear door to the post office. Note the bicycles and the push wagon among the children. *Image courtesy of Mickey Smith.*

Post Office, Rosenhayn. *Image courtesy of Mickey Smith.*

High School (left), School House (right), Rosenhayn, c. 1907. *Image courtesy of Mickey Smith.*

High School (left), School House (right), Rosenhayn, c. 1907. *Image courtesy of Mickey Smith.*

The Norma Athletic Association's baseball team, 1904. Front row (left to right): Sam Curlett, Joe Doran, Toots Peterson; middle row: Andew W. Beebe, Israel Goldstein, Jacob D. Spiegel, Emanuel Doroshow, Moe Spiegel; back row: Nathan Spiegel, Jacob Dittus, George H. Beebe. *Image courtesy of Marsha Levin Schumer for the Judge I. Harry Levin collection*.

Landis Avenue looking east at the dam for Frank Parvin's gristmill, present-day Rainbow Lake, Pittsgrove Township, Salem County, c.1900. Third from left identified as Earl Parvin; fourth from left, George H. Beebe; sixth from left, Jacob D. Spiegel. *Image courtesy of Marsha Levin Schumer for the Judge I. Harry Levin collection.*

Allivine Canning Company, Norma, New Jersey. The factory's relatively new appearance suggests this view dates to between 1903 and 1908. *Image courtesy of Marsha Levin Schumer for the Judge I. Harry Levin collection.*

Brotmanville, 1901. Brotmanville factory encompassed by the tailoring settlement. *From* William Stainsby, *The Jewish Colonies of South Jersey* (Camden, N. J., 1901).

250

FURTHER READING

Bayuk Rappoport Purmell, Bluma and Felice Lewis Rovner. *A Farmer's Daughter: Bluma* (Los Angeles, CA: Hayvenhurst Publishers, 1981).

Brandes, Joseph. *Immigrants to Freedom: Jewish Communities in Rural New Jersey Since 1882* (Philadelphia: University of Pennsylvania Press, 1971).

Eisenberg, Ellen. *Jewish Agricultural Colonies in New Jersey 1882–1920* (Syracuse, NY: Syracuse University Press, 1995).

Goldstein, Philip Reuben. *Social Aspects of the Jewish Colonies of South Jersey* (Philadelphia: University of Pennsylvania Ph.D. thesis, 1921).

Herscher, Uri D. *Jewish Agricultural Utopias in America, 1880–1910* (Detroit: Wayne State University Press, 1981).

Joseph, Samuel. *History of the Baron De Hirsch Fund* ([Philadelphia]: Printed for Baron De Hirsch Fund by the Jewish Publication Society, 1935).

Meyers, Allen. *Southern New Jersey Synagogues: A Social History Highlighted by Stories of Jewish Life from the 1880s–1980s* (Sewell, NJ: Allen Meyers, 1990).

Brotman, Richard. *First Chapter in a New Book: a Documentary Portrait of Brotmanville and the Alliance Colony.* DVD documentary (New York: Richard Brotman, 1982).

WHYY. *It's a Mitzvah!: Jewish Life in the Delaware Valley.* DVD documentary (Philadelphia: WHYY, narrated by Larry Kane, 2002).

Yoval. A Symposium upon the First Fifty Years of the Jewish Farming Colonies of Alliance, Norma and Brotmanville, New Jersey (Philadelphia: Westbrook Publishing Co., 1932; republished 1982).

LIST OF IMAGES

INDEX

COLOPHON

Devyn Brown and Sara Brown are primary editors for *Migdal Zophim*. Secondary editors for *Migdal Zophim* and *Farming in the Jewish Colonies of South Jersey* include Momtahina Afrin, Kelly Burns, Angela Capella, Joshua Champlin, Daniel Cordero, Bradford Cress, Jessica English, Brendan Helm, Sarah Holt, Haylee Korbobo, Alexandra Llerena, Jessica A. Lyon, Claire Riley, Kailey Romero, Gabriela Siwiec, Shannon Stolz and Pablo Tavarez.

Special thanks to Jay Greenblatt, Jay Einstein, Mark Demitroff, Mickey Smith, Marsha Levin Schumer, Nechama Rapoport, Aurora Rose Landman, Rachel Kirzner and Paul W. Schopp; each aided in the development of this text.

Tom Kinsella completed the final editing and supervised publication.

The text is set in 13-point Adobe Garamond Pro; chapter titles are set in 22-point Berkley Oldstyle.

South Jersey Culture & History Center

Advertisement for the sale of farms in Rosenhayn, dated c. 1890s. *Courtesy of the Paul W. Schopp collection.*